President & —

Thank you for your
faithful Service — May
this book confirm your
Testimonies of The mission
of the Prophet Joseph —
We love you both

Dud & Joan
Flanders

JOSEPH SMITH
AMERICA'S GREATEST EDUCATOR

*A Monograph Commemorating
His Bicentennial Birthday*

"The responsibility entrusted to this 'Minister of Education' had to accommodate interested learners from every dispensation of time—from Adam and Eve to his own day and beyond. . . . Imagine the responsibility: . . . to establish educational foundations of *content, structure, function, and context* that could accommodate all who were or would be involved. This task must have seemed ominous to a young man on the frontier of nineteenth century America. Consider the ultimate purpose: it enveloped all the people who ever lived— included every mortal living upon the earth, all who had suffered physical death but now existed in another spiritual domain, as well as all those who were yet to be born. Imagine the student body; imagine the faculty; imagine the curriculum he had to contemplate. The purpose, scope, and location are immense. He served as an educational architect of singular significance. . . . Joseph's vision of an educated people was contagious and many caught this spirit." (See page 68.)

What was it about this man who:

Inspired and energized marginally literate pioneer parents to study and learn, then teach and instruct their children to do likewise?

Continues to motivate, equip, and commit professional educators to improve their performance in the classroom, on the field, at the library and in the laboratory?

Intrigues and challenges theoreticians, mathematicians, scientists and artists in various fields to contemplate and explore the boundaries of their conceptual islands of knowledge?

[signature] Neil J Flinders
Brigham Young University
Joseph Smith Academy
Nauvoo, Illinois
2005/2014

ISBN-13: 978-0-692-21230-1

ISBN-10: 0692212302

Library of Congress Control Number: 201490930

Acknowledgements

Front Cover Art	D.J. Bowden, Photo of his Joseph Smith Sculpture by permission
Elijah in the Kirtland Temple	Daniel A. Lewis, Photo of his painting by permission
Records in Heaven and on Earth	Photos courtesy of "Snapshots" by Karalee
Comparative Architecture	
19th Century	Photo courtesy of "Snapshots" by Karalee
21st Century	Photo courtesy of Los Angeles Unified School District
Sacred Space	
Nauvoo Temple	Photo—Nauvoo Mission Collection
Kitchen Table	Photo—"Snapshots" by Karalee
The Long Trek West	
Wagon Train	Getty Images—North America
Handcart Family	Franz Mark Johansen, Photo of Sculpture at Winter Quarters Visitors Center by permission
Ship in a Bottle	Don "goaly" at instructables.com
Empty Bottle	Source unknown
Ten Commandments Tablets	Source unknown
Tower of Babel	Pieter Bruegels, Illustration by permission

The author (see page 209 for information about the author) expresses sincere gratitude to all those who read and shared their observations, insights, and encouragement at various stages in the preparation of this document. Particular appreciation is extended to Don Norton, Scott Flinders, and Kaitlin Zeller who shared their editing and layout skills in making the manuscript suitable for publication.

Abbreviations

BM	Book of Mormon
CR	Conference Report
D&C	Doctrine and Covenants
HC	History of the Church
JD	Journal of Discourses
JSH	Joseph Smith History
MS	Millennial Star
PGP	Pearl of Great Price
PWJS	Personal Writings of Joseph Smith
TPJS	Teachings of the Prophet Joseph Smith

TABLE OF CONTENTS

Supplementary Sources of Information Related to Joseph Smith's Views on Education

Note: Numerous articles and reports regarding Joseph Smith's views and activities are related to education. The purposes of these articles and reports are varied. Extensive studies, however, that specifically address Joseph Smith's views of, and activities related to, education are quite limited and usually unpublished. Examples are:

Milton Lynn Bennion. *Mormonism and Education*. Salt Lake City: LDS Dept. of Education, 1939.

Wendell O. Rich, *Distinctive Teachings of the Restoration*, Salt Lake City, 1962. (Based on his unpublished Doctoral thesis, Utah State Agricultural College, Logan, Utah, 1954)

Arthur C. Wiscombe, "Eternalism—The Philosophical Basis of Mormon Education" (unpublished Doctoral thesis, Colorado State University, 1960)

Garland E. Tickemyer, "The Philosophy of Joseph Smith and Its Educational Implications" (unpublished Doctoral dissertation, University of Texas, Austin, Texas, 1963)

James Roy Harris, "A Comparison of the Educational Thought of Joseph Smith with that of Certain Contemporary Educators" (unpublished Doctoral dissertation, Brigham Young University, Provo, Utah, 1965)

Orlen Curtis Peterson, "A History of the Schools and Educational Programs of the Church of Jesus Christ of Latter-day Saints in Ohio and Missouri, 1831-1839" (unpublished Master's thesis, Brigham Young University, Provo, Utah, 1972)

PROLOGUE

The Story of Human Education

The story of human education is the story of life itself; it is the story of every child and every family. To live is to experience *learning and teaching, following and leading.* Where these are not, we are not. Living is experiencing. This is a domain shared by everyone; it is the substance of all that we think, feel, and do. Education is the core of every person's life; it is both unique and something that can be shared without fear of depletion. The more we give, the more that what we have is enhanced.

Like life itself, the most useful, enduring, and desirable origin for personal education is in the *family* and *the culture that sustains the family.* Wherever there are humans, there is education, and the vastness of that story is hard to imagine—let alone encompass. And history suggests that the story of education can only be told in fragments and with limited illustrative commentary. Nevertheless, the topic is a vital story that needs to be told over and over again because we are all part of the story. Nothing is lost by this continual endeavor, and there is much to gain.

The story fragment in this document focuses on Joseph Smith, a boy born in eighteenth century frontier New England, who came into the world amidst poverty, humble circumstances and without fame or fanfare. His life, like all others', was shaped by *education;* but in his case the consequences of his education are particularly unique. What Joseph Smith was and is, and what he did are potentially relevant to the lives of all those who have been or are yet to be born on this planet. The nature of what he did, how he did it, and the way his education affected the education of others is certainly worthy of serious consideration. His personal story envelops the process of educational thought and practice that continues to grow and mature. He sought, received and acted upon "wisdom from God." It is an ever-developing saga. He initiated in his day a view of *where we came from, who we are* and *what our potential destiny might be.* He laid the foundation and prepared the platform for an educational enterprise that continues to expand in the twenty-first century, and is destined to continue to unfold into the millennial era.

vii

His impact began in a day where there was no electricity, no motors, no radio, no TV, no airplanes, and no Internet; yet his educational influence continues to thrive in a day of computers, cell phones, iPads, Facebook, Skype, Twitter and all manner of digital apps. It is this proposition that sustains the title given to this document: *Joseph Smith – America's Greatest Educator*.

Here and Now

At first glance, the title *America's Greatest Educator* might seem ill-advised or even vain. A Google search of this phrase reveals that nearly 8,000 citations reference these three words. However, the first ten windows suggest that no one has been granted this title. Of a myriad of articles, applications, etc., of related subject matter, none designate evidence that any person has been so crowned. I suppose one could imagine a person or persons that might be deserving. Consider the great Christian educator Noah Webster. His contributions are both extensive and admirable. His 1828 dictionary and the "blue back speller" span more than a hundred years of early American education. Or a justifiable case could be made to ascribe the worthy record of Moses Waddell, the southern educator who has actually been called "America's greatest teacher" (as measured by the illustrious achievements of his students). But even the author of that article admits it may be "audacious," if not "ludicrous," to designate that title for a man who has now been dead for nearly two centuries—"who virtually few if any have ever heard of." Other writers point out that John Dewey, a popular twentieth century personality and a leader in the modern secular education movement, has received considerable notoriety. But when one considers the title, just how much evidence should we expect in order for this recognition to be bestowed on an individual? That is what this monograph is about—the evidence; the title is simply ancillary. You, the reader, can be the judge to determine if the evidence presented justifies that the title be given to Joseph Smith.

Part of the task is to consider the history of Joseph Smith— where he came from, what he did as an educator, and what influences he set in motion. What ideas and practices, what context, content and process continue to set him apart as one who did invoke adequate remarkable and significant outcomes that continue to bear quality fruits? Have the educational seeds he planted grown into perennial plants of renown? Have his efforts blossomed into worthwhile, relevant, and useful elements that meet the challenges of a continually changing and challenging world? Is the authority he was given, the counsel he used and proffered to others, proving to be worthy and worthwhile? Does his espoused structural format of the past match the needs of the present? Can it be blended to our benefit—to our protection and our preservation, temporally and spiritually? These are the kinds of questions that would need to be asked and answered in order to crown a person with the title *America's Greatest Educator*. Addressing these questions is the major aim of this monograph.

For example, it seems to me that when one considers how things were in times past, how they are now, and what they will need to be like in the future, such a task as this should be describable, applicable, and doable. As individuals and families develop, function, and become generational, their education should reflect a movement toward that which is good and away from that which is evil. Otherwise, how can there be faith, hope, or charity? And where there is no faith, hope, or charity, other less desirable factors will certainly fill the void. The framework for all of this is, it seems, self-evident: *True education must be individually satisfying and family friendly, and it must foster a fundamental socially helpful commitment.* Otherwise it will deteriorate and negatively infect all who embrace it; and it will ultimately induce self-destruction.

The people in Joseph Smith's day did what they did with what they had, or they didn't. People in our day do what we do with what we have—or what we don't have. This is the challenge that faces each generation in each era of time. Latter-day Saints are currently striving to embrace a new *format* for education designed to help *children, youth* and *adults* meet today's needs and opportunities. This adjusted *format* for learning and teaching has recently (2013) been introduced to members of The Church of Jesus Christ of Latter-day Saints. The intent is to "design all [curriculum] and church instruction for the home and family first, with Sunday instruction as a supplement."[1] This is simply an extension of Joseph Smith's vision being applied in the twenty-first century. It appears to come with an

---

[1] *Deseret News*, December 10, 2013. Section A pp.6–7

urgency that *now is the time* and *this is the day* in which there is a *hastening*.

The recent emphasis on instruction is not new doctrine, principles or content. It is a reformed *format—a format* that derives from content and principles introduced by Joseph Smith in his era—two centuries ago. The essential process was revealed long before that. The basic elements are embedded in the standard works of The Church of Jesus Christ of Latter-day Saints. Its purpose is to strengthen and promote personal conversion. The doctrines and principles should be the same as in Joseph's day and long before. The "new" approach is simply an adjusted *format* that has been tailored for our times and resources and is now being reemphasized. The *redesign* is to help us better understand and meet current challenges.

Properly understood, this book can be helpful in displaying the contextual wisdom of where people have been, where we are now, and what will be of greatest value to us if we choose to embrace and implement what is being offered. As always, personal agency will prevail. The opportunity to choose the most beneficial path is before us.

Look Back for Orientation—Look Forward for Direction

It may be helpful at this point to take a peek through the window of history regarding education. There is a rather *large picture of learning and teaching* that people in recent times have endeavored to paint—particularly through the eighteenth and and nineteenth centuries. The modern academic community has been diligently engaged in trying to better understand the origins and activities in which humanity has been engaged. Individuals have attempted to survey societies and civilizations and report these to the general public. Arnold J. Toynbee's 12-volume *A Study of History* (1934–1961) and Will and Ariel Durant's *The Story of Civilization* (11 volumes, 1935–1975) are two well-known examples. At mid-century Edward D. Myers headed an effort based on Toynbee's work to explain "how the various civilizations handed down from one generation to the next the accumulated experience, knowledge, and wisdom of the human race." His book *Education in the Perspective of History* was published in 1960. It examines nineteen civilizations and offers commentary on the role of education in these societies that pertained to their (1) origins, (2) growth and development, (3) "times of trouble," and (4) ultimate demise or disintegration.[2] I refer to these sources simply to acknowledge that our topic has been a subject of significant interest. Western culture has invested considerable effort in trying to understand itself.

The Pattern: Birth and Death of Civilizations

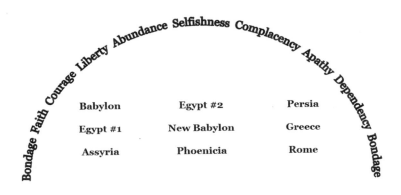

Babylon   Egypt #2   Persia

Egypt #1   New Babylon   Greece

Assyria   Phoenicia   Rome

---

[2]Edward D. Myers *Education in the Perspective of History* (New York: Harper and Brothers, 1960). The scope of the effort is impressive as it probes 21 societies: Egyptiac, Andean, Sinic, Minoan, Sumeric, Mayan, Yucatec, Mexican, Hittite, Syriac, Babylonic, Iranic, Arabic, Far Eastern (Main Body), Far Eastern (Japanese Offshoot), Indic, Hindu, Hellenic, Orthodox Christian (Main Body), Orthodox Christian (Russian Offshoot), and Western. See the chart on p. 332.

A more specifically focused example of seeking answers within the educational process can be viewed in other works, such as Larry Cuban's *How Teachers Taught: Constancy and Change in American Classrooms 1880–1920* (New York: Teachers College Press, 1993); Gibert Highet's *The Art of Teaching* (New York: Alfred A. Knopf, 1963); and E.C. Kelley & M.I. Rasey, *Education and the Nature of Man* (New York: Harper and Row, 1952). These are just examples of the continuing search and the *minimal finding* that characterize much of educational research in the "times of trouble" of our own civilization. Hundreds of volumes and thousands of articles have been and continue to be written on this subject.

It is not that people haven't tried to *comprehend and understand education and its role*; it's simply they have not succeeded as well as one might hope. This is one reason for taking a very careful look at Joseph Smith and what his life and experience contribute to this ongoing venture.

The observations on education which these explorations offer are quite interesting. The writers note that education is a matter of *perpetuating information.* They claim that the foundation of these efforts to educate can be reduced to three basic methods: (1) when one person *observes and then imitates* what another person does—the *apprentice* approach; (2) when one person *memorizes* then repeats to others that which was memorized—the *oral* approach; (3) when a person uses written words or symbols of information and passes them to another person—the *writing and record-keeping* approach. These respective *methods* often characterize a society and may influence its operation and destiny. Most people are quite familiar with each of these methods. Each one seems to have had its time of popularity in the panorama of history.

Another factor is also evident in these large research projects. Key figures in the educational process of any particular society can be identified. However, these personalities are often known primarily by what others say and do regarding what these individuals taught, rather than by direct information about that person's actual beliefs or educational thoughts or activities. For example, this was the case in Greece concerning the impact of *Socrates*, in China regarding the impact of *Confucius*, or in India relating to the impact of the *gurus*—their masters of instruction. Most of what is known about these "educators" derives from secondhand sources. The evidence of their influence is hardly in doubt, but not because of firsthand information. This dearth of primary information is also somewhat similar concerning the role of the traveling or wandering teachers in these societies. Groups of mercenary "educators" become quite prominent during the "times of troubles"—as societies break down into *conflicting factions* prior to their demise. This is part of what appears to be the cycle of the birth, life and death of most civilizations.[3] (It is also a sobering consideration when we view our present-day circumstances.)

There is a similar lack of specific and intentional application of Joseph Smith's personal educational practices. Like many who have gone before, his impact is most visible in

---

[3]Ibid. Competing schools emerge and itinerant teachers like the "sophists" in Greece flourish, pp. 37, 51.

how *what he taught* affected and influenced those *whom he taught*. It would be nice to have *more details* about Joseph's personal role in the learning/teaching process—day by day, week by week, and month by month, but not many of these kinds of records are now available. We are left with a limited variety of anecdotal examples. Those who knew Joseph by their own experience, and knew how he taught and related to others, are no longer with us. But there is an abundance of evidence of the secondary kind; accounts of the basics are evident in this monograph. Joseph did leave a rich and abundant record of principles and practices that defines what he believed, presented, and shared with others.

It is not difficult to see how Joseph Smith responded to many of the educational dilemmas that are yet left unanswered by the most serious and well intentioned students of the history of education. It is clear, by what Joseph thought and did, that he felt the role of education was central in the personal, family and social activities of humanity. The validity of Joseph Smith's teachings on these matters is consistent with the admonition expressed by Alma (a prophet/leader cited in the Book of Mormon record). He (Alma) indicated that the work of the ministry—the spiritual charge—includes *preparing a generation of parents who are capable of preparing a generation of children capable of preparing a generation worthy to receive the Savior at his coming* (Alma 39:16; also 16:15–16). This requires connecting *spiritual* and *temporal* instruction. Joseph Smith taught that this can be done if we seek to understand, embrace, and apply the truths we have been given. A simple chart portrays the principles to master in order to be the most successful in complying with this charge.

Preparing and Presenting Instruction that
Connects the Temporal to the Spiritual

TEMPORAL DOMAIN	*Procedures*	MORAL/SPIRITUAL DOMAIN
SHOW (Encounter Directly)	Concrete to Abstract	TEACH ACCORDING TO THE COVENANTS
TELL (Explain Simply)	Simple to Complex	TEACH BY THE SPIRIT
DO (Experience Personally)	Confirmation by the Learner	TEACH AS A WITNESS

Effective learning/teaching moves from the

Simulated a representation	to	**Real** actual object or ideal	to	**Ideal** temporal/spiritual together

Scriptural counsel regarding instruction is rooted in some very simple doctrines—doctrines that were clearly established by Joseph Smith. These doctrines might be expressed as:

Without *true priesthood*, there is *no true doctrine*
Without *true doctrine*, there is *no true morality*
Without *true morality, spirituality is in jeopardy*

The *scriptures* are a reminder that the doorway to the most effective instruction swings on at least *three simple hinges*—choices we all can make.

Place the *spiritual* before the *temporal* — because that *changes our priorities.*

Place *others* before *self* — because that *changes our attitudes.*

Place the *future* before the *present* — because that *changes our behaviors.*[4]

---

[4]A more detailed treatment of these principles is presented in parts XII and XIII of this book.

There and Then

This earth had a remarkable creation, and it will have a glorious conclusion. Between these two fascinating bookends, the world's history is linked by a series of dispensations of truth given by God to benefit humankind. The final dispensation of this divine story features a number of prominent personalities. Two individuals anchor the beginning and the end of this concluding dispensation—(a) Joseph Smith the Prophet, who was appointed to restore the fulness of the gospel of Jesus Christ, and (b) our Savior, Jesus the Christ, the son of God, who will return to this earth to complete His Father's plan in our behalf. He is and will be our advocate with Heavenly Father, a mission He received from the Father to prepare the members of the human family for their ultimate destination. Joseph Smith's mission was to serve under the direction of this most noble personality and leadership. It is vital to understand this relationship when considering Joseph Smith's views on education.

The connections between what Joseph Smith proclaimed and the mission of the Savior to this world are amazing. Joseph was taught, as were Adam, Noah, Abraham, Moses and others, that humankind, on their own without divine help, become an enemy to themselves and to their Creator (Mosiah 3:19; 5:2; 16:5). He learned that facts can flutter, personal concepts tend to waver, and human precepts are limited and temporary (2 Nephi 28:30–31; D&C 45:29). Only the precepts of God are permanent and priceless. It is in the context of these revealed truths that men and women may exercise their agency and bring to pass much that is good and useful. Joseph was shown why spiritual conversion is essential to physical, moral and social well-being. And the enabling power resides in the doctrines and ordinances that God reveals to humankind. Herein are housed the values, safety, and blessings espoused by the scriptural records that have been preserved for our benefit (D&C 132:7, 13–14). The records are available, and the story line is quite simple; they are now or will be, eventually, available to all who inhabit this earth.

Joseph Smith and Elijah—Companion Ministries for this Dispensation

Elijah Delivers the Priesthood Sealing Keys

Joseph Smith's initial introduction to his life's work was striking, unique and closely tied to these scriptural accounts. Moroni, the initial messenger sent to deliver Joseph's call to the ministry, explained that Joseph's assignment was linked to the remarkable latter-day work of Elijah, the Old Testament prophet of miracles. Elijah's restoration mission was to reconcile families—children to their fathers, fathers to their children—according to the divine pattern for eternal purposes. This ultimately requires priesthood sealing ordinances. Joseph would *learn* and then *teach* that sacred sealing ordinances were to connect families, both the living and the dead, in eternal relationships that would accomplish their personal destiny and fulfill our Heavenly Father's work (PGP Moses 1:39). He was told that it would be Elijah who would empower Joseph with priesthood keys and assist him in major tasks associated with this last dispensation of the Lord's work. (JSH 1:37–39; D&C 2:1–3.) Joseph was given *the message, the authority,* and *the educational mechanisms* for delivering this message. By the spirit of his calling, Elijah was to help *organize the genealogical records necessary for the population of the earth to act on the message.* Both are enabled to accomplish their missions through the influence and power of the Holy Ghost. (D&C 130:22–23) It was and is a miraculous process. We may not fully comprehend exactly how or even what is happening, but it is happening!

Looking back, it can be seen that Joseph's sacred "books" are the standard works of The Church of Jesus Christ of Latter-day Saints. Elijah's sacred "books" are the genealogical records that organize the families of the earth and enable them to receive the sealing ordinances. It is the "spirit of Elijah" that drives the genealogical interests that are currently manifest throughout the various nations and their inhabitants. Consider for a moment the present manifestation of this influence. Imagine the numerous genealogical societies, various organizations, databases, and collective family histories that would not exist were it not for the work of Elijah and his mission.

Elijah was to blend his spirit to a temple-based religious education work that operates on both sides of the veil. Joseph would also learn that he was to press for temples (sacred space) to be constructed, and family history records created, preserved, and shared. Thus the foundation for education was to be laid by Joseph to initiate the great work of providing information and ordinances that would engage with the worldwide family history and genealogical movement related to the spirit of Elijah. The success of these tandem efforts, rooted in the orientation of Joseph to his calling, and Elijah to his, remains so large as to seem incomprehensible to the mortal mind. Nevertheless, this quiet but world-encompassing process is spreading in every land and culture; it is a dual spiritual labor of the greatest significance. The evidence is available to all who desire to seek it.

Records in Heaven and Records on Earth

As this connecting task unfolded in Joseph's mind, the revelatory literature of the ages became more clear, simple and relevant. The Bible took on new meaning—both its strengths and weaknesses. The promise to Abraham that his seed would bless all the nations of the earth and the Apostle Paul's observation regarding baptisms by proxy for those who have died took on new meaning (Abraham 2:8–11; 1 Cor. 15:22, 29). It was obvious that parts of the basic curriculum for this enormous educational project were already at hand, and the promise was given that more would be made available as their combined missions rolled forth toward the *millennial era*. Part of Joseph's mission was to labor with the available scriptural library of information. He was to be an instrument in refining and increasing the knowledge base necessary to bring to pass the purposes he was called to accomplish. It was his task to provide in this final dispensation the path and the iron rod that could lead people from *biblical morality* to a *restored spirituality*. The assignment was both intriguing and daunting.

Joseph was informed that the first step was to translate and publish *another witness* for the work of the Savior: The Book of Mormon—a record of early inhabitants of the western hemisphere. He, a frontier boy from a poor family with limited educational experience or opportunities, certainly could not do this with his own intellect and skills. He would have to operate on a platform of faith, and not reason alone, because that was insufficient. He also recognized it was a beginning that would stretch into the future. He concluded, *"The ancient prophets declared that in the last days the God of heaven should set up a kingdom which should never be destroyed. . . . I calculate to be one of the instruments. . . . I intend to lay a foundation that will revolutionize the whole world"* (TPJS pp. 365–366). This was his mission assignment. He grasped the spiritual vision; the work, however, unfolded more slowly. It was miraculous in many ways, but it was also tedious and time consuming.

Joseph's initial training involved translating and publishing part of a sacred book of scripture. It was an abridged account of a thousand years of events on the American continents. The purpose of the publication was to provide a second witness to the mission of Jesus Christ. The entire record, he learned, also contained a revelation of "all things . . . which ever have been among the children of men, and which ever will be even unto the end of the earth." He was informed that eventually this complete revelation "shall be read upon the house tops . . . by the power of Christ" (2 Nephi 27:6–8, 11).

Meanwhile, Joseph was to see that the portion he was permitted to translate would enable "the deaf [to] hear the words of the book, and the blind shall see out of obscurity and out of darkness" (2 Nephi 27:29). This book—a book with a power of its own—was to be Joseph Smith's introduction to the world. And it came with a promise to every sincere and willing reader. The ancient keeper of the record offered this testimony:

> Behold, I would exhort you that when ye shall read these things, if it be wisdom in God that ye should read them, that ye would remember how merciful the Lord hath been unto the children of men, from the creation of Adam even down until the time that ye shall receive these things, and ponder it in your hearts. And when ye shall receive these things, I would exhort you that ye would ask God, the Eternal Father, in the name of Christ, if these things are not true; and if ye shall ask with a sincere heart, with real intent, having faith in Christ, he will manifest the truth of it unto you, by the power of the Holy Ghost. And by the power of the Holy Ghost ye may know the truth of all things. (Moroni 10:3–5)

Joseph Smith, young and inexperienced in the beginning, was not limited to his own capacities. The Lord gave Joseph commandments that inspired him, and he received power from on high; the means were prepared beforehand to translate the Book of Mormon. And this inspiration was confirmed to others by the ministering of angels, and is declared unto the world by them—all this to prove "to the world that the holy scriptures are true, and that God does inspire men and call them to his holy work in this age and generation, as well as in generations of old. Thereby showing that he is the same God yesterday, today, and forever" (D&C 20:6–12). The mission was large indeed; but the support was also more than adequate. Joseph was able to move forward with considerable confidence (D&C 128:19–25).

The Scriptures are Family Histories

The task of translation and publication gave Joseph a new appreciation for the sacred records that had been kept and preserved. He was informed that the Book of Mormon and the holy scriptures are given by God for instruction to his children on the earth (D&C 33:16). As his knowledge increased, it also became evident that *the scriptures are basically accounts of a few families and their descendants.* In these records, we are urged, invited and commanded to study and learn from the experiences of these families for our own well-being. They contain examples and warnings Heavenly Father has given to his children. They are filled with illustrations that can help us better understand and prepare for the circumstances we face while on this earth. Within these family stories is repeated counsel that, if followed, provides for our safety and well-being. The Lord said it this way:

> I will give unto you a pattern in all things, that ye may not be deceived; for Satan is abroad in the land, and he goeth forth deceiving the nations (D&C 52:14).

There is a common thread in these sacred records; and this thread is one of these grand patterns. It appears as a central theme in each of the six major accounts or genealogical stories:

1. Adam's family before the Flood	(Genesis 1-11; PGP Book of Moses)
2. Jared's family after the Flood	(BM Book of Ether)
3. Abraham's family after the Flood	(OT; PGP Book of Abraham)
4. Lehi's Family	(Book of Mormon)
5. Jehovah's (Spiritual) Family	(NT; BM 3 and 4 Nephi)
6. Restoration/Millennial Reign	(Doctrine and Covenants)

Each of these accounts describes a *pattern of the conflict* between *good and evil*—the conflict between Lucifer and our Heavenly Father and his Son, Jehovah. They emphasize our role as members of the human family in this ongoing drama. In every story the plot is the same. Reduced to its simple descriptive elements, the general pattern can be stated like this:

- Truth and promises are given to the people by Heavenly Father.
- The people reject the truth and his promises and substitute counterfeits.
- Adherence to these counterfeit beliefs and practices leads to destruction.
- A remnant of righteous people are protected and preserved within God's peace.

The basic strategies on each side of this conflict can be defined, described and compared. Nothing is really new—the driving forces and the structural strategies remain the same; it is only the wardrobe that seems to change. The critical variable is *informed commitment*. Joseph's personal conviction was apparent. The following expression illustrates the point when he said: *"The object with me is to obey and teach others to obey God in just what he tells us to do. It mattereth not whether the principle is popular or unpopular, I will always maintain a true principle, even if I stand alone in it"* (TPJS p. 332).

Consider how these scriptural sources of recorded family experiences enhanced Joseph's personal education—in his development of both content and literary skills. The labor of translating and interpreting provided *the sequential nature* and *enhancement* of Joseph Smith's education. As a child he learned the rudiments of literacy—mostly from his parents. He understood the alphabet, numbers, and some history and social patterns of his time and place. In his youth, his learning was enhanced in response to the intensity of his questioning mind regarding conflicting views about religion that existed in his home and community. Eventually, his deeply felt spiritual concerns were resolved by following the counsel of a biblical verse: *"If any of you lack wisdom, let him ask of God, that giveth to all men liberally, and upbraideth not; and it shall be given him"* (James 1:5; JSH 1:11–20). Joseph did seek that kind of help. He went into a local grove of trees near his home and prayed. He received the answer he sought and much more. From these small and simple acts a magnificent work began.

Subsequent to this experience he received further tutoring, was called to a mission, and eventually assigned a task that required an enormous amount of commitment and personal development. His enhanced education was now underway. Central to this learning process was the task he was given to translate into English a record prepared by an early historian and written in some form of Egyptian characters (Mormon 9:32–37; 1 Nephi 1:2; Mosiah 1:2–4). As mentioned, the account was of a group of early inhabitants of the Americas. The information associated with this translation provided Joseph with an abundance of patterns that formed a foundation for and the reinforcement of his expanding knowledge. The creation of this translated manuscript helped Joseph understand the essential conditions that frame the human experience in mortality. In the form of simple stories about a few families, numerous revealed truths appeared as he translated. These truths described the lives and events of a people who had lived on the American continents (between 600 B.C.–A.D. 400), and also a brief description of an even earlier group (ca. 2200 B.C.). These stories about parents and children made clear the concerns and consequences of humanity. They were simple and easy to understand—and so were the solutions offered.

For example, Joseph learned that the central theme and focus of the Book of Mormon is the experiences of a family divided between *believers* and *nonbelievers*—regarding the nature of God, and the validity of the commandments which He reveals to humankind. After translating 116 pages of historical context, which were lost to this generation, Joseph was instructed to continue the project by substituting a personal journal of a person named Nephi. His journal covered a similar period of time and with more intimate spiritual content.[5] Nephi was a son of Lehi and Sariah, who were the parents of this immigrant family that came from Jerusalem to the new world 600 B.C. It is their posterity that frames the story of the Book of Mormon—A Second Witness of Jesus Christ. Joseph Smith learned from this account that just before Lehi's death, the extended family was gathered in a family setting to receive instruction and blessings from their father. Grandparents, parents, and grandchildren engaged in a tender reunion to listen to counsel and receive blessings from their aging and ailing patriarch (2 Nephi chapters 1–4).

Joseph learned that Lehi called his family together to review sacred revelations and prophecies pertaining to their future. His desire was to explain one last time the principles and doctrines that could save not only his extended family from much of its turmoil and tribulation, but the human race. According to Nephi's journal, Lehi began his message to his family by emphasizing in some detail the following propositions:

---

[5] 2 Nephi 4:13–16.

God is a person; we are his children; he exists and interacts with his children if they will seek that relationship.

People can know good from evil.

There is opposition in all things; this is necessary in order for righteousness to prevail.

There are things that act and things that are acted upon.

People can act; they have their agency to choose.

There is a devil who seeks to do evil and entice others to do likewise.

There is a Savior who can save us from the eternal negative consequences of our sins and mistakes, and who can relieve much of our suffering, pain and illnesses.

People can repent, forgive and change from doing evil and embrace obedience.

Joseph learned that a prominent disposition existed in the minds of some of Lehi's family—those who *disbelieved* their parents' teachings. They felt that "spiritual" stuff was not all that relevant. They asked their father a basic question: Are the things you are telling us "to be understood according to things that are spiritual, which shall come to pass according to the spirit and not the flesh?" The response given them was, No!— "The things which [have been read to you] are things pertaining to both *temporal* and *spiritual*" (1 Nephi 22:1–3). Nevertheless, Nephi's record emphasizes that some family members continued to reject the truths Lehi taught and substituted other beliefs in the lives they lived. In one touching passage Nephi recorded, he said his father, Lehi, called together the children of those members in his family who chose to not believe the Lord's admonitions and said to these, his grandchildren:

Behold, ... I cannot go down to my grave save I should leave a blessing upon you; for behold, I know that if ye are brought up in the way ye should go ye will not depart from it. Wherefore, if ye are cursed, behold I leave my blessing upon you, that the cursing may be taken from you and be answered upon the heads of your parents. Wherefore, because of my blessing the Lord God will not suffer that ye shall perish; wherefore, he will be merciful unto you and unto your seed forever. (2 Nephi 4:5–7)

Soon after this meeting the record indicates that Lehi died.

Not long after this translation experience, Joseph learned that Adam had gathered his righteous descendants together in a similar meeting and given similar advice and counsel just before his death (D&C 107:53–57). It is evident that these stories and the principles associated with them continued to add to Joseph Smith's education. The family is significant.

Our Time, Our Day

It is apparent from Joseph Smith's experiences that a central challenge of mortality is how to utilize and manage the procreative powers of life—the need to develop the personal character necessary to do this according to eternal laws. Procreative powers are sacred. It's about *learning and teaching, loving and serving, giving and receiving, repenting and forgiving,* and doing so in ways that bring to pass the mercy and justice that make joy possible. Consider the following comparisons of the two major competing patterns. They form and frame the primary conflicts people inevitably encounter on this challenging trip through mortality:

Jehovah's Pattern for Protecting the People	Lucifer's Pattern for Destroying the People
True doctrines, principles, and ordinances are given to the people with a simple explanation and legitimate authority.	*False and counterfeit doctrines, principles, and ordinances are created and promoted without legitimate authority.*
Basic institutions to serve and protect the people are instituted and promoted:	*Basic ways to confuse and destroy the people are instituted and promoted:*
• Family • Church • Schools • Government	• Attack and destroy the family • Corrupt the Church and its teachings • Occupy and change the schools • Change the purposes of government
Basic strategies for survival are pursued:	*Basic strategies for destruction are pursued:*
A. Physically move a righteous remnant away from the wicked and establish a Zion community.	A. Destroy and change the form of government, then change and destroy the institutions and values of the people.
B. Spiritually gather the righteous into stakes and then strengthen and operate each Zion community. Nurture faith in Christ.	B. Change and destroy the institutions and values of the people, then destroy and change the form of government. Institute uncertainty.
The Culture of Saints	**The Culture of the World**
Peace, prosperity, service, and sacrifice	Eat, drink, and be merry, for tomorrow we die
4 Nephi 1:11, 15–18	*D&C 1:15–16; 2 Nephi 28:3–32*

In the world, the current statistics increasingly seem to favor Lucifer. The tendencies and temptations documented in the records are always similar if not the same: *reject the truth and substitute error.* Radicalize or denigrate religion. Abuse and prostitute the power of procreation. Marginalize and minimize marriage. Redefine and reconfigure the role of the family. Corrupt and contaminate the schools and their curriculum. Criminalize and misuse the government. Squander and waste resources. All of these practices and behaviors damage and destroy human relationships. It appears to be the historical pattern. They constitute the turf of tyranny, which is the fundamental platform for perpetuating evil. This is the ongoing saga of sacred writ—avoid the counterculture that has its own destiny. In frustration Joseph at one time, made this blunt but telling comment: *"There are so many fools in the world for the Devil to operate upon, it gives him the advantage oftentimes"* (TPJS p. 331).

In contrast, the culture of the Church he was authorized to restore moves forward; there is steady success, though there are too many casualties. The benefits and blessings of exercising self-restraint and compassionate service are evident. Faith and virtue, knowledge and temperance, patience and kindness, humility and diligence, charity and godliness produce personal and collective rewards. But as the records also show, these positive outcomes are not automatic. Each generation faces its own crossroads, not once or twice but many times—challenges are inevitable in each person's life, and family by family. Success or failure, as the records show, rests on the generational hinges that perpetuate *faith, hope,* and *charity.* This was the aim that engaged the Prophet Joseph Smith as he sought to magnify his calling and establish a process for delivering the assigned message. It was his task to set in place the elements that could empower not only those in his day, but in the unfolding times of all those who would follow; his work is particularly relevant to our day.

We face the challenge of dealing with a rapidly expanding deterioration of many cultures in a worldwide conflict between good and evil. It is our lot to cope with the disturbing incidents, trends and turmoil of societies in decline. We have the commission, the counsel, and the means to do this. We have the parents, leaders, teachers, resources, powers and tools equal to the task. We just need to become and to remain the kind of *learners* necessary to embrace and *teach* the mission to others. It is important to be involved and not apathetic.

We know about Adam's day, as well as Enoch and his city, Noah and the flood, Jared and his brother—and their families;

Abraham, Issac, Jacob and their posterity; Lehi and his family and the demise of many of their descendants. We know about Alma, the cities of Ammonihah and Zarahemla, and the Gadianton terrorists. We know about the Order of Nehor, the secular schools and an academic curriculum that taught only literacy and included nothing about (1) the existence of God, (2) His moral laws, or (3) the mission of Jesus Christ (Mosiah 24:4–7). And we also know that the gospel of Jesus Christ was restored in this dispensation to prevail over the evil of the Adversary. The outcome is clear, but the process to bring it to pass is personal; it is in the hands of those who live in these latter-days.

Now, as Latter-day Saints, we have both the commission and the curriculum. As Joseph recognized and taught, all of this is based on a basic principle of learning and teaching that begins in the family: *Children learn best when they do what is true, and they gain a witness and conversion by the Spirit when they teach others what they also can do that is true.* We know it is this simple. The plan is in place. We know the Lord is hastening his work at this particular time. He has made that clear:

> "Behold I will hasten my work in its time" (D&C 88:73—December 1832). [A year before, in 1831, the Lord had explained what he meant by *today*]—"It is called today until the coming of the Son of Man, and verily it is a day of sacrifice, and a day for the tithing of my people; for he that is tithed shall not be burned at his coming. For after today cometh the burning—this is speaking after the manner of the Lord—for verily I say, tomorrow all the proud and they that do wickedly shall be as stubble; and I will burn them up, for I am the Lord of hosts and I will not spare any that remain in Babylon. Wherefore, if you believe me, ye will labor while it is called *today*." (D&C 64:23–24, September 1831)

> Mine *indignation* is soon to be poured out without measure upon all nations; and this will I do when the cup of their *iniquity* is full. (D&C 101:11, December 1833)

The Lord's indignation refers to his anger, aroused by unjust and unworthy activities and attitudes, which come from the iniquity of the people. The Lord has worked diligently to prepare a way for all who will heed his counsel to join in bringing to pass the salvation of the souls of humankind. This involves learning and teaching. He has extended the invitation; it is the work in which the Prophet Joseph Smith enlisted. He it was who laid the foundation for the solution to most of the challenges we face in this last dispensation. It is always a matter of education.

This is the story that this book seeks to tell. It is one person's effort to view Joseph Smith and his work through the eyes of an educator, *which we all are* or *should become.* As the story unfolds, it will be obvious that a major challenge in this ongoing epoch is rooted in learning and teaching. And the primary effort, as always, begins and is intended to end in the home and the family circle. While succeeding generations face increasing forms of distraction and opposition, the principles of learning and teaching, following and leading revealed to Joseph Smith take on increased significance. Institutional and auxiliary efforts to support the family have in the past, are at present, and will continue to be given careful attention. New formats for the curriculum will be created and modified. Methodologies will become more focused and refined. Age-old revealed principles will become more clear and their application will be more effective.

After finishing the reading, one might be asked to respond to the question, *What was the book about anyway?* And one simple answer could be, *This book is about how to learn and teach like Joseph Smith was taught to learn and teach.* It's a very worthy endeavor and most certainly, it is timely.

This is the Time, Now is the Day
D&C 88:73; Alma 34:31–36

Master we hear Thee calling.
Thy voice is quiet and clear.
The time to hasten Thy work
Unfolding, both far and near.

Souls are yearning and searching,
Near home and in far away lands.
Parents are catching the vision,
Prophets extending their hands

This is the time, now is the day.
We are the one's called to care.
Help us prepare, show us the way,
Help us to live, so we can share.
This is the time, now is the day.

Teachers feel deeply His message.
The Spirit nudges each heart.
Despite our weakness or courage
There's blessings attached to one's part.
Conversion's the prize
for all who'll engage.

We are the ones called to care.
Help us prepare, show us the way,
Help us to live, help us to share.
This is the time, now is the day.
This is the time, now is the day.

NJF

A Brief Preface

This essay was written to all those who might find interest in exploring the relationship between American education and Joseph Smith the American Prophet. It is addressed to anyone who loves education and finds interest in the thoughts and writings of Joseph Smith, as well as to those who love Joseph Smith and also find interest in the theory and practice of education. My general observations are expressed in the text; more detailed connections to various aspects of Joseph Smith's ideas can be found in the footnotes, appendices, and references. As the reader may recognize, the breadth and depth of these topics far exceed an adequate treatment in a limited document by a single author. But what can be accomplished, hopefully, is to present enough of the story to demonstrate value in considering Joseph Smith as an educator worthy of critical study and relevant to all who live in the twenty-first century. Joseph Smith's life and message can contribute much to our understanding about education.

The footnotes and the appendices will signal to the serious reader, the pervasive and extended nature of this subject matter. The topical story line in the text itself is fairly simple; it should be accessible and of interest to even the casual reader. The scope and depth of the topics, however, are extensive and require thoughtful consideration. I begin with a brief commentary on two topics— (a) *education* and (b) *Joseph Smith* the person. It is vital to understand both the definition of education used in this document, and to sense the way this man's reputation spread throughout the world in such a rapid and remarkable manner. That is unique, and this phenomenon remains a mystery yet to be fully explained. His own explanation is fitting: *"No man knows my history. I cannot tell it: I shall never undertake it."* But he did labor to share that which he felt was most important: *"Would to God that I had forty days and nights in which to tell you all!"* (HC vol. 6, pp. 317, 313). Nevertheless, there is much about Joseph Smith that can be learned, and the value of this information may be both surprising and astonishing as well as helpful and valuable. It is certainly worth the effort of any who possess a curious and open mind.

Joseph Smith the American prophet and *education* are a natural fit. Like a hand in a glove, the two combined become an instrument of extraordinary potential. Serious students of either *education* or *Joseph Smith* will recognize that both subjects are much discussed, but seldom comprehended. I readily acknowledge that these topics are challenging, but that seems to be a common ailment in the human condition. Most of what is of value requires personal effort. Life itself is challenging, but life is also larger than its challenges. Like all children, each of us is worth far more than we realize, and we realize far less than we ought to—as we play out our days in this sandbox of mortality. So with the obvious limitations clearly in mind, I will try to sharpen and deepen our understanding of Joseph Smith as an educator. Whatever else Joseph Smith might have been, he was first and foremost an educator—a leader-like stewardship he shouldered with vigor and enjoyment, clothed in the mantle of *prophet, seer,* and *revelator.* This fact alone tends to set him apart.

What is Education?

I will begin with a word about my view of *education*: Studying the history, philosophy, and definition of education is something like studying the weather: it is certainly important, but seldom understood and hardly predictable. There are many theories why this is so, far more than can be addressed in a simple essay. What I will say, with some degree of confidence, is that my view of education, in its broadest sense, is *the acquisition and appropriate application of the truth—a knowledge of things as they are, as they were, and as they will be.* This is the sense in which I use the term. This definition also fits well with what Joseph Smith believed and taught. Further, it seems self-evident that learning and teaching are universal attributes. Professional educators have no corner on this market. Everyone is a learner, and everyone is a teacher. It is also a fact that in reality *the learner is in charge of learning* and *the teacher is in charge of teaching.* Much of today's education focuses more on the teacher than the learner. Too often, such expectations place the learner on educational welfare. The old axiom "If the learner hasn't learned, the teacher hasn't taught" is not a reliable assumption. This seems obvious, yet it is often misunderstood. *Personal agency* trumps nearly everything else in life. The sooner and the better learners realize this, the more effective education can become. It was certainly an emphasis of Joseph Smith. Education in this larger sense places parents and the family as the primary providers; other agencies and parties may be useful and even essential, but they are subsidiary.

Our social world is shaped and driven by how each person embraces, packages, delivers, and makes use of the foregoing function in learning and teaching. It is this universal *personal agency* that causes most of the fuss and a lot of the furor in our lives—at home, at work, and at play. Obtaining, organizing, and applying information or knowledge seems to be the basic quest of human life. When this complex process ceases, what is left? Education has to be a core consideration in every person's life, whether we realize it or not. This was the platform on which Joseph Smith based his life and his teachings. The unique intent of this monograph is the opportunity to explore education and how it fits into our daily lives when viewed through a lens of Joseph Smith's life and work. *The purpose and meaning of human life that he proclaimed were vast and comprehensive. As mentioned, they remain a standard against which all other educational philosophies and practices can be evaluated.* This is no small claim.

There is another important, often overlooked factor, in a review of any particular function of Joseph Smith's life and the work he performed. Joseph Smith was influenced by a *rural,* not an *urban,* social setting. This is the *environment* in which he lived and that *enveloped* the Church and its members during his lifetime. Nearly everything he did, from his birth to his death, took place in a raw frontier setting. The emergence of this gathering of people—known as Mormons—arose in a varied and loosely controlled social network. Diverse cultural, physical, and intellectual constraints were a common condition on the perimeter of much of nineteenth century America. Joseph Smith and his people moved from one rustic pioneering location to another. He and most of his followers moved out of upstate New York, to the Ohio frontier, on to the edge of the Indian land in Missouri, and finally to the coarse Illinois-Mississippi river culture. This meant repeatedly clearing land, building houses, and eking out a living by growing their own food, creating their own clothing and transportation, as well as getting along with new neighbors. Even at the time of his death

Joseph was planning for a further movement into the wilds of the Rocky Mountains. This document does not focus on the pros and cons of *rural* versus *urban* life, but there are significant differences, and the reader should keep this in mind. Joseph Smith did not pursue his mission in a neutral or particularly comfortable environment. It was physically a hard life, something difficult to appreciate by people who live in the comforts of our modern facilities and conveniences. Daily life was difficult and demanding; not soft or easy.

Joseph Smith's View of Education—a Snapshot

The author of one biography of Joseph Smith shared his perspective in these words:

> Joseph Smith was building, under God's direction, a Church for human joy. He understood that such joy requires more than temporal satisfaction. Economic security and social advantages, political protection, important as they are, do not of themselves provide full joy. Things of the mind and spirit, eternal truths, must be added. He was an intense lover of truth. He would have all men know the fierce joy of possessing and using truth—all truth in every division of human activity.

And then this author added that although Joseph himself had little *school* training, he made up for it by his *personal study*. Some people might ask: Considering he was a prophet of God, would this personal effort have been necessary? Could he not have appealed to divine sources and made that sufficient? In the face of these questions, the writer continues his explanation:

> That is an erroneous conception of revelation and education. The children of men are expected to use their own powers in all their affairs. The gathering of knowledge is no exception. Only when a man [or woman] has gone as far as they can, and more knowledge is required, does the Lord come with direct help.[6]

---

[6]John A. Widtsoe *Joseph Smith: Seeker After Truth, Prophet of God* (Salt Lake City: Deseret News Press, 1952, p.221).

These comments present a proposition that undergirds education as Joseph pursued it. By the end of his short life, he had developed *a good secular education* and *a superior spiritual knowledge*. He learned that wisdom can only come if it is sought by study and by faith. But there is no substitute for personal effort in either case. He diligently studied languages, law, history, literature, and many other subjects. In addition to personal study he also paid for formal instruction from others, and helped establish schools for both children and adults. When he was incarcerated for four months in a dungeon-like prison, he continued to exercise the "kingdom of his mind." Some have referred to this source of "light" as "the other window," in contrast to the two small barred openings in the rock structure of his prison. Under these nearly intolerable conditions, Joseph wrote a number of letters and dispensed inspired instructions; he also received numerous vital revelations which he shared with his followers. He displayed the example of a true educator: he lived what he taught.

What did Joseph think about curriculum? This question will be considered later, but his conception of what to study, learn and share was given to him by the Lord, who said:

> Teach ye diligently and my grace shall attend you; that you may be instructed more perfectly in theory, in principle, in doctrine, in the law of the gospel, in all things that pertain unto the kingdom of God, that are expedient for you to understand; of things both in heaven and in the earth, and under the earth; things which have been, things which are, things which must shortly come to pass; things which are at home, things which are abroad; the wars and the perplexities of the nations, and the judgments which are on the land, and a knowledge also of countries and kingdoms.[7]

Joseph believed that *"all the minds and spirits that God ever sent into the world are susceptible of enlargement."* He believed intelligence is light and truth; that we should seek learning out of the best books by study and by faith; that whatever knowledge we obtain in this mortal life will be to our advantage in the next life, and that it is impossible for us to be

---

[7]D&C 88:78–79.

saved in ignorance. He recognized that the most important education takes place in the home and that appropriate schools should also be provided for the benefit of the children because *"it is all important that children to become good should be taught [good]; . . . children soon become men and women. Yes, they are they who must follow us."* It is clear that he joined with Moses, who was commanded by God to instruct the parents to instruct the children of Israel in his day and to teach them diligently at home and away from home, and when they arise in the morning and when they lie down at night. (Deut. 6:4–8.) In Joseph's case he added an emphasis: the instruction of the young was important because they were to *"perform the duties which not only pertain to this world, but to the second coming of the Savior, even preparing for the Sabbath of creation, and for eternity."*[8] Education was an imperative.

Joseph Smith Taught

Whatever principle of intelligence we attain to in this life,

it will rise with us in the resurrection.

And if a person gains more knowledge and intelligence

in this life through his diligence and obedience than another,

he will have so much the advantage in the world to come.

(The Doctrine and Covenants 130:18–19)

---

[8]TPJS p. 354; D&C 93:36; 88:78–79; 88:118; 130:18–19; 131:6; 55:4; HC vol. 1, p.276–277; Deut. 6:6–7, 11:18–19.

PART I

INTRODUCTION: "WISDOM FROM GOD"

Joseph Smith introduced his account of his call to serve as a youth with this observation:

> I was deeply troubled by the "incessant . . . war of words and tumult of opinions" proclaimed by the "teachers of religion" of different persuasions. Their varied interpretations of scripture were so intense and different "as to destroy all confidence in settling the question" of who was right "by an appeal to the Bible."

He was also touched by the conflicting responses in his immediate family to these varied admonitions. He wrote in his personal history that

> while I was laboring under the extreme difficulties caused by the contests of these parties of religionists, I was one day reading the Epistle of James, first chapter and fifth verse, which reads: If any of you lack wisdom, let him ask of God, that giveth to all men liberally, and upbraideth not; and it shall be given him.

He said the feelings associated with his reading of this scripture caused him to "reflect on it again and again, knowing that if any person needed wisdom from God," he did.

At length, he came to the conclusion that he must "either remain in darkness and confusion" or do what James directed, "that is ask of God." So he retired to the woods near his home and proceeded to pray for direction. The result was an epoch change in the young man's life. He was visited by God the Eternal Father, who introduced His beloved Son to Joseph with the admonition to "Hear Him!" Joseph did! His response to the information he received, and to subsequent experiences set him on the course of an unusual and remarkably important education. This monograph is an exploration of that instruction.

1

(A summary of Joseph's early personal experience is available in The Pearl of Great Price, Joseph Smith—History or History of the Church, vol.1, Chapters 1–5.)

The exploration in this monograph of Joseph Smith's effort to seek the wisdom of God illustrates how Joseph spent the remainder of his life seeking and proclaiming that wisdom. Most readers will discover that the disturbing turmoil Joseph Smith felt two centuries ago has only increased and continues to trouble many concerned people today. The description he gave of his times and personal feelings seems even more evident and pervasive now than it was then. Only the wardrobe has been modified and modernized; the conflicts, darkness, and confusion remain. The tumult of opinions, contradicting responses, and dramatic consequences are alive and well. The urge to search for wisdom from God is as needful now as it was then. The intent behind this document is to nurture the urge to seek wisdom from God within all those who choose to read it and then are willing to embrace that wisdom. This search can be just as fruitful now as it was for Joseph Smith. The path has been well marked and the solutions are as available to seekers today as they were for Joseph and his generation. We have the same vital tools to work with that he did.

Let this adventure begin with the bicentennial celebration of his birth. The year 2005 was marked in some circles by a flurry of interest in the life of Joseph Smith. Two hundred years had passed since his birth in Sharon, Windsor County, Vermont. At the time, few, if any, would have expected that two centuries later, the Library of Congress would be sponsoring a two-day symposium (May 6–7, 2005) commemorating his life and contributions. In fact, thousands of people in numerous countries and a variety of publications would make him a point of focus on that bicentennial anniversary—a continuing trend that seems to be gaining momentum. This is evidenced by the recent focus on his life by the partnering in 2013 of the Abraham Lincoln Presidential Library and Museum, the Illinois Supreme Court on Historic Preservation, and the Church's History Department (*Church News*, September 29, 2013).[9]

---

[9]These events, held in Nauvoo, Springfield, and Chicago, Illinois during the year 2013, address two of the legal issues rooted in the U.S. Constitution that confronted Joseph Smith, viz. *Habeas Corpus*—the right of an individual to

Here was a man, born to poverty, who lived only 38 years. He, along with his brother Hyrum, was martyred by a mob of mutinous militia, June 27, 1844, in a tiny frontier jail in Carthage, Illinois. Why would such a person elicit this kind of attention over this period of time? What could be driving such an unusual phenomenon? What did he accomplish in less than 20 years? These questions and their answers appear to capture and sustain a continuing interest—an interest and an influence that grow ever wider and more intense as the years pass and the development of his influence expands. Why would one of his latest successors say in regard to Joseph Smith's view of Jesus Christ the Savior of the world: "At this time . . . in an age of skepticism and doubt, his witness [of Christ] is unequivocal and certain" (Gordon B. Hinckley, *Church News,* Dec. 31, 2005, p. 8).

Library collections continue to grow in an effort to answer the foregoing questions and assess their varying answers. The *Joseph Smith Papers* project provides 21 volumes that detail Joseph's history. This monograph focuses on only two examples of why this is happening. *First,* Joseph Smith articulated a *pattern of religious order and beliefs, principles, and ordinances* against which all other religious orders, beliefs, principles, and ordinances can be evaluated. *Second,* he proclaimed and implemented the *foundations for a living process of education* that defines and sustains the temporal and eternal nature of the religion he was commissioned to *restore.* These *educational* foundations are likewise a means by which all other *educational* organizations, beliefs, principles, and philosophies can be evaluated. It is this enterprise, educational vision, and process that are the object of examination in this monograph. Hopefully, it will provide the reader with improved insights regarding questions like, "What did Joseph Smith initiate in thought and practice that

---

be brought before a court to hear the charges against him or her and to present his or her defense, and the state's right of *extradition*—the right of a given state to request that another state transfer a criminal defendant to its jurisdiction where the crime allegedly occurred. Joseph Smith's life was intertwined with both of these fundamentals. These critical issues extend from the English Magna Carta through the U.S. Constitution to the current conflicts involving prisoners at the Guantanamo Bay facility. It is interesting that Joseph Smith's circumstances would be used to highlight such central concerns in today's public debates on such civil matters.

continues to find such practical, useful, effective and satisfying applications—particularly in our ever-changing social and institutional environment?" "What is it about the *learning and teaching*, the *following and leading*, which Joseph espoused that continues to have such impact?" This is the point of focus in what follows. The story has an eternal context. It is much more than a parochial or provincial concern.

Joseph Smith as a youth was troubled by honest and personal questions. These concerns led to penetrating answers that pertain to every person. He wanted to know what he should do about his unsettled feelings toward the people he knew who were promoting very conflicting responses to his basic concerns. He discovered the path to a solution of his quandary in the scriptural exhortation of James 1: 5–6. If you lack wisdom, ask God! Following this advice, he received answers, not only to his immediate concerns, but additional knowledge. He learned what God the Father and His Son, Jehovah, looked like. He learned of other simple, pervasive, and surprisingly expansive information, such as that God will speak to his children. He also learned there are settling explanations to the great, and some say "terrible" questions— *Where did I come from? Why am I here? What is my ultimate destiny? Is there a plan?* This knowledge gave him comfort and confidence, but also led to disturbing persecution.

These questions have always troubled humanity. Modern mankind seeks to answer these questions with reason, science, and ofttimes various traditional religions—even superstition. The answers from these sources are very different from the ones Joseph Smith received, and much less comprehensive. The contemporary response to questions regarding a person's existence before one's birth, during mortality, and what life will be like after death, is fragmented and contradictory. *Science* offers multiple *theoretical guesses but no promises* about where we came from or what happens after our death. *Traditional religion* suggests that some mysterious "power" known as "god" created us—perhaps out of nothing (*creatio ex nihilo*)—and proposes that an *individual's life may continue after death in some ways that remain consensually undefined.* The lack of adequate answers to these questions is why they have been referred to as "terrible."

4

The revelation received by Joseph Smith offers much more than this. We are the offspring of Heavenly parents who gave each of us a spiritual body. This spiritual body inhabits the earthly body created by our earthly parents. After birth in this mortal state we experience the learning and teaching and following and leading that occur here, then we die. Death is not the end of our personal existence, it is a new phase of our eternal existence, which has been prepared for us by our Heavenly parents. The "mystery" is incidental, meaning it dissolves as a result of our own experience; and the plan is inclusive and comprehensive. The issues we each encounter are certainly personal; but we have been empowered with the agency to participate in the outcomes according to our desires. This is a far different pattern than what the world has to offer. It is a platform that adds truth to truth.

Can what Joseph initiated help us discern between right and wrong, truth and error, better and best, appropriate and inappropriate, good and evil, constructive and destructive, desirable and undesirable? A brief monograph cannot hope to cover all of the relevant issues enveloped by this question. But I believe it is possible to provide a descriptive, useful, and insightful exploration of much that will be of value to all who are involved with *learning, teaching, following,* and *leading.* This is essentially what life is about. These four elements affect almost everyone and everything they do. I trust that those who seek will be appropriately rewarded for their efforts. The *intent* of this document is simple and direct: *to review how Joseph, as an educator, unveiled his views; how those views relate to the cultures that now envelop us; and the way those who followed his counsel continue to apply his views to meet contemporary needs—the needs of children, youth, parents, teachers, and others who act to support individuals and the family.* Like the man himself, interest in what Joseph initiated as an educator continues to expand far beyond what was originally envisioned. The connections between what Joseph proclaimed and the mission of the Savior to this world are indeed amazing. The organization that has been restored by divine means is an astonishing educational enterprise.

PART II

WHO WAS JOSEPH?
WHAT OTHERS SAID ABOUT HIM

Consider the following regarding Joseph Smith the person. His name is well-known to members of The Church of Jesus Christ of Latter-day Saints; others may be more or less familiar with the man and his mission. In terms of notoriety, however, his name is extraordinary; it pervades every continent. Joseph Smith is a man whose name is spoken in tones of both good and evil throughout the world. The number and the variation of these descriptions are exceptional and informative. A sizable library of books, pamphlets, and articles has been written about him, perhaps as many as, or more than, about any other American. Consider the range in perception of just five selected excerpts from recorded observations by his contemporaries. Then ponder the question, *Why did this young man from such obscure origins, who lived just thirty-eight years, evoke such an immediate and widespread interest—a fascination that continues to expand with time?* The answer to this question could illuminate the title of this presentation and help frame the relationship between education and Joseph Smith the person.

Selection One. Thomas Hamilton, a writer from England, visited America in 1831. He published a travelogue entitled *Men and Manners in America* (1833). Mr. Hamilton never personally met Joseph Smith but willingly expressed his opinion as if he had. He relates his own experience of traveling toward the Ohio frontier in the early 1830s. He describes the village of Canandaigua at the edge of a beautiful lake, viewing Niagara Falls, where the eccentric Sam Patch jumped 125 feet to his death from a rock below the Horseshoe in 1829, and notes in detail the variety of human traffic he encountered while moving along the Erie Canal. He writes:

> We passed also several parties of . . . Mormonites, going to a settlement established by their founder, in Ohio. [He acknowledged that he had never heard of this sect before, but he willingly passed on

7

considerable imaginative, here-say commentary, such as] I gleaned the following particulars from one of [my fellow] passengers. A bankrupt storekeeper, whose name I think was Smith, had an extraordinary dream. It directed him to go alone to a particular spot . . . where he was to dig to a certain depth. This dream was of course treated as a mere delusion, and, as is usual in such cases, was thrice repeated. . . . Having dug to the requisite depth, . . . he found a book with golden clasps and cover, and a pair of elegantly mounted spectacles, . . . astonishing magnifiers. . . . Smith had some difficulty in undoing the clasps of this precious volume, but on opening it, though his eyes were good, it appeared to contain nothing but blank paper. It then occurred to him to fit on his spectacles, when, lo! The whole volume was filled with certain figures and pothooks to him unintelligible. Delighted with his good fortune, Smith trudged home with the volume in his pocket and the spectacles on his nose, happy as a bibliomaniac, . . . lucky enough to purchase a rare [document] dog cheap from an ignorant proprietor.

In the same vein Mr. Hamilton continues his explanation of the coming forth of the Book of Mormon, which he attributed to "a converted Rabbi, who flourished in the days of our Saviour, . . . that continues to puzzle theologians" (pp. 310–313). This is one view of Joseph from the perspective of a rather flippant, wayfaring soul intent on entertaining his readers.

Selection Two. A second, more serious view of Joseph Smith appears in the *Dublin University Magazine* of March 1843. This article from a venerated Old World academic institution is entitled "Mormonism; or, New Mohammedanism in England and America." The treatise begins,

We are accustomed to boast of the intelligence of the nineteenth century. . . . Mormonism is a bitter reply to our self-laudation; . . . it exhibits to us a convicted swindler received as a prophet by thousands in both hemispheres—a literary forgery so thoroughly absurd . . . yet recognized as revelation, and placed on the same level of authority as the Bible itself. . . . Hundreds of our countrymen annually quit their homes to join the ranks of the impostor in the wilds of

Illinois. . . . We have conversed with these deluded men; on all subjects, save religion, we have found them shrewd, clever, and well-informed; but, when reference was made to Mormonism, they at once became insensible to reason and argument; neither clergymen nor layman could turn them from their error, or convince them of the absurdity of their proceedings." (p. 283)

Consider the overt implication of these two accounts. They demonstrate that in both hemispheres, less than 20 years after he became known beyond his hometown village, people in very common walks of life as well as highly esteemed social circles, felt compelled to say something about Joseph Smith—whether they had met him in person or not. And this was in a day when communication was very slow, sometimes dangerous, and often difficult and expensive.

Selection Three. A third observer, Samuel A. Prior, a Methodist minister, visited Nauvoo, Illinois in 1843. Reverend Prior writes that he "left home with no very favourable opinions of the Latter-day Saints," thinking of them "as being of quite another race from the rest of mankind and holding no affinity to the human family." He speaks of his disappointment when he arrived in Nauvoo in 1843. Instead of finding a few "miserable log cabins and mud hovels," as he expected, he was

> surprised to see one of the most romantic places that I had visited in the west. . . . I heard not an oath in the place, I saw not a gloomy countenance; all were cheerful, polite, and industrious. I conversed with many leading men—found them social and well-informed, hospitable, and generous. (Samuel A. Prior, "A Visit to Nauvoo," *Millennial Star* IV, #7, (Nov. 1843), pp. 105–08)

Nowhere, reported Reverend Prior, did he find evidence of the deprecation and villainy he had heard applied so often to this people.

Selection Four. A fourth witness was Josiah Quincy, a well-educated attorney from Massachusetts, who served as the mayor of Boston (1845–1848). Mr. Quincy, in company with Charles Frances Adams, made an unintended visit to Nauvoo, Illinois in May of 1844. Josiah was impressed with what he saw and marveled that a frontier city of 15,000 or more could be built in less than half a decade. The location and setting was striking: a mile-long Main Street that began and ended on the same river—a fact as unique as the city's name. These two visitors saw a university in the making; a large, imposing temple under construction; and some 2,500 log, frame, and brick buildings on the edge of a wilderness. Mr. Quincy said he felt the energy of a peculiar people. The site and the circumstances amazed this politician, a man very familiar with America in her infant state. But more than anything else, he was struck by the founder of this unusual enterprise. As viewed by Josiah Quincy, Joseph Smith was an admirable mystery.

Four decades later, after due reflection, this prominent legislator was still inclined to write: "Joseph Smith, . . . a rare being" has exerted a "wonderful influence"; and notwithstanding unsavory criticisms, he is a "phenomenon to be explained." The mayor went on to project that the day may come when Joseph Smith, the American Prophet, could be recognized as the historical figure of the nineteenth century that "exerted the most powerful influence upon the destinies of his countrymen." Mr. Quincy asserted that "the most vital questions Americans are asking each other today have to do with this man and what he has left us . . . [and admitted that] a generation other than mine must deal with these questions. Burning questions they are." Mr. Quincy noted that Joseph Smith "talked from a strong mind utterly unenlightened by the teachings of history." Though not always complimentary of the Mormons, Josiah was careful to state, "I have no theory to advance respecting this extraordinary man." (Josiah Quincy, *Figures of the Past: From the Leaves of Old Journals*, pp. 376–400).

Selection Five. Finally, an observation from a man who, in June of 1844, shared the tiny room in Carthage Jail where Joseph and his brother Hyrum were murdered by an angry "mob"—or more accurately a corrupt militia. John Taylor testified of the victims' innocence and proclaimed: "Joseph Smith, the Prophet and Seer of the Lord, has done more, save Jesus only, for the salvation of men in this world, than any other man that ever lived in it" (*The Doctrine and Covenants* 135:3). John Taylor delivered his personal witness of Joseph Smith, and it is thus recorded:

I testify that I was acquainted with Joseph Smith for years. I have traveled with him; I have been with him in private and in public; I have associated with him in councils of all kinds; I have listened hundreds of times to his public teachings, and his advice to his friends and associates of a more private nature. I have been at his house and seen his deportment in his family. I have seen him arraigned before the tribunals of his country, and have seen him honorably acquitted, and delivered from the pernicious breath of slander, and the machinations and falsehoods of wicked and corrupt men. I was with him living, and with him when he died, when he was murdered in Carthage Jail. . . . I have seen him, then, under these various circumstances, and I testify before God, angels, and men, that he was a good, honorable, virtuous man—that his doctrines were good, scriptural, and wholesome—that his precepts were such as became a man of God—that his private and public character were unimpeachable—and that he lived and died as a man of God and a gentleman. This is my testimony. (John Taylor, *The Gospel Kingdom,* p. 355.)

His testimony includes the observation that Joseph Smith is to play a great role in the grand council to be held at Adam-ondi-Ahman prior to the return of our Savior at the beginning of Jehovah's millennial reign (Ibid. pp. 216–17, 357).

So here we have a range of views—from the ridiculous to the sublime. At one end Joseph is disparaged and on the other he is eulogized. It is the making of an enigma, a puzzle caused by an inscrutable and mysterious personality. Why is Joseph not just summarily dismissed by his peers? Why, after two hundred years, did America's Library of Congress co-sponsor a symposium in honor of his bicentennial birth? These are among numerous questions that have yet to be adequately resolved in the minds of many people. Perhaps these and other questions, if we had appropriate answers, could shed some light on this quandary. Consider just these six selected from an extended parade of legitimate queries:

Why did this young, unschooled, energetic, frontier boy, who grew to be such a charismatic man, attract so much positive and negative attention?

Why did his notoriety spread worldwide in less than two decades?

What did he do or say that impacted so many individuals so deeply?

Why did the established social order react so violently toward him?

Why did the Church he founded evolve from a small persecuted band to a major religious influence in the United States and the world?

What did Joseph Smith learn and teach that has had such a powerful impact?

This list of questions could be expanded many times over. My immediate interest, however, is the central element of the last question: *Does what Joseph Smith learned and taught qualify him to be considered America's Greatest Educator?* In response, I propose that Joseph be viewed as a *Minister of Education* and let his record speak to the question. No other educational title seems to better describe his mission. Any serious review of his life and experience quickly reveals Joseph Smith's intuitive nature, and this is evident in various educational matters by what he did and what he encouraged others to do. John Taylor, one of Joseph's most intimate associates, a powerful intellect in his own right, punctuated the significance of this topic when he declared: *"Joseph Smith knew more in regard to true education than all the philosophers and scientists of the earth; and he knew it by the revelations of God"* (JD vol. 20:179).[10] Joseph laid the foun-

---

[10]Full quotation: "There is another class of people among us doing a great deal of good; that is our Mutual Improvement Associations; both Young Men's and the Young Women's. How much more pleasant it is to see our youth grow up in the fear of God, *trying to instruct one another in the principles of life and salvation,* than to see them ignore the laws of God. How pleasing to God and the holy angels! Let us encourage these things and instruct our sons and daughters, that they may grow up in intelligence, virtue, purity and holiness before the Lord. And then we want to study also the principles of education, and to get the very best teachers we can to teach our children; see that they are men and women who fear God and keep his commandments. . . . Hear it

dations and those who followed have built upon them in rather remarkable and timely fashions. He began an educational endeavor that continues to unfold in the lives of millions of people and has a future that is yet to be comprehended.

---

you fathers and you mothers! *Talking about education, as I said before, Joseph Smith knew more in regard to true education than all the philosophers and scientists of the earth; and he knew it by the revelations of God.* We want to get together to train our children up in the fear of God, to teach them correct principles ourselves, and place them in possession of such things as will lead them in the paths of life." (General Conference address, April 8, 1879)

PART III

JOSEPH SMITH AS MINISTER OF EDUCATION

Joseph Smith fits well the definition traditionally applied in many lands to ministers of education. Ministers in government organizations are persons chosen and assigned to be the facilitators of various services. *Socially,* a minister is one who attends to the needs and wants of others. He looks, sees, and then does what is necessary, considering available resources, to respond to the welfare of those whom he is appointed to serve. *Legally,* in the historical sense, a minister is a person responsible to the king who appoints him. He is the highest officer over the stewardship bestowed upon him; he represents the sovereign and is invested with the authority to implement the benefits of his ministry among the people.

Joseph Smith certainly fits both the social and legal descriptions of a *minister of education.* His appointment came from a Heavenly King.[11] He worked with the resources at hand and carefully bestowed them for the benefit of the people he served. His entire life was devoted to learning, teaching, ministering, and organizing others to do the same. He did what he wanted others to do. He was an example. He was what he wanted others to become. He never compromised his mission or violated his office.

As a minister of education, Joseph Smith can be defined and ranked both in terms of (1) the propositions he espoused, and (2) the ongoing consequences of what he initiated. These matters may be compared to a variety of elements associated with educational endeavors in human society. This task is a little spongy because education is such an amorphous subject; it is real but has no definite form. People view education in a wide variety of ways and with remarkable degrees of difference.

---

[11]See Joseph Smith's "History" in the Pearl of Great Price. This account describes in his own words his appointment to teach the people. Many volumes have been written about the subsequent developments that followed this initial commission.

Nevertheless, some common categories exist. Among these would be:

History:	How education came to be and what it is
Authority:	By what power education functions
Philosophy:	What education entails
Nature:	The quality and design of educational experience
Purpose:	The general intent of educational effort
Focus:	The specific point of the effort
Scope:	The breadth and depth of the effort
Sequence:	The order of the process
Method:	How education is implemented
Location:	The place of delivery
Results:	The outcome of the investment and labor

Every family, church, and school has its own version of these elements. But the extent to which they become formal and explicit varies dramatically. Nevertheless, these are among the fundamental criteria by which one can assess an educator and his or her educational efforts. It is with these elements in mind that I make a few cursory comparisons. A book or several books would be required to treat all the relevant topics as they might apply to Joseph Smith. What follows is only a snapshot of Joseph Smith as a minister of education; a brief description of his ideas and performance compared to some other beliefs and practices. The contrasts are rather stark, but they help illustrate the uniqueness of Joseph's educational thought.

In order to appreciate the significance of these contrasts, it is necessary to recognize two or three of the most fundamental assumptions driving educational thought in western society—particularly as they are manifest in America. Several basic educational squabbles have been etched on the American scene since the birth of Joseph Smith. They each emerged from serious questions about *what is real, who should be in charge,* and *why people act like they do.* Joseph had considerable to say about such notions. His views were often at variance with what was commonly accepted at the time, and they remain so today—notwithstanding how the popular options change from time to time. His insights are unique and sometimes disturbing to the status quo. To some people, they may appear uncomfortable, if not heretical; for others, they can be considered standards for evaluation—foundational elements on which to build.

Recognizing different and often conflicting answers to the foregoing questions and propositions helps one understand Joseph Smith's views of education, and to the foundations upon which these respective views rest. It will be well to keep this in mind as our story unfolds and we consider the role authority plays in that portion of our story.

PART IV

AUTHORITY

At the very root of all educational processes lies the question of authority. When authority raises its head, all other issues tend to pale into insignificance. The presence and acceptance of power is essential to the longevity of any educational effort. The modern world cites a variety of "authorities" for its educational programs: the individual, the family, a particular group, the state, society at large, a governing person—king, ruler, and magistrate—have all been mentioned. The person or group that fashions the critical decisions in an educational endeavor is central to nearly all the other functions that could or do occur. Authority is the fuel that sustains the function of education in human society. Where there is no authority there can be no formal, definitive education—there can only be confusion and chaos.

Western culture can be viewed as generating four general responses to the question of authority. These perspectives are like platforms upon which people have stood to launch their respective programs and proclaim the reasons for pursuing education the way they do. The basic assumptions people make regarding education are not in agreement. Education in America has been and still is shaped by four rather distinct approaches. Each of these views can be easily envisioned in principle by considering two basic axes of concern. These beliefs are relevant to every person, family, and most social entities. They have an influence; they deserve consideration. It is best they be not ignored, because that will not minimize their consequences.

The *first axis* contrasts the view that there is a *supernatural* and a *natural* dimension to reality, with the notion that there is *only a natural domain* and nothing else. In other words, there are people who believe the universe is composed of two building blocks—spirit stuff and physical stuff, to put it bluntly. Then there are people who believe there is no spirit stuff, only physical stuff. The result is somewhat like the two ends of a teeter-totter: there is a continuum along which degrees of differences have been strongly expressed. But at center point the issue shifts, the basic assumption changes, and the difference is exclusive.

Supernatural		No Supernatural
and a	———————	only a
Natural Domain		Natural Domain

Joseph Smith learned early in his experience the importance of understanding that there is a supernatural, spiritual dimension to our existence, as well as a physical, natural domain. While translating the Book of Mormon to English he learned of a man named Korihor who lived in this ancient culture. This individual challenged the established doctrines of belief in that day—by claiming there is no God. He argued that religious doctrines are the foolish traditions and superstitions of our unenlightened ancestors. He taught the people who listened to him that you cannot know what you cannot see. Thus you cannot know that God exists. Religious convictions are the result of a frenzied and deranged mind. There is no God to intervene in our behalf; we survive in life by our own efforts. Churches and religions place people in bondage chaining them to ideas and authorities. Joseph also learned from this manuscript that this philosophy was also introduced into some of the educational programs of that day. They taught the rudiments of reading, writing, and arithmetic but they removed from the curriculum all references to God, the Ten Commandments, and any references to the mission of Jesus Christ.[12]

The implication of embracing the belief that there is *only* a physical dimension of reality is that this notion is an *exclusive* and not an *inclusive* idea. People who believe there is only a physical dimension are prone to think that people who believe there is also a spiritual and supernatural order are stupid, deluded, even insane. And there is a tendency to avoid, shun, or make laws that punish or eliminate such people. After all, if a person believes something exists that does not exist, are they not a threat to a healthy society? Joseph read in the material he

---

[12]Alma 30 and Mosiah 24. See Appendix B for a comparative chart to modern thought.

was translating that this distinction became so intense in this ancient society that at times it sentenced such people to death.

Second, there is another *axis* of belief that views the individual as the primary authority in educational matters, versus the notion that the society or the group is the primary source of authority in these endeavors.

Individual  Society

When these two axes are diagrammed to intersect at the center, one vertical and the other horizontal, *four quadrants—* directions or domains—for the development of contrasting educational programs become visibly evident. The quadrants of belief formed by these differing assumptions drive people in different directions when they pursue education or create and operate a school. It doesn't require a great deal of probing to discover a person's preferences. Proponents and opponents to these differing views have been very active in the history of American education, as well as in other nations. Notwith-standing the considerable variety of programs that may appear in each of the quadrants, the basic premises are easy to discern. We have a long history and many examples of schools that fall roughly into these four different categories. People cannot escape seeing the differences created by these conflicting assumptions if they are willing to face their own preferences. This can be visualized in a simple chart. (A more detailed explanation of these factors is found in Appendix A.)

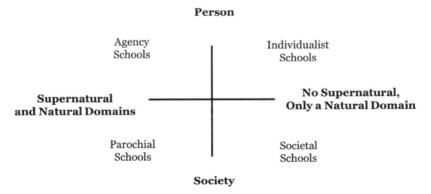

1. The *lower left quadrant* of authority sponsored the traditional form of schooling in early American history. It was religious or *parochial* in nature. This was a dominant pattern for education in Joseph Smith's day. Those who favor this realm believe there is both a natural and supernatural dimension to existence. They also presume that the authority of the church or some similar social institution takes precedence over the preferences of the individual. These assumptions are manifest in the organization, implementation, and methodology of instruction that are created, promoted, and used. *The church, not the individual, controls education.*

God	(empowers the church or social order)
↓	
Church	(empowers the school, selects curriculum and teachers)
↓	
Teacher	(directs and evaluates the student)
↓	
Student	(is accountable to the line of authority)

2. In the *lower right quadrant*, people reject the notion of a supernatural dimension to existence and presume reality to be simply a natural or physical domain. The assumption is clothed in a purely secular, naturalistic wardrobe. In this realm society also prevails over the individual as the primary source of authority. *The society, not the individual, controls education.*

Society	(empowers the government and the school)
↓	
School	(selects the curriculum and the teacher)
↓	
Teacher	(teacher directs and evaluates the student)
↓	
Student	(student is accountable to the line of authority)

3. In the *upper right quadrant*, people also reject the notion of a supernatural dimension to existence and presume that reality is simply a natural or physical domain. In this realm *the individual, not the society, is the primary source of* *authority.* The individual dictates education. The function of the child is to live his or her own life, not the life that his government, anxious parents, or some teacher who thinks he knows best, feels the child should live. The teacher, school, and government exist to serve the individual's desires. Autonomy and self-determination reign supreme. This type of education is often discussed, occasionally pursued, but seldom established.

Student   (directs his or her own learning)
↓
Teacher   (serves and enhances the students
↓   interests)
School   (provides teacher facilities and
↓   resources)
Society   (endorses and supports the
               educational program)

4. In the *upper left quadrant,* people accept the reality of both a supernatural and a natural domain. They may also acknowledge that each individual is composed of both a spiritual and physical dimension. In this realm, *primary authority and responsibility for personal education reside with the individual, but limitations and external expectations need to be acknowledged.* The individual is subject to and has an imperative interactive relationship with God. The individual may also have a vital, interactive, and responsible relationship with other persons who may assist in the teaching/learning process. Individuals also may have an interactive relationship with society—but society exists to serve and support rather than dictate in educational matters. Authority is derived from and manifest through each of these relationships. The family institution may play a vital role in this approach to education. (D&C 68:25–34). *It is in this quadrant that Joseph Smith's views of education fit most comfortably.*

In this quadrant, the individual is viewed as an *agent* with inherent freedoms for self-determination. But he or she also acknowledges a *supernatural influence* that gives context to his or her actions. Individuals are not autonomous; they are independent but have a shared relationship with authority. An individual in this domain accepts and honors the fact that others who may be the teachers also are accountable as individuals to the superior influence of supernatural authority. Therefore, all individuals stand on equal ground—each perceiving that social institutions exist to serve the interests of the individual, and not the other way around.[13]

Recognizing different and often conflicting commitments to these propositions helps one understand Joseph Smith's views of education and the foundations upon which these respective views rest. He was aware that no educational enterprise can safely extend beyond the foundation upon which it is built. The foundations of an educational program do invite inevitable consequences; they are significant. And in the final analysis it is *authority* that *validates* or *invalidates* the presuppositions that frame the foundations. It is folly to assume otherwise. *Joseph Smith was well aware of this phenomenon in all aspects of our lives.* All who are involved in education should give serious consideration to where they really stand on these basic matters. It is an important facet of personal integrity and helps shield one from hypocrisy.

The concept of authority is simple. For example, if a person has authorized access to a valid bank account that contains legitimate funds, they have legitimate monetary resources at their disposal. If they are not authorized, they do not have legitimate access to these funds.

---

[13] Joseph Smith endorsed the belief that "governments were instituted of God for the benefit of man; and that he holds men accountable for their acts in relation to them, both in making laws and administering them, for the good and safety of society. We believe that no government can exist in peace, except such laws are framed and held inviolate as will secure to each individual the free exercise of conscience, the right and control of property, and the protection of life" (D&C 134:1–2). It is evident that Joseph believed institutions exist to serve the individual; people are the end, organizations are the means to that end, and care should be taken not to confuse the two. See Appendix A for additional explanation.

Legitimate authority connects us to legitimate resources.

The opposite is also true. The potential consequences change.

Illegitimate authority connects us to illegitimate resources.

Likewise

Divine authority connects us to Divine resources.

Eternal authority connects us to Eternal resources.

"And [if] ye know the truth, . . . the truth shall make you free." (John 8:32)

PART V

HISTORICAL OPTIONS

The foregoing issues generally shape the educational efforts of humankind. What people believe about *God, Nature,* and *Man* dictate in one way or another how education is perceived, designed, and delivered. It is these three timeless pillars that Joseph Smith redefined for our day and then used to form the way he perceived and applied education. The consequences are numerous and significant. The most obvious is the way his views can chart a course through the general historical confusion that has filtered into our modern society and its various institutions. The history of education is long but its modern forms are not difficult to understand when one considers their origins. It makes a difference which ideas and assumptions a family or a school uses to direct the education of a child.

Three prominent historical examples that have influenced American society illustrate this point. (a) The ancient *Hebrews* had their views, as did (b) the *Greeks*, and so does (c) our *Modern Society*. The differences in these three worldviews are fundamental and often dramatic. All three have had a significant impact on American education and its practices. Each one has played an important role. Each one has characteristics that deserve to be understood.

Joseph Smith's roots, both genealogical and intellectual, were firmly planted in the Hebrew perspective, but his spiritual experiences led to significant refinements of this tradition. And these same roots helped him discern the nature of the Greek and Modern influences that were prominent in his day. When one understands the underlying premises it is unnecessary to get lost in the details that often promote confusion. Preoccupation with methods and subject matter is not the best place to begin in evaluating educational choices—despite the current tendencies of many people involved in education today.

Western culture is at present a social conglomerate of all three views vying for attention and allegiance. Some people would say our contemporary society is a hodgepodge of various combinations of these three intellectual tributaries. Contemporary American education emerged out of this multi-dispensational drainage of ideas. This was true in Joseph's day as well as our own. There has been a flood of conflicting notions then and now—many have come, and gone, and been recycled—which probably adds to the confusion. Compulsory apprenticeships, the "hickory" stick, required memorization and recitation, penmanship, cursive writing, rhetoric, Latin, one-room schools, consolidated schools, home schools, slates, blackboards, whiteboards, textbooks, laptops, smartphones, tablets—and the list goes on and on and on. Each of these has had its time in the limelight; each has its proponents and opponents. What is a person to do? Which of all the "schools" is true or most true? There seems to be no end to the educational revivals—with their various proponents crying "Lo here" or "Lo there." Educators today seem to have their modern "burned over districts," just as sectarians had their revivalist periods in previous centuries. Joseph Smith was confronted by this in spiritual matters. *Which church was true?* Modern conflicts over *temporal salvation* are quite similar in nature. *Which schooling is the best?*

This ongoing debate has washed over but failed to erode the educational premises held by Joseph Smith. He refined and perpetuated the views of his Hebrew heritage in both thought and act. The principles he espoused are recorded and the efforts to implement them continue to this day and time. The encompassing propositions he restored and instituted continue to stand as an ensign against which one can evaluate the respective elements of each of these three dominant tributaries to modern educational programs and practices. Without such standards of evaluation it is difficult to discern what is *good, better,* and *best* from that which is *dangerous, bad,* and *destructive.* The Hebrew, Greek, and Modern views are not the same. There is a difference between truth and substitutes for the truth. The challenge is to discern these differences.

People find it helpful when they understand the basic ideas underlying each of these major divergent historical traditions of belief. Each one has tumbled down through time and ended on our doorstep. Adherents to one or the other abound. A basic perception of these traditions sets in relief and highlights the unique significance of Joseph Smith's view of education. A brief summary of some of the conflicting elements could read like this:

The *Hebrew* premise is that God created (1) man and woman, (2) the world on which humankind lives, and (3) the universe in which Earth is situated. Contemporary Western culture has now essentially rejected these three premises because the primary referent is God. Joseph Smith was alerted to this impending condition when he translated a prophetic warning in the Book of Mormon text. He learned from this document that an early writer had seen in vision our day. This early historian offered the following description of our culture that God had given to him:

> Behold, in the last days . . . all the nations, . . . those who come to this land and those who shall be upon other lands, yea even upon all the lands of the earth, behold, they will be drunken with iniquity and all manner of abominations. . . . This people draw near unto me with their mouth, and with their lips do honor me, but have removed their hearts far from me, and their fear towards me is taught by the precepts of men. . . . They shall contend one with another . . . and they shall teach with their learning, and deny the Holy Ghost, which giveth utterance. . . . they deny the power of God; . . . and they say unto the people: Hearken unto us, and hear ye our precept; for behold there is no God today. . . . Yea and there shall be many which will say: Eat, drink, and be merry, for tomorrow we die; and it shall be well with us. And there shall also be many who will say: Eat, drink, and be merry; nevertheless, fear God—he will justify in committing a little sin; yea, lie a little, take the advantage of one because of his words, dig a pit for thy neighbor; there is no harm in this; and do all these things, for tomorrow we die; and if it so be that if we are guilty, God will beat us with a few stripes, and at last we shall be saved in the kingdom of God. Yea, and there shall be many which shall teach after this manner, false and vain and foolish doctrines, and shall be puffed up in their hearts, and shall seek deep to hide their counsels from the Lord; and their works shall be in the dark. (2 Nephi 27 and 28)

The *Modern* view, which seems to be a major object of the warning given above, is very different. It rejects the Hebrew premises of a personal God who is the father of our spirit body and substitutes another path. Modernism offers several evolving options: ranging from the traditional (a) "God" is a mystery, to god is an un-embodied force; (b) then the option moves toward God is nature; and (c) the current promoted notion that perhaps Man is god—if one has to apply the title. The educator John Dewey, for example, expressed this latter view when he said "god" is the power to create mental images and convert those images into action.[14] This premise makes man's intellect "god." Whatever path was followed, modern American education no longer holds to the *prime educational value* of the Hebrew, which is to become as God is, by *doing what God says and does.* Many people still favor this view, but it is no longer acceptable as a national ideal or an educational objective in the public domain. These modern views make a big difference. Once embraced, they can lead to rejecting or changing the God-given institutions of moral standards and the role of marriage and the family. When man presumes to be "God," then everything tends to become relative and not imperative. People do whatever they want to do, when they want to do it, and how they want to do it—with little regard for the consequences. Order is lost; confusion reigns, and suffering increases. Life without God is life with less meaning when compared to Joseph's views.

The ancient Hebrew notion that God is a person—an immortal being, our Father, the same yesterday, today, and forever—has now essentially been replaced with *secular humanistic policy* in popular and political circles. The old Hebrew view was significantly blurred: first, by the people's rejection of authorized prophets and apostles, then by substituting a merger of Christian theology with *Greek philosophy* during the early centuries A.D. The Hebrew/ Christian concepts of Sin, the Fall, a need for a Redeemer, an Atonement, a physical Resurrection, and God as a person with body parts and passions—all became debatable. The original concepts of marriage and the family were abused and misused (Romans 1:16–32). These topics were repeatedly fashioned and

---

[14]See John Dewey *A Common Faith*, pp. 48, 51.

refashioned over the centuries and continue to be. Subsequently, such doctrines have essentially been distorted or set aside in American public discourse. Court rulings during the twentieth century separated religious doctrines from government-related practice. America's "Christian" heritage is now increasingly disavowed in public education, state, and federal institutions. The notion of Providence has largely evaporated from public discourse. It is an old story with familiar outcomes.

Today's social secularization of education would have troubled Joseph as deeply as did the conflicting creeds of the religions during his day.[15] Joseph saw education as a way to honor, not avoid, God's role in human affairs. Compartmentalizing one's beliefs by using the shield of "separation of church and state" does not change the consequences of educational outcomes. When the idea of God is distorted or eliminated from education, there are consequences. This is not the first time this evasive strategy has been invoked. It's an ancient issue in many cultures. Such is evident in the storyline of ancient Greece, which has largely evaporated from modern texts and discourse. The serious study of history is no longer a popular part of our public curriculum, unless it has first been or is now being *revised*. Revisionist history does seem to be *increasingly prevalent* in modern textbooks. Without belaboring the point, consider the following paragraphs as a historical brief. This summary illustrates how much like our day were the process and the conditions that contributed to the demise of ancient Greece—then Rome. Sometimes a little history can bring a helpful clarification to modern concerns.[16]

---

[15]Joseph Smith clearly understood the warning that was issued by God regarding America as a land of promise. "And now, we can behold the decrees of God concerning this land, that it is a land of promise; and whatsoever nation shall possess it shall serve God, or they shall be swept off when the fullness of his wrath shall come upon them. And the fullness of his wrath cometh upon them when they are ripened in iniquity. . . . And this cometh unto you, O ye Gentiles, that ye may know the decrees of God—that ye may repent, and not continue in your iniquities until the fullness come. . . . Behold, this is a choice land, and whatsoever nation shall possess it shall be free from bondage, and from captivity, and from all other nations under heaven, if they will but serve the God of the land, who is Jesus Christ." (Ether 2:9–12)

[16]Appendix B exhibits a chart of prominent personalities who have promoted the same arguments Korihor espoused in the material which Joseph Smith

For example, our modern transition from a *sacred* to a *secular* perspective in western culture was a rerun of a similar change in ancient Greek society. However one may view the imperfect supernatural characters described in the *Iliad* and the *Odyssey*—Zeus, Hera his wife, and their twelve children, the gods of Mt. Olympus—they did represent a cultural image of supernatural authority; an image that was ultimately rejected by the intellectual community. The philosophical ideal expressed in Plato's *Republic* and the works of other Greek enlightenment theorists moved people away from the concept of Deity as a person. The Golden Age of Greece embraced a new view of authority, a type of *secular psychology* founded on reason and rhetoric. Basically, it was the notion implied in the Greek word *encyclopedia*: put your foot in the center of the universe and seek *knowledge*, in order to *admire, appreciate, and celebrate* the Cosmos.

Knowing became the *prime educational value for Greek intellectuals*. The Sophists, a new vocation of teachers, made a lucrative profession of promoting this emerging view in their society. The celebration and appeasement of the traditional anthropomorphic "gods with bodies" faded. The idea of "God" was no longer conceived as a person. Greek culture was effectively "modernized." And the concept of human destiny changed. The new idea of the individual was that a person is to become a disembodied transient intellect, capable of fusing with the Cosmic Mind, rather than an eternal embodied personality. This concept flourished.[17] Society changed because

---

translated and is found in the Book of Mormon.

[17]The story of Greek influence on early Christianity and later western education is long and tangled. It involves the shifting views attending the Greek Enlightenment (500–300 B.C.) and the merging of Greek philosophy with a struggling Christian population's ideology following the death of Jesus Christ and his twelve apostles. An extensive examination of these matters can be found in *History of the Church*, vol. 1, Introduction (written by B.H. Roberts); Friedrich Solmsen, *Intellectual Experiments of the Greek Enlightenment*, in which he notes that "the result was a psychology established on a purely secular basis, with no need for divine causation"; all of Werner Jaeger's *Early Christianity and Greek Paideia*, 1961, particularly pp. 30, 90; Augustine's *Confessions* and *On Christian Doctrine*; P.E. More, *Hellenistic Philosophies*, 1923; *The Anti Nicene Fathers* (9 volumes); W.H.C. Frend, *The Rise of Chrisitanity*, 1984; J. L. Barker, *Apostasy from the Divine Church*, 1960; Edwin Hatch, *The Influence of Greek Ideas on Christianity*, 1957; Hugh Nibley, *The World and the Prophets*, 1960, p. 35.

basic beliefs and education changed. This seems always to be the case, whether those beliefs were considered mythological or real. Once it starts, it's difficult to stop.

The new view for the Greeks was exhilarating; secular excitement in Greek culture stimulated admirable temporal achievements that dazzled not only themselves and later Rome, but ultimately modern Western education. Science, art, music, and a great variety of divergent schools of thought flourished. The power and the fruits of the human intellect were compelling. As a consequence, influential people reveled in the idea that man's ultimate positive destiny was to *abandon his or her personal identity* and become one with the *Cosmic Mind.* For the Greek intellectual community, it was the Cosmos that was eternal—the same yesterday, today, and tomorrow—not the individual or a personal God. This was apparently a byproduct of the idea that Paul, the Hebrew apostle, challenged when he visited Athens and tangled with the doctors at the Parthenon on Mars Hill.[18] The devotions of the Greeks were in shambles. They even sought to cover their concerns about the future by constructing an altar to THE UNKNOWN GOD—who Paul said was a product of superstition and ignorance.

This fits well with the secular mood of that day. It sustained the Platonic notion of *philosopher/kings* and complemented the science of the day. *Knowledge based on reason* was the key to this eternal connection; everything else seemed temporary. Crime was possible. People could commit errors. But there was no word in their language for *sin.* The idea of a fall, a redeemer, an atonement, or physical resurrection, simply didn't fit into the mindset of Greek education or the Roman version that followed. Centuries later, the merging of this Greco-Roman perspective with early and late medieval Christianity was indeed *philosophy mingled with scripture.* The basis of transition from the past to the then unforeseen future was set in motion. An influence that was to tantalize *modern education* was born. Joseph Smith did experience some of the impact of this movement in his day; and we are experiencing a subsequent and more pervasive and intense version in our day. The consequences are real and seem to be almost unavoidable.

---

[18]See Acts 17:16–34.

33

The seemingly random merging of these two old contradictory worldviews with the added and conflicting perspective of the modern post-industrial world, has created an indescribable tangle of educational ideas. An intellectual trip through modern educational thought for many, if not most, people creates a distinct, unsettled feeling. It is akin to viewing an old house composed of multiple and indiscriminate add-ons—a room here and a room there. There is a sense of ongoing striving to assemble something from a loose assortment of rather jumbled factors. For serious seekers, it can be somewhat like a stroll through an *intellectual junkyard*—looking for something of value to retrieve. Once one enters the realm of abstraction, what is real and concrete can become increasingly blurred. The clearly documented history of modern education makes it evident why such could be the case. The traditions from which many aspects of modern systems of education are formed constitute a jumble of ideas and practices that were not derived from, or even associated with, the same basic assumptions. It's more like an impulsive structure formed from salvage. When that becomes the constructed vehicle it can leave much to be desired.

Little wonder that our dominant educational edifice looks like it does—a structure without an architect, and competing contractors vying for recognition. The resulting sense of existing uncertainty alone offers a fairly compelling reason for one to wonder how we got from where we came from to where we are now. At least it seems so. That is one very good reason to consider Joseph Smith's views, and to recognize that *reconstruction* is not the same as *restoration* when it comes to truth—particularly in matters of education. When it comes to learning and teaching, it is worthwhile to consider whether there is something better than what we have and particularly what might be popular at the moment in educational practice.

Lest we forget, the foregoing picture is not new. The records of antiquity (life on earth before the great flood) indicate that many similarities and practices were common to that era. People rejected God and substituted knowledge and theories of their own. Deeming themselves very much in control, they advanced many theories for honors, power, and gain. The focus became:

34

Creating military hardware and rule by force.

Manufacturing jewelry, cosmetics, and fashionable dress.

Presenting scientific formulas to explain nature and the universe.

Controlling the environment.

Pursuing gold, silver, and precious stones.

Engaging in all manner of licentious indulgence.

Establishing synagogues, schools, and museums.[19]

Joseph Smith, Columbus, and George Washington

If one desires to retain clarity in educational matters, it is helpful to keep in mind that basic "plain and precious truths" can easily be ignored, distorted or lost. Joseph Smith was given the advantage of exposure to some of these fundamentals when he translated into English the information contained in the Book of Mormon: Another Testament of Jesus Christ into English. A prominent theme in that book details, in clear and simple language, the discovery of a promised land and the story behind the creation of a divinely shaped nation based on freedom for its citizenry. This is the story of America—its discovery, development, and opportunity for prosperity or destruction (1 Nephi 22:7; 13:14; 2 Nephi 26:15; 27:1–2; Ether 2:8–12; 8:20–26). The account specifically explains how a man from the Old World would be inspired to set in motion the factors that would lead to a New World settlement. This person was Columbus, an imperfect but religious man who said of himself,

> God made me the messenger of the new heaven and new earth of which he spoke in the Apocalypse of St. John after having spoken of it through the mouth of Isaiah; and he showed me the spot where to find it.[20]

---

[19]See Hugh Nibley, *Enoch the Prophet* (Salt Lake City: Deseret Book, 1986, pp. 184–186); Also PGP Moses 5, 6, 7, 8.

[20]Quoted in Pauline Moffitt Watts, "Prophecy and Discovery: On Spiritual Origins of Christopher Columbus's 'Enterprise of the Indies,'" *The American*

35

A twentieth century successor of Joseph Smith, Ezra Taft Benson, confirmed Columbus's personal explanation with his witness when he said:

> God inspired "a man among the Gentiles" (1 Nephi 13:12) who, by the Spirit of God was led to rediscover the land of America and bring this rich new land to the attention of the people in Europe. That man, of course, was Christopher Columbus, who testified that he was inspired in what he did. "Our Lord," said Columbus, "unlocked my mind, sent me upon the sea, and gave me fire for the deed. Those who heard of my enterprise called it foolish, mocked me, and laughed. But who can doubt that the Holy Ghost inspired me?" (Jacob Wasserman, Columbus, Don Quixote of the Seas, pp.19–20). It is assuring to know that this nation has a prophetic history, that all of the great events that have transpired here, including the coming of Columbus, the Pilgrim Fathers, and the War of Independence, were foreseen by ancient prophets (1 Nephi 13:10–19).[21]

These kinds of statements may make some modern historians nervous; nevertheless, they do exist—to be heeded, ignored, or denied. Meanwhile, the evidence of their validity continues to increase in kind and exposure. And the message they express is part of Joseph Smith's view of what the curriculum should contain, and it fits into the larger explanation of the kind of education he preferred that the people have. It is information that indicates God's role in what is happening to his children.

The records associated with the founding of this nation attest that under the influence of persecution, many of the early American settlers came here because they felt this land was a

---

Historical Review, February 1985, p. 73.

See also a contextual examination of Columbus's life and mission in Neil J Flinders' "Christopher Columbus: 'The Spirit of God . . .Wrought Upon the Man,'" paper presented at the Quincentennial Lecture Series Celebrating the Arrival of Christopher Columbus in the Americas, Brigham Young University, Provo, Utah. November 18, 1992.

[21]Ezra Taft Benson *The Teachings of Ezra Taft Benson* (Salt Lake City: Bookcraft, 1988).

blessing from God—a covenant place of refuge. The Puritans in England, for example, became Separatists, then exiled Pilgrims. They sought diligently for relief. William Bradford, long-time governor of "Plimmoth Plantation" [Plymouth Colony], expressed the spiritual feeling of his group when he said they came with

> great hope and [the] inward zeal . . . of laying some good foundation . . . for the propagating and advancing of the gospel of the Kingdom of Christ in those remote parts of the world. Yea, though they should be even as stepping stones unto others for the performing of so great a work.[22]

The story continues to unfold as the Founding Fathers of this nation led the fight for independence and won, largely thanks to supernatural assistance. The recognition of this "firm reliance on the protection of Divine Providence" enabled our forebears to declare themselves to be free and independent. George Washington was so committed to this concept that he led his congressional associates through a *covenant-making* sequence at his first inaugural ceremony. The Father of our country placed his hand on an opened Bible, opened to Genesis 49:22–26. This is the passage where Joseph (who was sold into Egypt) is promised that his posterity, as part of the House of Israel, would inherit a promised land and receive God-given blessings. (This account is consistent with the prophecy of this same Joseph that is recorded in the Book of Mormon, who foretold the mission that his descendant, Joseph Smith, would fulfill in this nation.) Following the inauguration ceremony in New York, President Washington "led his congress to St. Paul's chapel, where they prayed and asked God to accept their offering and invoke the New American Covenant just as ancient Israel had made their covenant thousands of years earlier."[23] Federal Hall and other locations in the early colonies contain

---

[22]V. M. Hall William Bradford's History (1901 edition) as quoted in *Christian History of the Constitution*, pp. 191–93.

[23]Ryan Fisher, "The Nephite Explorer," Part 4. (Documentary; see www.nephiteexplorer.com). See also Timothy Ballard, *The Covenant: America's Sacred and Immutable Connection to Ancient Israel*, Salt Lake City: Deseret Book, 2012; *The Covenant: One Nation Under God*, vol. 1, Salt Lake City: Deseret Book, 2013; *The Covenant: One Nation Under God*, vol. 1, Salt Lake City: Deseret Book, 2013.

additional signs and symbols of the strong connections between ancient Israel and our covenant-making founding fathers. The origin of this nation was not a historical accident, it was a divine venture. And education was an important aspect of that venture.

Joseph Smith certainly captured and promoted this spiritual connection between America, its founding documents, and the competing counterforces at work in this enterprise. In 1833, Joseph Smith reported a revealed endorsement by the Lord regarding the significance of

> the laws and constitution of the people, which I have suffered to be established, and should be maintained for the rights and protection of all flesh according to just and holy principles. That every man may act in doctrine and principle pertaining to futurity, according to the moral agency which I have given unto him, that every man may be accountable for his own sins in the day of judgment. Therefore, it is not right that any man should be in bondage one to another. And for this purpose have I established the Constitution of this land, by the hands of wise men whom I raised up unto this very purpose, and redeemed the land by the shedding of blood. (D&C 101:77–80)

According to Joseph Smith, this is the perspective of the nature and purpose that should drive our educational efforts. When the citizenry stray or depart from this perspective, the welfare of our society is in jeopardy.

While living in Nauvoo and perhaps elsewhere, Joseph frequently expressed his concerns about how this nation was being governed. He was very familiar with political persecution. One sentiment regarding this nation he is ascribed by various people as having expressed, is that

> even this nation will be on the very verge of crumbling to pieces and tumbling to the ground, and when the Constitution is upon the brink of ruin, this people will be the staff upon which the nation shall lean, and they shall bear the Constitution away from the very verge of

destruction.[24]

Character rooted in righteous principles was a cherished theme. There is little doubt that Joseph had premonition-like feelings regarding the fragile nature of freedom and liberty. He was personally sensitive to the abuse and selfish application of power, the inevitable consequences of apathy and misguided intent, and the potential cruelty inherent in political control of centralized authority. The role for a benevolent Providence was an imperative element in the personal welfare of both individuals and institutions. Without such, a stabilizing influence and presence the consequences are undesirable, if not dire and destructive. America, like ancient Israel, is dependent upon Divine Providence for its safety and prosperity. And, like ancient Israel, the inhabitants of this promised land are bound by a covenant that has both positive and negative stipulations. There is abundant evidence this is not a secret; it is a truth that is only hidden by ignorance, apathy or willful disdain (see BM Ether 2:7–12; numerous Biblical references; and even in fictional literature, e. g. Jonathan Cahn's *The Harbinger*).

---

[24]July 19, 1840, as recorded by Martha Jane Knowlton Coray; ms. in Church Historian's Office, Salt Lake City; Joseph Smith Papers, LDS Church Historical Archives, Box 1, March 10, 1844

PART VI

FROM THERE AND THEN TO HERE AND NOW

The larger historical path that led from the ideological conflicts of antiquity, to the perplexity in Joseph Smith's day, and on to present-day educational concerns is quite clear. The trek was away from (a) revealed *doctrine, principles, and practices* through (b) *philosophy, logic, and rhetoric* to (c) *hypothesis, experiments, and scientific theory.* The intellectual divide over which education passed was precarious; it traveled through deep canyons between three great peaks: the *Reformation, Renaissance*, and *Enlightenment.* These three monuments to change emerged from the landscape of Western culture during the fifteenth through the eighteenth centuries. They created striking alterations in the cultural landscape, the results of socially seismic activity, and influenced the formation of modern education. Reasons for sending children to school changed and changed and changed. So did the nature of their schooling—as it happened then and as it is happening now. The various developments created and continue to create an exciting epoch of both positive and very questionable outcomes. Certain basic issues, however, remain.

For example, these three great movements that spawned the modern world sufficiently uprooted traditional autocratic and dictatorial rule to lay a foundation for individual freedom and forms of liberty-driven democratic social order. This kind of liberty was new. The leverage for such change was provided by a spirit of personal exploration, a remarkable increase in literacy, an advanced vision of human transportation, and inventions that make our physical lives much easier. The printing press was invented, explorers seemed to go in every direction, and individuals flexed their capacity to decide for themselves in both religious and secular matters. As noted, the real but battle-scarred result was the discovery of a new world, new opportunity for individual growth, and a redistribution of governing powers from birthright, wealth, and brute force to the population at large. A major impetus for these activities

41

seemed to be a pervasive spiritual exhilaration not associated with any particular religious organization. Just as desires for personal freedom emerged from the cracks and crevices to challenge slavery and demagoguery, so a similar battle persists in various forms today.

The previously mentioned Greek influence, among others, is evident in our modern history. Change continues to be with us. It is an ancient pattern, like a larger-than-life rerun of the Golden Age of Greece (ca. fifth century B.C.). As it had in a past era, western culture experienced an energetic *Enlightenment* that pushed forth a modern *science*; an exhilarating *Renaissance* provided a new *humanities*; the liberation of a *Reformation of protest* in personal belief gave birth to a multitude of new religious sects and a powerful urge for civil freedom. Elements of the past became deeply entwined with concepts of the future. The tension lines tightened, and when plucked vibrated with violence. Wars and rumors of wars proliferated. This seems to be our social order now. Internal and external enigmas abound. The body politic is quivering. Economic confidence is hardly what one would call stable.

Looking back, education seems hardly equal to the task of establishing order, equity, or justice. In some ways the gateways to greater civilized conduct burst open, but people were hardly prepared to do unto others as they would have others do unto them. Temporal prosperity overran moral discipline. As it had been, so it was again; a flood of freedom carried with it a significant amount of chaotic debris and collateral confusion. The social order grew and expanded as the moral order wobbled with a new form of dizzy indifference. The fresh options in religion, the professions, and social relations ironically seemed to invite new forms of apathy. Sound familiar? It should, because we continue to feel the aftershocks decade after decade. The daily deluge of media places before us a continuous display of ideas in conflict.

This is not unlike the world into which Joseph Smith was born (1805)—nineteenth century America. In his day, the great shift that moved people away from a belief in a universe created from two building blocks—spirit and matter—to a belief that all reality is simply physical matter, was just an embryonic image in the New World. It was still in incubation. But the stage was clearly being set in American culture for the birth of *secularism*;

a monumental transition in the power structure was about to occur. Co-religionists in Joseph's day could not explain what *spirit* was and they did not agree on how to define an abstract God. This deficiency was eventually to prove largely indefensible in the face of a rapidly changing scientific and technological world. The conflict between *faith* and *reason* expanded and intensified. Temporal progress tested spiritual tradition. Machines to do our labor produced a prosperity that dimmed the need for saving souls. Prosperity had a numbing affect. What we had and now wanted more of, blurred the sense of who we were and what our future might become. The prize being sought was here and now, more than there and then what? Conventional religion became suspect for many.

Consequently, a monumental shift occurred during the late nineteenth and early twentieth centuries, first among academic intellectuals and subsequently on Main Street USA. Between 1880 and 1920 a transition in thought became comfortably entrenched among a critical mass of intellectuals. A new set of assumptions were being embraced. Control of higher education changed hands; a new administrative order moved into the old educational buildings. The stone, wood, brick, and mortar structures built with consecrated funds for moral and spiritual purposes over many centuries were confiscated in a few decades by nonbelievers. Institutions of learning founded on religious premises became agnostic and atheistic. As one writer put it, our *cathedrals of learning* turned into *citadels of secularism*. The nature of the schools and universities changed. *Secular humanism became a new religious order for those who embraced modern skepticism.* It was now convenient to believe and teach that *creation* could be viewed as spontaneous, accidental, evolutionary, or benevolent chance. To the skeptical mind this view was more persuasive than belief in a mysterious, incomprehensible power that fashioned the universe out of nothing.[25] The roots for traditional morality were severed.

---

[25]Medieval Christianity developed a philosophical theory of creation known as *ex nihilo*, meaning "out of nothing." The popularity of Greek Platonic philosophy in the schools of the third and fourth centuries created a number of serious doctrinal conflicts. Among these were (a) the nature of creation, (b) God not having a physical body, and (c) the impossibility of a physical resurrection. Consider three examples: (1) Because matter was considered corrupt (imperfect), it was unthinkable that God would have created the

"Cathedrals of Learning" – 19th *Century High School*

---

world from physical elements. Thus Augustine would write, "God made all things which he did not beget of himself, not of those things that already existed, but of those things that did not exist at all, that is, of nothing. . . . For there was not anything of which he could make them." (St. Augustine, *Concerning the Nature of God*, ch. XXVI.) (2) Because matter was considered corrupt, it was unthinkable that God would take upon himself a physical body. Therefore, the early church fathers would write, "And if God is declared to be a body, then He will also be found to be material, since every body is composed of matter. But if He be composed of matter, and matter is undoubtedly corruptible, then according to them, God is liable to corruption." (*Anti-Nicene Fathers* vol. IV, p. 277). (3) Because matter was considered corrupt it was unthinkable that God would provide that man be eternally united to a resurrected body. So Celsus would argue, "Who beheld the risen Jesus? A half frantic woman, as you state, and some other person, perhaps, of those who were engaged in the same system of delusion, who had either dreamed so, owing to a peculiar state of mind, or, under the influence of a wandering imagination, had formed to himself an appearance according to his own wishes, which has been the case with numberless individuals." (Celsus. See Origen, "Against Celsus," ii, 55, A.D. 170). J. R. Dummelow also asserts that "Many who reject the traditional belief in a corporeal resurrection . . . find a mediating position . . . [in the] theory . . . of a 'spiritual resurrection'." (*Bible Commentary*, p. cxxvi).

"Citadels of Secularism" – 21st Century High School

Joseph Smith's educational position, preserved and protected by others long after his death, confronted these very questionable options with a viable alternative. And this position was articulated with an incredulously simple clarity. [26] The contrast was stark then, and became even more visible as the years rolled on. The Church and its functions were to become, as he was told, "independent" of all other systems "beneath the celestial world" (D&C 78:14).

Religious instruction and belief in Joseph's day were poised on the edge of this turmoil. He lived on the cusp of the great change that was destined to spawn a full-fledged *secular*

---

[26]In contrast to these three positions, Joseph Smith wrote: (1) Regarding creation, "We [the gods] will go down, for there is space there, and we will take of these materials, and we will make an earth whereon these may dwell." (Abraham 3:24). "Now, the word create . . . does not mean to create out of nothing; it means to organize; . . . God had materials to organize the world, . . . which is element . . . which can never be destroyed; they may be organized and re-organized, but not destroyed. They had no beginning, and can have no end" (*Teachings of the Prophet Joseph Smith*, pp. 350–52; see also D&C 93:33). (2) Regarding God having a physical body, "The Father has a body of flesh and bones as tangible as man's; the Son also" (D&C 130:22). (3) Concerning the resurrection, "notwithstanding they shall die, they shall also rise again . . . [and] receive the same [but immortal] body" D&C 88:27–28; see also D&C 93:33).

society in America—a society based on what has been called the *secularization hypothesis: the more we learn about the secular, the less need there is for the spiritual.* And this brings us back to the issue of *authority,* which can now be considered within a context that displays greater clarity and appreciation for what Joseph Smith espoused as a minister of education. His views were radical to the educators and co-religionists of his day. Now, two centuries later, they appear even more sweepingly prophetic, and perhaps to some, frustratingly enigmatic—hard to accept, difficult to ignore. Today's theory and practice of education are considered by many to be a quivering structure, increasingly fragile. When placed next to the propositions Joseph Smith put forth, the modern enterprise fades in comparison, seemingly ignoring crucial issues. Both in its scope of purpose and its vision for learning and teaching, contemporary American education falls dramatically short due to one major flaw: *Current educational methods, media, technology, and achievements, admirable as they may seem, increasingly appear out of touch with a viable moral order.*[27] This breeds uneasiness, civil unrest, a growing public concern and incessant conflict.

Ironically, much of the good gained by modern society has been lost or remains in jeopardy because *moral imperatives* were freely exchanged for *ethical relativism.* In street language that means *there are no absolutes;* anything goes if it feels good or if some group says it's okay. *"When in Rome, do what the Romans do" drives much of contemporary behavior.* Ease of life and a number of positive benefits (great developments such as motor-driven machinery, the waning of official oppression upon women and children, movement away from politically endorsed slavery, and increased longevity, economic prosperity, among other things) have been accompanied by various fundamental *moral cancers.* Marriage and the family are ignored, redefined, or dismissed as irrelevant. Dramatic and disturbing statistics tell the story. It seems that the better off society has become *temporally,* the worse off it has become morally and *spiritually.* As is overtly manifest in our schools, America is increasingly turning away from God and his purposes to a variety of alternatives. At its core this is the

---

[27]See Appendix C.

46

classic educational issue: *Does man need God to help him (her) define and sustain a viable moral order? Or can man do this by his own power?* In light of current evidence, the ancient question returns, "What shall it profit a man, if he shall gain the whole world and lose his own soul?" (Mark 8:36) Joseph Smith offered a clear and simple solution. He was taught and believed in the messages delivered to him by remarkable tutors. These tutors will be identified in the next section. First, consider one other aspect of Joseph's insight into the process of education as it relates to maturation.

A Glimpse into Joseph Smith's View of Youth

In addition to the forgoing large cultural waves of change, there are the more intimate, less theoretical, social realities that also impact learning and teaching. Joseph did not overlook these. One example, among many that defined people's lives differently in Joseph's day is the transition from childhood to adulthood. There was no adolescent peer group, as such as developed in the twentieth century. The so-called teenage years of junior high and high school age group (13–18) did not have the group identity that now exists. A child's physical development and the needs of his or her family for labor dictated the expectations—not age or grade in school. Yes, puberty is a significant part of life—it always has been—but in the 1800s it did not bring with it much in the way of temporary privileges like it does today. There were few, if any, child labor or mandatory attendance laws to provide youth the opportunities to develop their talents, engage in education, seek social experiences, or just hang out as a group. If you were a child you were treated as a child; if you were not, you were essentially treated as an adult. The variable was simply what kind of work are you capable of doing. In a nontypical way Joseph Smith seemed to have a sensitivity to both the strengths and weaknesses of this common cultural reality. He had a concept of "youth." He recognized adolescence but also understood its vulnerable characteristics.

Youth were not just children or adults, and they were not to be abused, doted on, or coddled. They were to be serious, productive, and respectful. In the midst of exercising their abundant youthful energy, self-discipline remained a justified expectation. Joseph wanted the youth to make a contribution while they were growing and developing into adults. One writer who studied life in Nauvoo relates the enthusiastic praise Joseph Smith expressed to Heber C. Kimball, who developed the *Young Gentleman's and Young Ladies Relief Society of Nauvoo.*

> It began simply as a small and casual chit-chat gathering. But week by week more youth came and bigger and bigger meeting places were arranged. Once when the group met in the large room above the Prophet's store, he came to speak to them. He praised Elder Kimball for helping organize this "good and glorious work," complimented the youth on their good conduct, "and taught them how to behave in all places, explained to them their duties, and advised them to organize themselves into a society for the relief of the poor." Specifically, he asked them to fund and then build a house for a brother who was lame. In response, the youth drew up a constitution, elected officers, called monthly meetings, and opened their membership to anyone under age thirty in Nauvoo— LDS or not, including young men and "the tender, lovely and beautiful females of our city.[28]

This report seems to capture Joseph's uncommon perspective regarding the youth. Many other accounts exist of how he felt about and related to children and youth. But we do not have in the records that are available as much as it would be nice to know. What we do know is that Joseph was not trapped by some of the less desirable beliefs and practices that were common in his day. He seemed to be intuitively ahead of his times in matters of positive human relationships.

---

[28]William G. Hartley "Joseph Smith and Nauvoo's Youth" *Ensign,* September 1979.

PART VII

JOSEPH SMITH'S TUTORS

No person can become a truly great educator without first becoming an effective student worthy of becoming authorized. *Learning is equal in importance to teaching.* Joseph learned this lesson early. Learners cannot remain on *educational welfare* and succeed; nor can they flourish without the input of qualified tutors. The willing student needs the assistance of qualified teachers—those who can empower his or her qualification. Joseph Smith was a focused learner; his deepest desire was to become a qualified teacher and perform well. He had an extraordinary preparation, as well as remarkable and continuous in-service training suitable for his personal mission. This exceptional instruction is obviously an important key to the unique educational enterprise he initiated. In just twenty-four years he laid the foundations and sketched the future pattern for a remarkable learning/teaching institution upon which his successors continue to build. This was no ordinary venture; it was an endeavor that not only spanned the continents of this world, but extended into eternity. This is why he needed a special faculty to prepare him to be a *minister of education*—a minister who perceived and pointed toward an expanding program of education defined as

An individual function

A family obligation

A church responsibility

A state interest

When these factors are jumbled, educational chaos is inevitable.

Joseph was born into a supportive family. Whatever his native talents, they were enhanced by the love and emotional support of his immediate family. The social and financial circumstances of his parents, however, restricted his exposure to formal education. His boyhood schooling was limited or shielded, whichever one chooses to believe. But during his teenage years, the desires of his heart led him into a vital and unique personal experience. He sought and received an

49

audience with God the Father, his Son, Jesus Christ, and the distinct influence of the Holy Ghost. This experience was followed with numerous tutorials by former prophets and servants of God who had long since passed beyond the veil of mortality. This cadre of teachers constituted the faculty from which he obtained his knowledge and direction. They were individuals with divine commissions to prepare him for his work. Though Joseph sought no personal recognition by identifying himself with his teachers, the recorded impact of their influence remains. In Joseph's case, these mentors seem to have had a very good influence.

Among the additional personalities, beyond those already mentioned, who enriched his knowledge were Adam, Seth, Enoch, and Noah; Moses, Elias, and Elijah; Peter, James, and John; John the Baptist, others of Jesus's Twelve Apostles in the Holy Land, and the Twelve appointed disciples in the New World; Paul the apostle, Moroni, Abraham, Isaac, Jacob, and apparently many others. These were instructors who understood humankind. They knew the origin, nature, and destiny of God's children and all that pertained to them. A primary result of this process of preparation was, as Joseph Smith could say to his earthly associates, *"I have the whole plan of the kingdom before me, and no other person has."* This was not an expression of braggadocio, it was for him simply a statement of fact. Not only did it reflect his knowledge, it revealed the authenticity of his *authority*.[29] It was an authority he seldom referred to but always seemed to emulate.

An elusive benefit Joseph did receive from his angelic mentors, besides information, is sometimes overlooked. This is the *confidence* he gained from his personal contact with these personalities and what they represented. However brief or extensive these contacts may have been, they had a significant, if subtle, impact. They not only made a difference in Joseph's life, they made a difference in Joseph—what he thought and the way he felt. Consider the appeal that drives people to seek autographs from famous personalities. Why does this happen?

---

[29]See HC 5:139; *Joseph Smith–History*; John Taylor JD 21:94; D&C 128:20–21; 110:1–16; Truman Madsen, *Joseph Smith the Prophet*, p. 44; D&C 13, 27); H. Donl Peterson in his article "Moroni," cites 59 different personalities who actually appeared to Joseph Smith or communicated with him in vision.

Is it because there is something of potential value in a personal contact with another person? This may be subtle and difficult to define, but evidence suggests it is also real and may be significant. When that person has attained and exhibited accomplishments worthy of recognition or fame it can have considerable value. The list of names cited above is surely qualified to fit in this category. There is some truth in the old saying *"It isn't what you know, it's who you know."* Yes, such experiences can be misused—even abused; vanity can distort a good thing by corrupting it with wrong and self-serving applications. But quite the opposite can also be the outcome. The influences can be for good. They can enhance a person's motivation, self-identification, and self-confidence. Would you like to meet with the above named group?

As most educators learn—sooner or later—acquiring *confidence* is essential to becoming successful. The experiences Joseph had with these personages had a positive influence on his *motivation* and *commitment* as well as his knowledge. Later, he would hear and record this concept explained in the form of a universal promise from Deity to humankind:

> Let thy bowels also be full of charity towards all men, and to the household of faith, and let virtue garnish thy thoughts unceasingly; then shall thy *confidence* wax strong in the presence of God; and the doctrine of the priesthood shall distil upon thy soul as the dews from heaven. The Holy Ghost shall be thy constant companion, and thy scepter an unchanging scepter of righteousness and truth; and thy dominion shall be an everlasting dominion, and without compulsory means it shall flow unto thee forever and ever. (D&C 121:45–46, emphasis added).

Joseph didn't flaunt his credentials; he simply loved and served the people because of them. This is apparent in the views of those who knew him personally. For example, as one witness observed, he was a man filled with the love of God and was not content with blessing his family alone but all people throughout the world. He was anxious to bless the whole of the human family (PWJS, p. 481). One Church member who stayed at the Smith home witnessed and reported the Prophet's "earnest and humble devotions, . . . nourishing, soothing, and comforting his family, neighbours, and friends." This person apparently found the observation of his private life a greater witness of Joseph Smith's divine calling than observing his public actions. (JD 7:176–77) It is good to keep such an image in mind as one reviews the extraordinary nature of Joseph Smith's personal education and its application.

In a reflective epistle he wrote in 1842, Joseph exhorted the Saints of his day to appreciate and not lose sight of the great blessings they enjoyed because of the restoration of the gospel of Jesus Christ. He called attention particularly to the mission of Elijah and explained how "it is necessary . . . in the dispensation of the fulness of times . . . that a whole and complete and perfect union, and welding together of dispensations, and keys, and powers, and glories should take place, and be revealed from the days of Adam even to the present time" (D&C 128:18). It was this process, Joseph said, that enabled those who so desire to become instruments under the Lord's direction to share these blessings with their kindred dead who never heard the gospel while they lived on the earth.

All of this was possible because of his tutors who prepared the way for the priesthood authority and the ordinances to be restored. In his poetic expression he reminisced about how all this came to pass:

> And again what do we hear? Glad tidings from Cumorah! Moroni, an angel from heaven, declaring the fulfillment of the prophets—the book to be revealed. A voice of the Lord in the wilderness of Fayette, Seneca county, declaring the three witnesses to bear record of the book! The voice of Michael on the banks of the Susquehanna, detecting the devil when he appeared as an angel of light! The voice of Peter, James, and John in the wilderness between Harmony, Susquehanna county, and Colesville, Broome county, on the Susquehanna river, declaring themselves, as possessing the keys of the kingdom, and of the dispensation of the fulness of times!

> And again, the voice of God in the chamber of old Father Whitmer, in Fayette, Seneca county, and at sundry times, and in divers places through all the travels and tribulations of this Church of Jesus Christ of Latter-day Saints! And the voice of Michael, the

archangel; the voice of Gabriel, and of Raphael, and of divers other angels from Michael or Adam down to the present time, all declaring their dispensations, their rights, their keys, their honors, their majesty and glory, and the power of their priesthood; giving line upon line, precept upon precept; here a little, and there a little; giving us consolation by holding forth that which is to come, confirming our hope. (D&C 128:20–21)

Joseph then concluded his letter with this admonition:

Let us therefore, as a church and a people, and as Latter-day Saints, offer unto the Lord an offering in righteousness; and let us present in his holy temple, when it is finished, a book containing the records of our dead, which shall be worthy of all acceptation. (D&C 128:24)

PART VIII

FUNDAMENTAL PROPOSITIONS

The uniqueness of Joseph Smith's view on education is rooted in the dramatically different perspective he expressed regarding the nature of *God, spirit, matter, space,* and *light.* His proclamations on these fundamental issues struck like lightning through a dark sky. They still do. These elements have a significant place in the foundations of Joseph Smith's perception of education. Educators who ignore them are misguided and shortsighted at best. Particularly when one views what they offer as a substitute. Consider the following partial descriptions:

Who or What is God? The discussion of God in America has flourished under a canopy of abstraction. Amidst the conversations appear such phrases as

Unmoved Mover

Undefined being with certain described qualities

A Mystery

Nature

The Universe or Cosmic Mind

A transcendent influence that created the world but does not intervene

Incomprehensible perfect being

The human power that transforms thought into action

Love

A spirit, an essence, without body parts or passions

An absentee Landlord

Most of these ideas had been circulating for hundreds of years. None of them were really definitive; applied to God, they are mental abstractions. The terminology offers word symbols, but nothing concrete and unifying. They were *naming explanations,* not *explaining explanations.* People talked about God. They gave him descriptive names, but who claimed to know who he was or what he looked like? God was a mystery—even to those who proposed to represent him. If there is an eternal God and if it is the key to eternal life to know him, knowing what and who he is must be important. (John 17:3) The resolution is not settled by reason alone. History makes that notion quite clear. There is certainly a lot more written about what God is not than what God is—and there is no clear consensus in either of these domains.

Joseph Smith erased this quandary in simple, straightforward behavior and language. He did what the scripture advised. He received the answer he sought. He taught what he knew by his own experience: God is a person; he is our Father, the literal father of our spirit bodies. His name is Elohim and he has a resurrected body of flesh and bones as tangible as man. Jesus Christ is his Son, who also has a resurrected body just like the Father. The Holy Ghost is a person, but does not have a body of flesh and bone. This personage of Spirit is suitable to perform a particular mission. They are all separate beings; they constitute the Godhead, and all share in the same purpose—bringing to pass the immortality and eternal life of all who reside on this earth, which they created and maintain for us. Humankind existed as individuals in a pre-mortal estate with God. And all this can be known by anyone willing to seek this knowledge for themselves. This information sent shock waves through the theological world that continue to this day. "It can't be," the critics cried! *Why not?* It was only what sacred scripture had proclaimed from the very beginning. (Genesis 1, 2; D&C 130:22–23) "It is the first principle of the Gospel to know for a certainty the character of God," said Joseph (TPJS p. 345). This should be the most treasured knowledge of all. What could be of greater value?

What is spirit? The term *spirit,* frequently used by theologians and early philosophers, also comes on the scene trailing conceptual uncertainty. Spirit is mentioned in a variety of ways, for example:

Thought

Air set in motion by breathing

Conscience, fellowship, and intuition

Life, living substance

Immaterial, immortal part of man

A disembodied soul

A supernatural being

Energy

A disposition of the human mind

An organ that receives and contains God the spirit

Principle of conscious life

The incorporeal part of humans as opposed to matter

Again, in this case, there was and is an intellectual reach, but little or nothing to grasp.

Joseph answered the question simply and directly: "*All spirit is matter*, but it is more fine or pure" than physical matter "and can only be discerned by purer eyes. . . . We cannot see it, but when our bodies are purified we shall see that it is all matter" (D&C 131:7–8, emphasis added). This concept alone would revolutionize most contemporary education; the implications for perceiving the student and constructing an appropriate curriculum are immense. Joseph's proposition can be accepted or rejected. But if it is rejected what is there to take its place? And is this more true or useful?

Along with the fundamental questions about God and spirit, Joseph also spoke out on the ambiguity associated with *matter, space,* and *light,* issues that also relate to deeper educational concerns. He explained that light from God's presence fills the immensity of space. And all existence is subject to law. There is no space in which there is no kingdom; and there is no kingdom in which there is no space, either a greater or a lesser kingdom. And unto every kingdom is given a law; and unto every law there are certain bounds also and conditions. All beings who abide not in those conditions are not justified. He was given to understand by his teachers that only that which is governed by law is also preserved by law and perfected and sanctified by the same. (D&C 88:34–39) Light is a necessary companion to the truth, and truth is a knowledge of things as they were, as they are, and as they will be. To seek the truth without the light is folly. Light enables a person to understand the proper application of knowledge—which is the beginning of wisdom. (D&C: 93:19–40) Concepts like these could and should influence how one views education. They did for Joseph.

Such thoughts as these, which were understood and used by Joseph, could also make the minds of the most gifted physicists and mathematical theorists tremble with curiosity.[30] Why shouldn't they? He was taught how God governs and what we should do in response to that divine governance. He revealed how God speaks, what constitutes his voice, how we may hear that voice, and what impact this can have on our personal being. (D&C 88:66–68) Joseph did not proclaim himself an elitist in his educational thought. What he was given, he offered freely to others. All who were willing to qualify themselves could know what he knew. This knowledge was not his creation; it was given to him, and his ministry was to share it with all who would accept. In fact, he said this was the purpose of education on this mortal sphere—"to know for a certainty the character of God, and to know that we may converse with him as one man converses with another," because "when we understand the character of God, and know

---

[30]Joseph's view of reality, knowledge, and value was not of the academic variety. He observed through the medium of revelation how the seen and unseen dimensions of existence function. He reported on what he saw, described aspects of these operations, and used that knowledge to discern truth from error *without presuming to proclaim these insights as a vocation to be marketed.* Divine revelation is not bound by the limitations of reason and empirical experiment, and Joseph did not subject his knowledge to those forms for the purpose of gaining acceptance. Modern theorists continue to wrestle with the enigma: What is real? How do we know? What is of value? This search, understandably, goes on. Contemporary views of the *macroscopic* and *microscopic* domains of existence have emerged through many participants seeking the truth. Historical figures like Galileo, Newton, Kepler, Maxwell, and Einstein are familiar names of those who strove to obtain a theory that explained everything. Astronomers and astrophysicists now speak and write of planets, solar systems, galaxies, and metagalaxies. They talk of black holes and dark matter, light years and cosmic webs, and novas and supernovas. Others, who probe the tiny building blocks called cells, speak and write of molecules, atoms, neutrons, electrons, quarks, and now strings that presume a multidimensional—six possible dimensions or more— existence in which people and things may dwell. As we pass through the premodern, modern, and postmodern epics of man-made theory, it is apparent that human knowledge is soft and ever-changing. We would like to know and know for sure, but that security seems to be just out of reach without divine assistance. Joseph Smith bridged that gap and invited others to follow. The more that people understand what he proclaimed, the more intriguing his knowledge becomes.

how to come to him, he begins to unfold the heavens to us, and to tell us all about it. When we are ready to come to him, he is ready to come to us" (TPJS pp. 345, 350).

Joseph Smith's view of education was not restricted to this exalted realm; he connected that lofty view to the common concerns of this earth and the issues of everyday mortal life. In addition to the eternal designs, Joseph proclaimed to his community that the purpose of education was to *"diffuse that kind of knowledge, which will be of practical utility, and for the public good, and also for private and individual happiness."* However, the view behind the application was "a marvelous work and a wonder." *One cannot fully appreciate what education is all about until one gains some truthful understanding of what life is all about.* When the two are separated confusion reigns and the seedbed for distortion is laid (*Times and Seasons*, vol. 2, January 15, 1841, p. 274; Isaiah 29:14). Joseph connected context, process, content, and method. Joseph knew and taught that "the exaltation and happiness of any community goes hand in hand with the knowledge possessed by the people in that community" (*Times and Seasons* vol 3, August 15, 1842, p. 889.). He knew and understood that knowledge is an essential key to power.

Man is Eternal. Joseph was taught not only that God was a person, the literal father of our spirit body—a being we can know and converse with—but that each human being is eternal. Death will not cause us to cease to exist; it will not result in our losing personal identity; rather, it is a doorway to a more exalted sphere of personal opportunity. Not only will this be the case individually, but it also comes with an invitation to preserve family relationships—husband and wife, parents and children, generation to generation. That which is on earth in its pure and undefiled pattern is and will be in heaven. This is the grand purpose that comprehends the ultimate aims of education. Education, for Joseph, was to be a means for perpetuating the existence of proper family relationships in the eternal context. Such vision puts the fundamentals of *reading, writing* and *arithmetic* into an entirely new role and elevates the significance of learning to a whole new level—one that is built upon and preserved by the development of *character*. Literacy and learning take on a whole new purpose. It was an extraordinary perspective then and remains so today.

Man is an agent, free to choose. The dominant teachings and widespread beliefs about the nature of humankind in his day were not consistent with the views introduced to Joseph Smith as part of the restoration project—nor are those that dominate today. They were and are substitutes that have long been objects of debate. Such "traditional doctrines" did not claim that humans were independent agents free to choose right from wrong under divine guidance. They pushed the definitions of human nature then, as they do now, in other directions. For example, it was then and is now, not surprising to hear such notions as

- Man is a fallen creature, predestined to either heaven or hell by an arbitrary God.
- People are essentially products of their social and natural environments.
- Humankind is shaped and controlled by genetics, which may be engineered.
- People are spontaneous accidents that are the beneficiaries of evolutionary forces.

Joseph proclaimed another view. He learned that humanity was, at its very core, unique from the rest of creation. People did not belong to the (a) kingdom of minerals, (b) kingdom of vegetables, or (c) kingdom of animals, as described in modern textbooks. Humans were of divine origin, children of God, inherently members of the *kingdom of God* and potential heirs to all its rewards. Joseph knew there were "things that act and things that are acted upon"; that humanity was created to act, not to be acted upon"—[except] by the law of justice according to the commandments of God (2 Nephi 2:26). People are free to act; God has given humankind to know good from evil and has made them free to act according to their own desires (Helaman 14:30–31). Hence, the most important of all *education* was the education of a person's *desires*. This was quite unique then and is now. Where are the documents that explain how to educate desire?

Joseph Smith's doctrine of human agency and freedom can be summarized in eight fundamental statements (see D&C 93:29–31):

60

1. Man was in the beginning with God.
2. Intelligence, or the light of truth, was not created or made.
3. All truth is independent in that sphere where God has placed it.
4. All intelligence is independent in that sphere in which God has placed it.
5. We are to act for ourselves in the sphere in which God has placed us.
6. Our capacity to choose within the sphere in which we are placed to act constitutes the agency of man; here is where our exaltation or condemnation will be determined.
7. The condemnation of man is to reject "the Plan," which was plainly manifest from the beginning.
8. The application and fruition of each of these elements are connected to the Atonement of Jesus Christ.

The attribute and realm of human agency were established to help us develop and fulfill our divine destiny. In a very practical sense, the attribute of human agency trumps everything except eternal Justice (2 Nephi 2:26). For Joseph Smith, these concepts should shape the structure and the function of educational endeavors. All other true educational principles are designed to complement these fundamentals of human nature. They form the very backbone of education, of learning and teaching. Educational strategies and policies that ignore these propositions or act as distractions to them are destined to produce only a shadow of what otherwise could be. These divinely revealed premises are the essential foundation of all other principles and practices of effective education. And they are the framework upon which Joseph built and upon which he instructed his followers to build. They did and continue to do this. The key is to receive what Heavenly Father has given and then act upon it; not to reject these principles and rely on the arm of flesh. (D&C 1:19; 2 Nephi 28:31)

Joseph Smith's premises flew in the face of the powerful, contradictory, and confusing doctrines regarding human nature prominent in his day. One view proclaimed man to be a fallen creature, evil by nature, and predestined to an awful destruction unless the Creator, by grace, arbitrarily plucked a sinful person from his or her otherwise inevitable destiny of eternal punishment. Others held an opposite view of this dark, human condition; it was that humankind is intrinsically and inevitably good—because they are God's creation, and God does not create evil. Any natural human activity, therefore, may be condoned and embraced; evil is not a product of nature, it is simply an unexplainable perversion. A great variety of enticing speculations arose between and among the proponents of these two diverse theological propositions in early America. Debates were common; they fueled the revivals of the period.

Joseph addressed the confusion and contradictions with a simple proposition: Mortals are neither inherently *evil* nor patently *good;* they are born *innocent* and become either good or evil by the choices they make and the actions they initiate. He recognized that "the natural man is an enemy to God, and has been since the fall of Adam, and will be, forever, unless he yields to the enticings of the Holy Spirit, . . . and becometh a saint through the atonement of Christ the Lord" (Mosiah 3:19). "For all have sinned and come short of the glory of God" (Romans 3:23). He saw clearly that everyone stands in need of God's grace.

Joseph recognized that it was a characteristic of fallen humankind, if they followed their unaided physical desires, to become *carnal, sensual,* and *devilish* (Moses 5:12–15). This condition would lead people to more *faulty thoughts*: (1) All reality is physical (*metaphysics*). (2) We can only know that which we apprehend through our unaided or aided physical senses (*epistemology*). (3) All thoughts and things are of equal value (*axiology*). Joseph made it clear to the common person as well as the philosopher that the solution to the problem was to embrace the Atonement of Jesus Christ. But he also emphasized specific obligations connected to that unearned, universally available, but conditional help; we are recipients of God's grace only as we comply with the requirements prescribed by him. Otherwise we suffer our own consequences. Yes, man's divine origin was good, but that was not sufficient to overcome the inevitable consequences of personal choice in a mortal estate. It was a matter of *freedom and grace, faith and works*—not either/or. Again, *education* was the key to this relief. The *atonement* made it possible. Revelation made it understandable.

In brief, Joseph's explanation might be summarized in the following manner. Said he, "We know that all men must repent and believe on the name of Jesus Christ, and worship the Father in his name to the end, or they cannot" fulfill their promised destiny. The opportunity to accept or reject is before each person, or will be at some time before the final judgment. We will be taught; but we are responsible to act. "We [can] know that *justification*"—the instruction from the Holy Spirit that enables a person to acquire the characteristics of godliness—comes "through the grace of our Lord and Savior Jesus Christ [which] is just and true. And we [can] know also, that *sanctification*"—the purity necessary to qualify for the Holy Ghost to be our instructor and companion—comes "through the grace of our Lord and Savior Jesus Christ, [which] is just and true, to all those who love and serve God with all their mights, minds, and strength" (D&C 20:29–31, emphasis added; PGP Moses 6:60–62). It is the Holy Spirit that enables us to separate ourselves from the consequences of our own bad choices—whether this occurs by prevention or correction.

Joseph knew, as Moses knew, that by the "*water* [of baptism] ye keep the commandment; by the *Spirit ye are justified,* and by the *blood ye are sanctified.*" It is in this manner, according to these witnesses, that people "obtain the Comforter; the peaceable things of immortal glory; the truth of all things; . . . this is *the plan of salvation* unto all men" (Moses 6:60–61, emphasis added). Just as each individual, in his or her premortal estate, had to meet the conditions established to obtain God's grace to have the privilege of coming to this earth, so it is necessary to *seek, knock, ask,* and *do* what is required in order to enter back into His presence. The issue over grace and works vanished. All of this process is a learner-driven enterprise. Each person must learn, accept and not reject the truth, and then do what needs to be done to implement that truth in his or her life. These fundamental ideas formed the backbone of Joseph Smith's perspective on education. Every means of education that would contribute to this defined end was enveloped in his perspective of the purpose and nature of education. It should be so today.

One illustration of this practical application is the way Joseph dissolved another common educational disparity of his day. *What is social refinement?* Sophisticated Europeans viewed Americans as crude, coarse, and vulgar—sorely lacking in social graces. Protestant preachers in America, on the other hand, condemned as vulgar, sinful, and evil much of what Europeans hailed as cultural refinement—dancing schools, boundless romantic literature, and flaunting opulence and debauchery. This difference between the old world and the new was one form of social conflict. Another schism emerged among Americans themselves. It was regional in nature.

Americans on the Eastern seaboard considered those on the Western frontier as woefully lacking in domestic civility, manners, and education. The division was partially related to whether one earned one's living by laboring primarily with the mind or with the hands. Joseph avoided these extremes. As a person he was neither crude nor polished. In his view, refinement was not merely centered in external appearances or social graces. The taproot of refinement in human personality was internal desires. Proper qualities of *character* were the true source of cleanliness, beauty, and deportment in daily life—not rudimentary manners, as useful as these might be. His exhortation to the Saints was this: *"Let honesty and sobriety, and candor and solemnity, and virtue, and pureness, and meekness, and simplicity crown our heads in every place."*[31] This is what fosters propriety in a society—it is more a matter of internal integrity than external conformity. This is the bulwark against hypocrisy that should be built into the curriculum of education at every level. Some things are primary; other things are secondary.

---

[31]Dean C. Jesse ed. *The Personal Writings of Joseph Smith*, p. 397.

PART IX

IMPLEMENTING RESTORED EDUCATION

Joseph's initial assignment, once his call to serve had been extended, was to create—to prepare, organize, and pursue—an expansive curriculum. The sequence went something like this:

- He was tutored and then assigned to translate the Book of Mormon. Questions that arose were answered by revelation. The revelations were generally recorded.
- He was given authority to organize a Church, receive and administer sacred ordinances, and distribute priesthood keys for others to assist in the work.
- He was admonished to clarify the biblical record by restoring many of the plain and precious truths that had been removed by previous generations. This included the translation of some writings on Egyptian Papyrus— the Book of Abraham; and receiving by revelation a more accurate account of antiquity in writings from the Book of Moses—including an extract from the Book of Enoch.
- He was instructed to build temples, keep sacred records, and publish selected revelations that were given to him pertaining to this enterprise.
- He felt an increasing responsibility to organize and implement ways to (a) proclaim the truths he received, (b) prepare and improve the circumstances and qualifications of his people, and (c) assist in sharing the knowledge and the ordinances with his followers, their progenitors, and their posterity.
- He was given directions on the nature of the curriculum to master (D&C 88:77–80) as well as the type of relationships and a format for the setting in which instruction was to take place (D&C 88:117–126).
- He received extensive information about principles related to the education of children, youth, and adults and how this related to the home and family (for example, PGP Moses 6; D&C 68:25–32; Mormon 8).

Joseph's personal possession of this information, plus the command to share it with the world, posed a significant challenge. By 1840 he clearly understood that the Bible, as it had been preserved, was an inspired and powerful *moral treatise*. He learned much from the Bible and used it to teach his people. It was a very useful instrument to train and sustain good and honorable people; a way to prepare and qualify them for a spiritual, *terrestrial* lifestyle. This sacred record was a witness that Jesus is the Christ, and there is a gospel, "good news," for mortals that will guide them to happiness in mortality. It is a record that proclaims the necessity and defines the *moral order* required to prepare a person for life beyond the grave. It describes the basic ordinances. It is a marvelous double testament to what is good. However, it does not contain a fullness of the gospel of Christ. There is additional truth to bless people's lives if they will accept it. Joseph learned and taught this additional truth to his people.

The Bible, without the doctrinal clarification provided by the Book of Mormon: Another Testament of Jesus Christ, the collection of revelations Joseph placed in The Doctrine and Covenants, and priesthood ordinances applied with proper authority, could not enable people to obtain a *celestial* lifestyle, the apex of human destiny. There was more to the story than what appeared in the sacred biblical record as it survived through many hands and centuries. Joseph was told by divine messengers that many "plain and precious" parts and covenants had been changed or removed (1 Nephi 13:26–29, 32, 34). The Bible in its present form could only hint at the "mysteries of godliness" (Matt. 13:11; Deut. 29:29). It did not explain these mysteries and their attendant ordinances, or provide the means for man to profit from them. Such authority and information had vanished from the earth. They had to be restored by those persons who last held the keys for the administration and dissemination of the doctrines and ordinances of exaltation. God's kingdom is indeed a kingdom of order and power (John 15:16; Titus 1:5; D&C 13:1; 27:12–13; 65:1–6; 132:8).

The burning question for Joseph seems to be "How can I distribute and implement this great *Plan of Happiness* among the people now that it has been restored?" Certain fundamental challenges were evident:

1. Possessing knowledge is different from sharing knowledge.
2. The desired learning and teaching must be consistent with revealed content, principles, and practices.
3. Whatever the course of action, it must be realistic and fit current circumstances.
4. How can we help people learn to teach according to the covenants (D&C 107:89), teach with the spirit (D&C 42:13–14), and teach as a witness (Mosiah 18:8–9)?

Joseph knew he had the authority to share the knowledge he had received. The intended scope required to deliver this information to the world, however, far exceeded any process to which he had been exposed in his humble origins. He knew it required more than the traditional *show*, *tell*, and *do*. His instructional challenge was how to adapt his efforts to the circumstances at hand, while at the same time continuing to plow new ground—to organize, expand, and refine an ever expanding population. His audience was unable to grasp all he had to offer. His approach of necessity had to be "line upon line, here a little and there a little" (2 Nephi 28:30; D&C 98:12; Isaiah 28:9–10). People had to be *prepared* in order to *perform* and *achieve*. This required both insight and patience. It required generational time. It was an educational challenge. He had to avoid the temptation of "looking beyond the mark" (Jacob 4:14). He had to honor the very truths and principles he was commanded to share.

The need to educate a very diverse and ever-increasing membership—perhaps 20,000 in just over a dozen years—was an ever-present reality. But this extraordinary growth rate was not the only difficulty. Joseph's followers suffered extreme persecution. They were driven from three states—New York, Ohio, Missouri, and into Illinois—in less than a decade. Of necessity, the setting in which he had to perform his task was both physically and socially primitive and antagonistic. Such trying circumstances were hardly conducive to formal and systematic learning and teaching. And he was aware that the sharing task would ultimately involve millions. Joseph remained undeterred; he retained his practical, unwavering convictions. He spoke with confidence to his people, citing the seemingly *"insurmountable difficulties that we have overcome in laying the foundations . . . of a work that is destined to*

67

bring about the destruction of the powers of darkness, the renovation of the earth, the glory of God, and the salvation of the human family."[32] He understood that he was involved in a work in progress.

His immediate strategy was simple: teach those who worked the closest to him how to teach others every needful thing. He organized conferences to discuss issues and establish policies of order. He identified, refined, and created appropriate curriculum. He ordered a printing press and set in motion a flow of information to people inside and outside his organization. He, and those whom he sent forth, sought audiences through other available media—newspapers, cottage meetings, lectures in rented halls, and lyceum-like instruction. He organized leadership training schools for adults and classes to prepare missionaries, encouraged public and private schools for children, and supported the establishment of a university. He recognized the family as the most fundamental institution and parents as primary educators.

He organized quorums of teachers to instruct and assist fathers in their homes to foster better training of their children. He created a woman's Relief Society to support the women in serving both spiritual and domestic needs. Youth groups were encouraged to seek moral and character education as well as the three R's. He stressed the importance of connecting the strength of families by linking generations and he identified the family as the primary center for fundamental education. Leaders were exhorted to set a proper example of furthering education in their own homes. However modest the extent of these early innovations may seem by today's standards, they were not common on the American frontier. But these principles and practices were uniquely foundational. They provided an invaluable basis for the mammoth educational enterprise that would follow, an expanding organization rendering service to millions. And above all this he encouraged every individual to be a willing, seeking learner.

The responsibility entrusted to this "Minister of Education" had to accommodate interested learners from every dispensation of time—from Adam and Eve to his own day and

---

[32]*Times and Seasons* vol. 3, p. 776, May 2, 1842, *emphasis* added.

beyond. True, he had been carefully informed that this task was not his alone. There were multitudes who would participate. Consider the responsibility, however, to establish foundations of *content, structure, function,* and *context* that could accommodate all who were or would be involved. This task must have seemed ominous to a young man on the frontier of nineteenth century America. Consider the ultimate purpose: it enveloped all the people who ever lived—including every mortal living upon the earth, all who had suffered physical death but now existed in another spiritual domain, as well as all those who were yet to be born. Imagine the student body; imagine the faculty; imagine the curriculum he had to contemplate. The purpose, scope, and location are immense. He served as an educational architect of singular significance.

Two major challenges from the very beginning were (a) lack of resources and (b) the educational readiness of the participants. Just because Joseph had the vision did not mean that the new converts were prepared and ready to understand and recognize how to appropriately fulfill their respective roles. The material resource issue was difficult because of continuous persecution and frequent changes in place of residence. Hence the saying "Three moves equal a burnout." The Saints repeatedly lost their material possessions to persecution. Most of the participants were poor as to the things of this world. Cultural diversity was often an obstacle; newer members came from a variety of cultures and native tongues. Language was a challenge. The majority had received limited formal education. Many lacked the training and literary skills to make learning easier and faster. Joseph's people were physically persecuted to such an extent that it was very difficult to acquire the physical and financial means to provide for their own livelihood, let alone generate what most educators would feel were sufficient rudimentary facilities and instructional materials.

Joseph encouraged a basic education for all, particularly in those areas that would increase the people's capacity to understand and fulfill their personal missions in this life. Evidence clearly suggests that he envisioned the need for five basic elements in the curriculum. (a) *The hub of the wheel was moral and spiritual education.* Extending outward from this core was a common curriculum; (b) language and the expressive arts, (c) mathematics, (d) social studies, and (e) science. Basic literacy, skills in computation, a knowledge of people, places, and periods of life, as well as the insights to understand the world in which people live, eat, drink, and create were an obvious necessity. The various schools, halls, shops, and skills apparent in the city of Nauvoo demonstrate that this type of education, in a very broad sense, was a central value. He and his people had a mission to perform. This mission demanded the training of hearts, minds, and hands, an objective that demanded persistent and diligent effort. His vision reached far beyond what the world was seeking. And with limited resources Joseph led his people to seek learning.

Joseph himself was surrounded by people who demonstrated the advantages of "an education." His maternal grandmother, his mother as well as his father, and his wife were all proponents and providers of educational skills. Many of the men who worked with Joseph in fulfilling his role and responsibilities were useful because of their educational skills. The work Joseph did as a leader and teacher was a constant reminder of the value and necessity of useful education. He responded positively to opportunities to improve his knowledge—he loved to study and learn. And the more he learned, the more he pushed for education among his followers. He organized a school for both youth and adults in Kirtland, Ohio. The Kirtland High School taught math, geography, grammar, writing, reading, and languages.

The Nauvoo City Charter, granted by the State of Illinois in December of 1840, contained a provision for the creation of a university. A Proclamation issued by the First Presidency [Joseph Smith, Sidney Rigdon, and Hyrum Smith] in January of 1841 states the hope and purpose of this institution:

> The "University of the City of Nauvoo" will enable us to teach our children wisdom, to instruct them in all the knowledge and learning, in the arts, sciences, and learned professions. We hope to make this institution one of the great lights of the world, and by and through it to diffuse that kind of knowledge which will be of practicable utility, and for the public good, and also for private and individual happiness.

The proclamation also mentions "common schools" and the need to establish "a regular system of education" which would "hand over the pupil from teacher to professor" as feeders to this university "until the regular graduation is consummated and the education finished."[33] The vision was commendable; the resources and circumstances severely limited and primitive. Matching the two was a serious obstacle to any form of success. It was a stringent test for a minister of education.

How to respond to such an enormous task with such limited resources was a difficult challenge for Joseph. The pattern he established under these circumstances appears to be twofold:

(1) *Do what you can with what you have.* This fit the economic realities of a frontier people who understood well the adage that they must learn to make it do or do without, use it up and wear it out, in many aspects of their lives. Avoid waste; foster conservation. From the beginning, the *basic solution* to the problem of resources was defined in the form of a principle: the participant's *voluntary* consecration of time, talent, and material wealth. It was a gradual compliance, however, based on learning correct principles and allowing individual agency to prevail—not by some compulsory means. And it depended on the organization and function of the family which formed the center for all the other organizational elements in these educational endeavors. Like a seed, this impetus for *learning in order to do what God desires, not just learning for the sake of learning,* or *making for the sake of gain,* grew and continues to grow. *He was building an educational philosophy on Hebrew—not Greek or Modern—assumptions.*

(2) *Do what you do with integrity to the truths being shared—not after the manner of the world.* This premise was clearly expressed as early as 1831 when Oliver Cowdery and W. W. Phelps, two of Joseph's more educated associates at the time, were instructed by revelation from God to select and write "books for schools in this church, that little children also may receive instruction before me as is pleasing unto me" (D&C 55:4). The sharp focus of this task remained intact following Joseph's death more than a decade later. Minutes of a conference in 1845 show the ongoing concern for developing

---

[33]HC 4:269–70.

71

proper educational materials. The same delimitation, set in place years before in Kirtland, was applied in Nauvoo. The curriculum had to be consistent with the mission—even in the face of another exodus. As the Saints prepared to move west, W. W. Phelps raised the concern in a conference: "There is another piece of business of great importance to all who have families; that is, to have some school books printed for the education of our children, which will not be according to the Gentile order" (*Times and Seasons* Vol. 6, No. 16, Nauvoo, Ill., Nov. 1, 1845. p. 1015). Again, the premise is clear: curriculum to support the educational aims revealed to Joseph must be distinctly different from those of the world. Integrity and clarity between educational means and ends are essential and should not be compromised.

Joseph's vision of an educated people was contagious, and many caught this spirit. The local paper in Nauvoo, citing evidence back to the Kirtland era, was comfortable with printing the positive declaration that *"the day is not far distant when all nations will marvel at the knowledge and wisdom of the Church of Jesus Christ of Latter-day Saints. . . . To this end let the Elders that go to the nations prepare accordingly"* (Ibid. p. 1079). Those sent forth were to gather knowledge they felt was useful, as well as to teach a message that was essential.[34] As Joseph's educational efforts developed, so did the people. Indeed, it was as if a stone had been cut out of a mountain and was rolling forth (Daniel 2:34). And at the very center of Joseph's educational vision was the temple—The House of the Lord—necessary sacred space. It was this structure that was to provide and symbolize the fundamental views, commitments, and expectations of education. What happens on earth is to be connected to what happens in heaven. The connecting link in terms of a structure was the temple.

---

[34]These commitments would continue to drive subsequent leaders. The *Quorum of the Twelve Apostles* issued the next *Proclamation*. It was published in New York City April 6, 1845 and in Liverpool England on October 22, 1845. Included in this admonition was the following: *"A great, and glorious, and a mighty work is yet to be achieved, in spreading the truth and Kingdom among the Gentiles—in restoring, organizing, . . . instructing, relieving, civilizing, educating and administering"* What Joseph initiated others continued to promote.

Temples Link Heaven and Earth

Kirtland Temple

Nauvoo Temple

Worldwide Temples Now

"When the Savior comes, a thousand years will be devoted to this work of redemption; and Temples will appear all over this land of Joseph. In North and South America and also in Europe and elsewhere; and all the descendants of Shem, Ham, and Japheth who received not the Gospel in the flesh, must be officiated for in the temples of God, before the Savior can present the kingdom to the Father, saying, 'It is finished.'" (Wilford Woodruff, *Journal of Discourses*, 19:229–30)

PART X

THE TEMPLE AS A SACRED SCHOOL

Unique to Joseph's educational enterprise was the temple. Here was the point of institutional connection between earth and heaven—both symbolically and temporally. Joseph established from the very beginning a *hierocentric* (temple-centered) society—and it was twofold: a mindset among the people and a physical dwelling place for God and his sacred works on the earth. The central notion was that truth and light come from God, are manifest through individual personalities, and requires personal covenant-making in order to lift man from earthly ways to heavenly ways. Husbands and wives, parents, and children are prepared for eternal relationships; associations that will exalt them above the carnal, sensual, and devilish natures so prevalent in a fallen earth and its corruptible societies. At every location where Joseph settled his people, the spiritual order of business was to identify a site on which to build a temple—a House of the Lord—a place of learning. It was essential that people understand that the *temple* was the center. The circles of learning and the teaching implemented must draw people toward—not away from—the temple. That which transcends time and earth is ultimately of the greatest value.

Joseph sensed a fundamental and practical association between the family and the temple that needed to be recognized and established. This connection might be reduced to a simple observation; something like this:

> *The kitchen table is the symbolic center of the civil order.* What happens or doesn't happen at the kitchen table will dictate the type of *temporal society* in which we live. Modern life tends to move people away from a regular pattern of eating together as a family; parents and children daily sharing each other's presence while preparing, cooking, and consuming food in the home. Circumstances have changed this experience for many people who now miss the bonding relationships that can be nurtured around the kitchen table. What was once a common practice has been replaced with

various forms of what has been called a *counter-top culture*. It is easy to cook a meal; to rely on the microwave and pre-prepared food; to just eat at the counter-top while on the go; it's a hurry-up world. Each member of the family is often on their own schedule and there is little time for routine interaction. Consequently, we can lose touch with some of our most valuable *sacred time and space*.

The temple is the symbolic center of the celestial order on earth. What happens or doesn't happen at the temple will dictate the type of *eternal society* in which we live. The family, guided by temple instruction and covenants, was the center from which education was to flow. The institutional scaffolding was to sustain and enhance these family-centered efforts. Schools were important, Church organizations essential, and government agencies helpful. But these secondary institutions would be valued according to their capacity to support and protect the family unit. It was the family that had an eternal role to play—not the educational programs established to serve its members. The temporal educational scaffolding was destined to fulfill an important but temporary role. The importance of the family and parental responsibility was and is critical—it is highlighted on earth and extends to eternity.[35]

---

[35]The day the Church was organized, the basic principles and ordinances of the gospel of Jesus Christ were introduced. As early as 1831, less than two years after the Church was organized, Joseph made clear that the basic unit of the Church was the family. He recorded and proclaimed the will of the Lord pertaining to parents: *"And again, inasmuch as parents have children in Zion, or in any of her stakes which are organized, that teach them not to understand the doctrine of repentance, faith in Christ the Son of the living God, and of baptism and the gift of the Holy Ghost by the laying on of the hands, when eight years old, the sin be upon the heads of the parents. For this shall be a law unto the inhabitants of Zion, or in any of her stakes which are organized."* Also emphasized in the same instruction was the fact that parents were accountable not only for teaching their children (1) faith in Christ, (2) repentance, (3) baptism for remission of sins, and (4) the reception of the gift of the Holy Ghost, but they were also to (5) teach their children to pray, (6) walk uprightly before the Lord, (7) keep the Sabbath day holy, and to do this (8) while accepting and magnifying their callings in the Church (D&C 68:25–30). This information was delivered with an admonition to the

Sacred Space
for

The Civil Order

Kitchen Table

The Celestial Order

Nauvoo Temple

For Joseph, the temple was the foundry in which eternal links are forged and tempered. Without temples and the ordinances and instruction that occur therein, the *exaltation* of individuals, the preservation of eternal family units, and the linking of these units to generations of extended family are not possible. It was necessary, Joseph taught, that for people to understand and appreciate the ultimate aim of education,

> a whole and complete and perfect union, and welding together of dispensations, and keys, and powers, and glories should take place, and be revealed from the days of Adam even to the present time. And not only this, but those things which never have been revealed from the foundation of the world, but have been kept hid from the wise and prudent, shall be revealed unto babes and sucklings in this, the dispensation of the fullness of times. (D&C 128:18)

He was adamant about the context in which these marvelous things were to take place and indicated that though

---

leaders in the Church to set their own houses in order by complying with these instructions (D&C 68:31–35). As fundamental as the doctrines of faith in Christ, repentance, baptism by immersion, and receiving the gift of the Holy Ghost by the laying on of hands are in the Bible, it seems that not a single denomination in Joseph's day believed in and practiced all these principles. Some sects embraced one or more, but not all. See also, *The Family: A Proclamation to the World* issued by the First Presidency and Council of the Twelve Apostles of The Church of Jesus Christ of Latter-day Saints (September 23, 1995) for a statement reaffirming Joseph Smith's teachings.

the nations of the earth may be at war, the servants of the Lord would lay the foundation of a great and high watchtower. This would be a vantage from which humanity could be viewed from an eternal perspective. It would enable the Saints to recognize that in spite of social turmoil, external persecution, and some difficulties with certain attitudes of a few Church members, the work would progress. Then Joseph reportedly made this statement:

> Even this nation [the United States] will be on the very verge of crumbling to pieces and tumbling to the ground and when the Constitution is upon the brink of ruin this people will be the staff upon which the Nation shall lean and they shall bear the Constitution away from the very verge of destruction—Then shall the Lord say: Go tell all my servants who are the strength of mine house, my young men and middle aged etc., Come to the land of my vineyard and fight the battle of the Lord—Then the Kings and Queens shall come, then the rulers of the earth shall come, then shall all Saints come, yea the foreign Saints shall come to fight for the land of my vineyard, for in this thing shall be their safety and they will have no power to choose but will come as a man fleeth from a sudden destruction. (Joseph Smith, July 19, 1840, ms D 155 Box 4, Church Historians Office, emphasis added; source also cited in Glen Leonard, *Nauvoo: A Place of Peace, A People of Promise* (2002), p. 303)

Joseph also mentioned that some of his friends would turn against him and seek his death. He exhorted the Saints to build up "cities of the Lord" and invited them to join him in the labor to construct a temple in the City of Nauvoo [as they did in Kirtland]; expressing the hope that he would live to see its completion (a desire not fulfilled in mortality). The focus on a temple, as it had been in Ohio and Missouri, was launched in Illinois July 19, 1840—only months after the Saints began to arrive on a swampy peninsula at a bend of the Mississippi River called Commerce. These physical circumstances punctuate the intensity of Joseph's conception of education. It was fundamental, extraordinary, and temple-centered, notwithstanding difficulties of the time or place.

Now brethren, I obligate myself to build as great a temple as ever Solomon did if the Church will back me up, moreover, it shall not impoverish any man but enrich thousands, . . . and I pray the Father that many here may realize this and see it with their eyes, [stretching his hand towards the place on the brow of the hill] and if it should be the will of God that I might live to behold that temple completed and finished from foundation to the top stone I will say–Oh Lord it is enough, let thy servant depart in peace which is my earnest prayer in the name of the Lord Jesus, Amen. (Ibid.)

In the same discourse, Joseph addressed additional educational matters, suggesting that although the temple was the center of his thoughts, there was more: "school houses shall be built . . . and high schools shall be established, . . . and many . . . even noble men shall crave the privilege of educating their children . . . with us, which hold the keys of entrance into the Kingdom." (Ibid.)

Homes, schools, and universities offered preparation in temporal skills and knowledge. But the education which linked families together, generations to each other, and earth with heaven was to be obtained in the Temple. All roads that lead to the life God lives go through the doors of His temples. There are no exceptions. He has many other kingdoms for those who choose a different life, as Paul the Apostle stated and as Joseph Smith was taught (1 Cor. 15:40–42; D&C 76:89–92). Jesus shared this same observation with his disciples while he was on the earth (John 14:2). It was this perspective that pushed Joseph to pursue the educational paths that he did and in the way he did. His effort was to bring to pass the purposes that had been placed before him. And in the final period of his life, he passed the responsibility and the authority to build on the foundation he laid to those who would follow. In March of 1844, Joseph conveyed full authorization to the Quorum of Twelve Apostles to lead and direct in the affairs of all he had initiated. Prior to his death, he said, "I roll the burthen and responsibility of leading this Church off from my shoulders on to yours, . . . for the Lord is going to let me rest awhile." Collectively, the authority then resided in the Quorum of the Twelve Apostles, who held the office next in succession to care for all matters pertaining to the Kingdom after Joseph's death.[36]

The conscious transition of authority and responsibility from Joseph Smith to the Quorum of Twelve was a careful and directed event. It was not impulsive, sudden, or devious. This pattern of delegation was rooted in the process evident in the Church that Jesus Christ established while he was on the earth. Like then, this action involved a transfer of keys and instruction similar to that which transpired on the Mount of Transfiguration (Matt. 16:13–18: 17:1–9; *HC* vol. 3, p. 387). As was the case anciently, the membership in the restored Church was rapidly expanding—from hundreds to thousands and then tens of thousands in the coming decades. Continuation of leadership in the absence of the central figure was clearly needed. It was provided.

The impact of Joseph's teachings during the final two years of his mortal life was detailed, sacred, and visionary. His disclosure of additional personal covenant-making required covenant-related instruction, some of which had to occur in *sacred space.* Because the curriculum was designed to connect the *temporal* to the *spiritual,* the veil between the two domains had to be both thin and porous and the focus pure and personal. The learning and teaching had to be *temple worthy.* The distribution of this work was now Joseph's educational preoccupation. He was blessed with a miraculous gathering of willing learners who were eager to study, embrace and apply the expanding vision of who they were and what they could become.

Joseph introduced these faithful converted followers to new, astonishing, and exhilarating concepts about families, responsibilities, powers, promises, and opportunities. They were invited to develop relationships in marriage and generational families that could be eternal, not just temporary associations that ended with the death of one or the other party. He also introduced the revealed structure for governing the society that will prevail during the *millennial era*—the

---

[36]Glen M. Leonard, *Nauvoo: A Place of Peace, A People of Promise* (2002), p. 260.

"Kingdom of God" on the earth, with its title, constitution, and rules of order.[37]

---

[37]"Joseph Smith said he had gone before the Lord [on 7 April 1844] and had received the constitution for the 'Kingdom of God' [not the Church] by direct revelation. He then gave the text of the revelation as follows: 'Ye are my Constitution and I am your God and ye are my spokesmen, therefore from henceforth keep my commandments' (461). The brevity of this constitution did not mean that the Council of Fifty [as the organization was then called] operated in a loose or chaotic fashion. The Council was guided by certain parliamentary procedures that were also finalized in this 18 April 1844 meeting. Since the constitution of the 'Kingdom of God' was essentially an 'unwritten constitution,' the following parliamentary procedures consequently took on constitutional status. The Rules of the Kingdom: **1.** The Council is convened and organized by the President of the Church subject to the rules of the Kingdom of God. He is elected standing chairman upon convening of the Council. **2.** Members of the Council sit according to age, except the chairman. **3.** According to the order of voting in the Council, a recorder and a clerk of the Kingdom are elected. The clerk takes the minutes of the meeting and the recorder enters the approved minutes into the official records of the Kingdom. They are voting members though they do not occupy a seat in the circle. **4.** All motions are presented to the Council by or through the standing chairman. All motions must be submitted in writing. **5.** To pass, a motion must be unanimous in the affirmative. Voting is done after the ancient order: each person voting in turn from the oldest to the youngest member of the Council, commencing with the standing chairman. If any Council member has any objections he is under covenant to fully and freely make them known to the Council. But if he cannot be convinced of the rightness of the course pursued by the Council he must either yield or withdraw membership in the Council. Thus a man will lose his place in the Council if he refuses to act in accordance with righteous principles in the deliberations of the Council. After action is taken and a motion accepted, no fault will be found or changes sought for in regard to the motion. **6.** Before a man can be accepted as a member of the Council his name must be presented to the members and voted upon unanimously in the affirmative. When invited into the Council he must covenant by uplifted hand to maintain all things of the Council inviolate agreeable to the order of the Council. Before he accepts his seat he must also agree to accept the name, constitution, and rules of order and conduct of the Council. **7.** No member is to be absent from any meeting unless sick or on Council business. If this were not the case, rule five could be invoked to invalidate any action of the Council. **8.** A member can be assigned to only one committee of the Council at a time. **9.** Adjournment and specific date of reconvening the Council are determined by vote. The Council may be called together sooner at the discretion of the chairman. If the Council adjourns without a specific meeting date (sine die), it next meets only at the call of the standing chairman (or new President of the Church, if applicable) (462). Naturally rule number five was the heart, the soul, the beauty of the 'Kingdom of God.' To Joseph Smith it was the answer to the inevitable clash between minority and majority rights. It was the guarantee of freedom of speech and the right of peaceful dissent in Council meetings. If the true spirit

Lest some may think this talk of temples and glorious anticipations is a form of arrogance or even delusion, Joseph made it clear that such feelings were unacceptable. *Reverence* and *humility* were to rule, not pride or self-aggrandizement. With remarkable insight, he once explained the danger of prideful behavior resulting from thinking too highly of one's self because of the acquisition of knowledge. This was his explanatory instruction regarding the consequences of *knowing* and *not knowing*:

> If we get puffed up by thinking we have much knowledge, we are apt to get a contentious spirit, and correct knowledge is necessary to cast out that spirit. The evil of being puffed up [even] with correct (though [often] useless) knowledge is not so great as the evil of contention. Knowledge does away with darkness, suspense and doubt; for these cannot exist where knowledge is. There is no pain so awful as that of suspense. This is the punishment of the wicked; their doubt, anxiety and suspense cause weeping, wailing and gnashing of teeth. In knowledge there is power. (TPJS pp. 287–88)

The greater one's knowledge, the greater should be one's reverence and humility. This was to characterize all that transpired in the temple.

---

of the constitution were followed, the Council would be the 'spokesmen of God' in their political deliberations." [style as quoted] Andrew F. Ehat, *Joseph Smith's Introduction of Temple Ordinances and the 1844 Mormon Succession Question,* BYU Master's Thesis. December 1982, pp. 90–91.

PART XI

HELPING CHILDREN, YOUTH, AND ADULTS LEARN

Imbedded within the general considerations of Joseph Smith's view of education there is considerable that is practical, universal, and essential. Joseph learned much about what and how education related to the individual. He learned what was expected of parents. He was taught and reminded that parents were the primary ones commissioned to bring useful education into the life of a child. He recognized that the family unit was the institution that safeguarded this process. The elements involved in helping youth and children learn that which was most important to their welfare were quite simple and they were to be the framework for what adults needed to learn. Temporal means for accomplishments were to be guided by spiritual ends essential to human welfare and eternal destinies.

Joseph was shown a pattern for creating relationships that would bring success in these endeavors: *Love them, correct them, and provide a way for them* (D&C 95:1). This is to continue until they can love, protect, and provide for themselves. The process for helping children is so natural that it is almost self-evident. Yet these simple functions are often ignored, neglected, or abused. Parents are to help their children learn to *walk, talk, write, and read*. This fundamental literacy is the bridgework from dependence to independence. They are to teach them where they came from, who they are, and what they can become. The key to doing this is to listen, share, care, and be self-reliant so they can acquire these attributes—not only by precept but by example. This work all begins soon after birth. Parents have to be dedicated to these responsibilities and most seem to intuitively sense this is what should happen. We naturally want our children to do for themselves many of the things which initially others have to do for them, like feed themselves, put on their own clothes, and avoid dangers that cause injury and pain. Little children are not accountable until their development enables them to become accountable.

83

Meanwhile, parents are responsible. These are fundamentals of life.

When childhood becomes adolescence, new responsibilities and opportunities arise. Puberty releases the power of procreation in a person's life. It is a powerful force in need of control if its purposes are to be fulfilled with satisfaction, joy, and no regrets. Most of the standards given to Joseph Smith were directly or indirectly related to properly governing this great power that is bestowed temporarily upon humankind. There has to be order in the use and preservation of this procreative power. Much, if not most, of the pain and suffering that occurs in humanity can be traced to the misuse, abuse, and prostitution of this gift. The preservation and perpetuation of the human race depend on the powers and proper functions of reproduction. Few if any things are more vital to correct education than understanding and properly using this power. A major aim of education should be to establish the personal character in each individual to properly utilize and manage this power in his or her life.

A prime time for addressing this challenge is related to the period in life when puberty arrives. Joseph Smith was taught, and he instructed others to understand and clearly teach, this because great blessings are attached. The wheelhouse in which this can best be done is the home and family. His successors have endeavored to carry this teaching to succeeding generations and to share its importance to the world. Evidence to this end is apparent in two current documents. One entitled *For the Strength of the Youth,* and a second *The Family: A Proclamation to the World.* Compare the content of the counsel in these documents to what the worldly philosophies, advertisements, and admonitions are now pushing into the lives of people in many cultures. Here is an example:

The Family: A Proclamation to the World

The statements in column one are quoted from the Proclamation.

Column two cites views strongly advocated by many in contemporary society.

Proclamation Statement	**Alternative View**
Marriage between a man and woman is ordained of God.	Marriage between "consenting adults" is both traditional and optional. It is a personal matter.
The family—father, mother, and children—is central to human destiny.	The family—"a group of people living together"—can be socially convenient but it may also be supplanted.
All human beings—male and female—are created in the image of God.	All human beings are mammals that evolved by natural selection from simpler life forms and are formulated by chemically based genetic codes.
Each human being is a spirit son or daughter of heavenly parents with a divine nature and destiny.	Each human being is a physical organism—the sole product of genetic and environmental histories.
Gender is an essential characteristic of individual premortal, mortal, and eternal identity and purpose.	Gender is an arbitrary characteristic derived from biological urges and socialization.
In the premortal realm spirit sons and daughters knew and worshiped God as their eternal Father and accepted his plan of progress and fulfillment.	There is insufficient consensual evidence to support the premortal existence of human life. "Science affirms that the human species is an emergence from natural evolutionary forces."
The divine plan of happiness enables family relationships to be perpetuated beyond the grave.	There is no personal life beyond one's mortal existence. "We can discover no divine purpose or providence for the human species. . . . Promises of immortal salvation or fear of eternal damnation are both illusory and harmful."

Proclamation Statement	Alternative View
Sacred ordinances and covenants available in holy temples make it possible for individuals to return to the presence of God and for families to be reunited.	"We find insufficient evidence for belief in the existence of a supernatural; it is either meaningless or irrelevant to the question of the survival and fulfillment of the human race. . . . Institutions, creeds, and rituals often impede the will to serve others."
We declare that God's commandment for His children to multiply and replenish the earth remains in force. We further declare that God has commanded that the sacred powers of procreation are to be employed only between man and woman, lawfully wedded as husband and wife.	"Orthodox religions and puritanical cultures, unduly repress sexual conduct. The right to birth control, abortion, and divorce should be recognized." "There should be no criminal restraints on any homosexual behavior or public solicitation for private sexual behavior between or among consenting adults of the same sex."
Husband and wife have a solemn responsibility to love and care for each other and for their children.	Cohabitation without legal ceremony, responsibility or the encumbrance of children is valid and useful; it is an expression of personal rights that may foster optimum satisfaction.
Husbands and wives—mothers and fathers will be held accountable before God for the discharge of these duties: to provide for their children's physical and spiritual needs, to teach them to love and serve one another, to observe the commandments of God and to be law-abiding citizens.	Parents or the government should provide children with food, shelter, clothing, and education sufficient to make them contributing members of the society. This is temporal and intellectual task.
The family is ordained of God.	Families are temporary social conveniences.

Proclamation Statement	**Alternative View**
Children are entitled to birth within the bonds of matrimony, and to be reared by a father and mother who honor marital vows with complete fidelity.	Matrimony is a social tradition and children may be conceived and given birth with or without this tradition depending on individual choice.
Happiness in family life is most likely to be achieved when founded upon the teachings of the Lord Jesus Christ.	Happiness in family life is relative and is most likely achieved when the needs of each person is met in an atmosphere of peace and prosperity.
Successful marriages and families are established and maintained on principles of faith, prayer, repentance, forgiveness, respect, love compassion, work, and wholesome recreational activities.	Successful marriages are based on mutually accepted patterns of communication, sexual activity, division of labor, and sufficient financial resources to satisfy personal values.
By divine design, fathers are to preside over their families in love and righteousness and are responsible to provide the necessities of life and protection for their families. Mothers are primarily responsible for the nurture of their children. Disability, death, or other circumstances may necessitate individual adaptation.	There are no set gender roles in families; they are a matter of personal preference, mutual acceptance, and convenience. To stipulate specific roles for the man or woman is unacceptable.
Extended families should lend support when needed.	Once children become of age or leave the home they are on their own. The government is responsible if they need assistance.
We warn that individuals who violate covenants of chastity, who abuse spouse or offspring, or who fail to fulfill family responsibilities will one day stand accountable before God.	There may be some social standards but these are relative, not absolute. There is no supernatural dimension to life. "There is no credible evidence that life survives the death of the body." "No deity will save us; we must save ourselves."

Proclamation Statement	**Alternative View**
We call upon responsible citizens and officers of government everywhere to promote those measures designed to maintain and strengthen the family as the fundamental unit of society.	"To enhance freedom and dignity the individual must experience a full range of civil liberties in all societies." "The right to birth control, abortion, and divorce should be recognized." "A civilized society should be a tolerant one." We should "not prohibit by law or social sanction, sexual behavior between consenting adults." "The many varieties of sexual exploration should not in themselves be considered evil." "Short of harming others, . . . individuals should be permitted to express their sexual proclivities and pursue their life-styles as they desire."

The forgoing comparative columns highlight the significance of preserving the original, natural intent of the family—which is and always has been *to properly use and safeguard the primary purpose of the power of procreation.* No society can long exist in health or safety that consistently ignores, tolerates, or abuses the sacred nature of the primary purposes of procreation. The very purpose of gender—male and female—is to create, protect, and provide for children and to honor parental trust in their respective relationships. Men and women were endowed with this shared responsibility. It enables and sustains the human race. It provides for the birth and protection of children. It protects and enhances the proper relationships that are essential to family stability and function. It cannot be redefined with immunity. When this foundation is violated or eliminated, social order crumbles. History is a testament to the inevitable demise and destruction that occurs to any society that intentionally violates the sacred nature of the family—the victims will be both adults and children. Whatever auxiliary roles might exist or be desired, they cannot take the place of the original nature and purpose of the family. And without that family structure, deterioration and debilitating confusion are inevitable.

It was no accident that Joseph Smith was born at second light—during the sunrise of American freedom.[38] Through him, a shining light now filtered slowly over the shadowed land of a largely incarcerated world. Under the favorable conditions of this free nation, he struck the burning flame of restored truth, an act destined to illuminate a coming millennium with a miraculous education. In Joseph's mind, it seems, the future was not *in mortality*; the future is *through mortality into eternity*. His labors represent a work in progress that continues unabated. So what educational actions due to his initial efforts have transpired since Joseph's day? A few examples of such activities would be a fitting way to *link this essay from what has been, to what is now unfolding, and is yet to come.* Everything is not clear, but some things are. And those who read this monograph are invited to participate; each will have the opportunity to play an important part if they so desire. The remainder of this monograph seeks to explore these continuing and unfolding aspects of his work as a Minister of Education.

---

[38]The First Great Awakening (1735–1743) is well known. The trigger that released the American Revolution could well have been the impetus of this period of religious revival. American colonists were motivated to establish their right to separate the church and state, sufficient to allow the citizenry to create or embrace the church of their choice, among other issues related to individual agency. The Second Great Awakening (1815–1830) is also well known. This revivalist fervor spawned an intense debate over free will and predestination (determinism). It was during this period that Joseph Smith entered the scene. The Bible emerged as being more fundamental than church structure or social practices, and a sense of an imminent millennium surfaced. The stage was set for the impending battle between traditional Christian belief and modern secular philosophy, which flowered during the twentieth century and rages on to the present day.

PART XII

BUILDING ON FOUNDATIONS LAID BY JOSEPH SMITH

Much has been written and much more could be written to describe what has transpired in the two centuries since Joseph Smith established his views of educational fundamentals. Many people embraced and nurtured these principles. This monograph cannot envelop so large a task; the volume of information is far too immense. The very nature of the project would require multiple volumes and a great deal more talent, time, and resources than this writer possesses. What is doable is *first,* to call attention to a bridge of selected personalities that embraced and carried Joseph's educational thought from the nineteenth century into the modern era; *second,* to illustrate, with the briefest outline, the nature of the superstructure now operating on Joseph's inspired foundation. Of necessity this, too, will be selective. There is much more to the story than can be allotted in this essay as is signaled in the footnote below.[39]

---

[39]What one must not lose sight of is that Joseph Smith's educational influence moved West with the Saints. His foundational principles and policies have continued to shape the nature of *educational goals* wherever the Church has been established. A lucid, explicit example is manifest in the *"Articles of Incorporation"* written for the association formed to sponsor the building of the Manti Utah Temple. This document was signed on June 26, 1886 by John Taylor, George Q. Cannon and 48 other men from the Temple District. Article Two in part reads*: "The objects of said incorporation, are religious, scientific, social and educational, as well as for the practice of religious ceremonies and sacred ordinances, and not for pecuniary profit. It being the purpose of the incorporators to found and maintain a place for the administration of religious ordinances and a school of science in a Temple at Manti, Sanpete County, Utah Territory, for the practice of religion and for the promotion of learning and scientific knowledge, said school to include departments devoted to Theology, Astronomy, Mathematics, History, Languages, Laws, Natural Science and all other principles of true knowledge pertaining to the growth of infidelity which pervades so many departments of science as now taught, we enter into this agreement with the distinct understanding that nothing shall ever be taught in said school of science which will throw doubt upon the existence of the Supreme Being, or that will detract from His glorious majesty, or that will lessen in the least degree the most exalted faith in His divine doctrines."* (Manti Centennial Committee, *The Manti Temple,* Provo, Utah: Community Press, 1988, p. 146.

91

The building on the foundations laid by Joseph continued and is expressed in the actions initiated by subsequent leaders in the Church. In a sense, Joseph provided a blueprint for those who would follow him in continuing to shape the message he was inspired to deliver. The changing of times, resources, circumstances, and personalities have enhanced rather than eroded the fundamentals that he established in the early 1800s. The larger society has changed, but the needs of the people have remained quite constant (so have Joseph's educational views)—because they are basically eternal.

Moving Joseph's Views from the Nineteenth into the Twentieth and Twenty-First Centuries

The actions of four major players that followed Joseph Smith illustrate how others were helpful in the transmission of Joseph's views of education to the present day. Each of the subsequent Church leaders made their contributions, but the actions by these four demonstrate this point: Brigham Young, John Taylor, Joseph F. Smith, and David O. McKay. Like major pillars, these men anchored the preservation and promotion of the principles and practices that sustained Joseph's view of learning and teaching. And they did this in the face of powerful counter-forces. Each of them served as the senior leader in the Church—prophets in their own right—between 1850 and 1950. During the hundred years of their collective service, numerous counter-currents in western culture rose, fell, and swirled amidst confusing and enticing social changes. Pressures to modify revealed principles and practices were intense in both

---

Although subsequent growth and development in the Church permitted the building of significant educational facilities separate from the temple, the principles and philosophy established by Joseph Smith remained foundational in the Church. *Sometimes members struggle with his premises due to their excessive allegiance to secular influences.* Most, however, resonate with John Taylor's revealed witness, that it is *"in these houses* [temples] *which have been built unto me"* that I the Lord will reveal *". . . those things pertaining to the past, the present, and the future, to the life that now is, and the life that is to come, pertaining to law, order, rule, dominion, and government, to things affecting the nation and other nations; the laws of heavenly bodies in their times and seasons, and the principles or laws by which they are governed, and their relation to each other, and whether they be bodies celestial, terrestrial or telestial, shall all be made known, as I will, saith the Lord."* (Revelation given to President John Taylor, Logan, Utah. May 16, 1884. Church Archives.)

Europe and America. In many, if not most, government systems and religious organizations, these pressures prevailed; changes did occur. Schooling was in flux both in purpose and practice. The pre- and post-periods of the industrial revolution were turbulent and disruptive. The rise of *leisure* created new challenges—particularly in *character and values education*.[40] Personal role definitions were modified, and divisive debates continue today without resolution. The conflict over *imperative* and *relative* values has not diminished.

The demise of the old world kingdoms and the emergence of personal freedom in thought and act flourished; so did personal interpretations of what was acceptable to think and do. For example, the excessive liberality of literary salons among France's opulent elite embraced debauchery; Germany's structures of rigid and controversial institutionalism nurtured worldwide wars; Protestant liberal theologies reduced much of "Christianity" to social "ethics"; America's dominant agnostic and humanistic secularism moved God out of public education; are typical of a myriad of movements that impacted schools and educational practice. There was much to embrace and much to resist. Temporal progress was exhilarating; *populations were busy nearly everywhere rejecting revelation and offering substitutes for what God had revealed.* As the decades unfolded mid-century to mid-century, the four men mentioned held fast to what Joseph Smith had taught and pushed for the better way. Meanwhile, the divisive debates persisted in an ever evolving search for acceptable answers. The discussions were largely devoid of consensus at home and abroad. A variety of conflicting options were promoted. These discerning men consciously resisted the enticing diversions and encouraged their followers to do the same. They carefully embraced what fit Joseph's pattern and avoided what did not.

Brigham Young

After the martyrdom of the Prophet Joseph, Brigham Young, then president of the Quorum of the Twelve Apostles in this dispensation, assumed leadership of the Saints. By their

---

[40]See for example: Kraus's *Recreation and Leisure in Modern Society* (Jones & Bartlett Publishers) – (Paperback version of the original (2011) by Daniel D McLean, Amy R Hurd.)

vote according to the law of common consent, Brigham was chosen to preside over the move of thousands of the Latter-day Saints from Illinois to the Rocky Mountains. The move was necessary because of the difficult and deadly persecutions waged against them in and around Nauvoo, Illinois—as well as in a number of countries in Europe. Sitting governors of the States and territories of the Union refused the Latter-day Saints asylum in their borders; and some members of congress even met with Brigham and urged him to take his people and leave the United States.[41] Under these trying conditions, education remained a central theme in the preparations, journey, and establishment of these people outside the boundaries of the United States. Notwithstanding the temporal hardships, the learning/teaching emphasis of Joseph Smith continued and expanded. Schools were soon established in the new settlements of the West.

Brigham Young clearly explained the role of the gathering of the people. *"Joseph Smith has laid the foundation of the Kingdom of God in the last days; others will rear the superstructure."*[42] This was to be a central theme. Brigham was one who devoted his life to establishing the framework of education—both temporal and spiritual—on those foundations. His personal view of Joseph was as an extraordinary teacher. He once summarized the nature of Joseph's teachings in these words:

> The excellency of the glory of the character of Brother Joseph Smith was that he could reduce heavenly things to the understanding of the finite. When he preached to the people—[he] revealed the things of God, the will of God, the plan of salvation, the purposes of Jehovah, the relation in which we stand to him and all the heavenly beings, he reduced his teachings to the capacity of every man, woman, and child, making them as plain as a well-defined pathway.[43]

---

[41]*Journal of Discourses* 11:17–18.
[42]Ibid. 9:364.
[43]Ibid. 8:206.

The story of the westward movement in America and the role Latter-day Saints played in that dramatic era is well known. Hundreds of communities were established in the western wilderness. Teachers were appointed. Schools were built. A university created and academies in various localities were formed. The shared worldview of these people required that the educational vision of Nauvoo be realized in the lives of individuals and families, even though they were preoccupied with pioneering and physical survival in this wilderness. Volumes have been written regarding Brigham Young's perceptions of life and learning. Briefly outlined in one chapter of his collected comments is the way he viewed education. These headings indicate how devoted he was to what he said Joseph had taught him regarding education.

Knowledge and Intelligence

A Religion of Improvement

Continuous Education

Effects of Education

What to Study

Religious Education

The Body and the Mind

Wisdom

Brigham Young had a lot to say about each of these and other categories. His commentary in these areas was dependent upon and in harmony with what Joseph Smith had established as the foundation of education. Brigham actively nurtured education when the acquisition of food, shelter, and clothing was the primary necessity for survival.

John Taylor

John Taylor, an intimate friend to Joseph, was in the same room of Carthage Jail when Joseph was murdered by a mutinous militia in Illinois. This future leader of the Church was an intimate friend to Joseph. He admired his unique gifts as a teacher and leader and sought to be tutored by him. John Taylor served as an editor of the *Times and Seasons* newspaper in Nauvoo, as well as in many of the town's activities and educational endeavors. He traveled the world sharing the message of the Restored Gospel and was familiar with international happenings around the world. While in France he interacted with the worldly intellects of that nation, and had his own responses to what he considered the frivolous philosophies being espoused. On one occasion he said this, speaking of the philosophies he encountered in Paris:

> There they had a sort of exceedingly light cake. It was so thin and light that you could blow it away, and you could eat it all day . . . and never be satisfied. Somebody asked me what the name of it was. I said, I don't know the proper name, but in the absence of one, I can give it a name—I will call it philosophy, or fried froth, whichever you like. It is so light, . . . eat it all day, and at night be as far from being satisfied as when you began.[44]

John Taylor made quite clear the reason why he was often troubled by the philosophies concocted by men.

> One great reason why men have stumbled so frequently in many of their researches after philosophical truth is that they have sought them with their own wisdom, and gloried in their own intelligence, and have not sought unto God for that wisdom that fills and governs the universe and regulates all things. That is one great difficulty with the philosophers of the world, as it now exists, that man claims to himself to be the inventor of everything he discovers. Any law and principle which he happens to discover he claims to himself instead of giving glory to God.[45]

In contrast to this is his description of interacting with Joseph Smith.

> He introduced principles which strike at the root of the corrupt systems of men. This necessarily comes in contact with their prepossessions, prejudices, and interests; and as they cannot overturn his principles,

---

[44]John Taylor *The Gospel Kingdom*, p. 78.
[45]Ibid., p. 47.

they attack his character. And that is why we have so many books written against his character, without touching his principles, and also why we meet with so much opposition. But truth, eternal truth, is invulnerable. It cannot be destroyed, but like the throne of Jehovah, it will out-ride all the storms of men, and live for ever. . . . Many a time I have listened to the voice of our beloved prophet while in council, . . . his eyes sparkling with animation, and his soul fired with the inspiration of the Spirit of the living God. It was a theme that caused the bosoms of all who were privileged to listen, to thrill with delight. . . . My spirit glows with sacred fire while I reflect upon these scenes, and I say, O Lord hasten the day![46]

It was John Taylor who eventually became the owner as well as editor of the *Times and Seasons*, Nauvoo's Newspaper in 1844. He understood and was acquainted with many of the new theories emerging in and gaining popularity among the intellectual community in western society. He pushed for establishing Sunday School for the youth of Nauvoo and later in Salt Lake City oversaw the creation of a Primary Mutual Improvement Association. His concern for the youth and the responsibility for parenting them were significant. He linked this feeling to the revelation given to Joseph Smith which exhorted parents to teach their children, see that they receive the priesthood ordinances, and teach them to "pray, and to walk uprightly before the Lord" (D&C 68:25–32). While in Nauvoo he wrote:

> To see children break the Sabbath by running about and playing on Sunday; to see them saucy too to persons of riper years; to see them filling up the streets to play upon week days, and to hear them swear and use vulgar language, is a disgrace to their parents; a stigma upon the neighborhood; and a slow poison to themselves, that will eventually corrupt and ruin their reputations, unless cured by virtue and reason.[47]

---

[46]John Taylor, *The Gospel Kingdom*, p.356.
[47]Glen M. Leonard, *Nauvoo: A Place of Peace, A People of Promise*, p. 227.

John Taylor's interest in education as Joseph taught it, however, went beyond the local and practical levels. He exercised his capacity to comprehend the worldly philosophies and to shield the saints from being diverted by them. He often referred to the various political and philosophical shortcomings in world events, and warned of the *myth of modernism.* For example, he understood the failings of the utopian socialists like Robert D. Owen, Charles Fourier and Ettiene Cabet. In fact, he was very familiar with the Icarian movement which occupied Nauvoo after the Saints were driven out. These French immigrants bought the homes and land the Saints had abandoned for back taxes, and sought to establish a communal society, but it failed. Commenting on the likes of such movements while in France, John Taylor said:

> If Owen, Fourier, Cabet, and other philosophers have failed—if all the varied schemes of communism have failed—if human philosophy is found to be at fault, and all its plans incompetent, and we [Latter-day Saints] have not failed, it shows there is something associated with this people and with Mormonism that there is not with them.[48]

John Taylor was a person who, in his day, envisioned the temples being constructed as a type of university—a center for education that encompassed both a temporal and spiritual curriculum (as noted in footnote 39 in this document). He was a diligent and qualified protector of the educational views of Joseph Smith and strongly resisted insidious movements. John Taylor was convinced that education was essential to develop character. He understood this could not happen by separating the temporal from the spiritual; they had to be connected or morality in life would suffer and so would the people. Character was crucial. He made this point with great clarity and in a single sentence when he declared, *"Honorable men will be governed by constitutions, and laws, and principles, but dishonorable persons will not."*[49]

---

[48]John Taylor, *The Gospel Kingdom*, p. 327.
[49]John Taylor, JD vol. 23, p. 34. March 5, 1882. Assembly Hall.

Joseph F. Smith

The mother of Joseph F. Smith was Mary Fielding Smith, the widow of Hyrum Smith, the Prophet Joseph's brother, who was also martyred in the Carthage, Illinois Jail. This widowed woman of fierce independence crossed the plains and reared a son who became a champion of the importance of the role of the family. What John Taylor did to help the Saints understand and avoid *external cultural threats*, Joseph F. Smith did to help the members of the Church turn their focus inward to dangerous *internal forces* that needed attention. Forces were at hand to destroy the family and divert its functions elsewhere.

Joseph F. Smith was the impetus behind efforts to *protect the family* and to *correlate* educational curriculum and organization in the Church to better serve its members. He organized committees and created priorities that fit the model Joseph Smith, his uncle, had proclaimed was necessary, if the people were to accomplish their primary purposes for coming to this earth. The compilers of his writings and sermons noted that these messages "teach, in wisdom and moderation, practically every essential doctrine of the Latter-day Saints concerning the present life and the life hereafter. . . . They abound in helpful counsel and advice on everyday practices in right living, stated in simple and persuasive language."[50] These efforts are manifest in the origins of the Family Home Evening program instituted under his direction.[51]

Although Joseph F. Smith's recorded works are compiled under the title *Gospel Doctrine*, the focus of his efforts seemed to always stress the necessity of making that doctrine apply in the home and family. He stressed holding family home evenings and often explained the nature of proper marriage, home, and family relationships. His teachings regarding the

---

[50]Joseph F. Smith, *Gospel Doctrine*, Introduction, p. vi.

[51]In 1903 Joseph F. Smith emphasized the central role of the family in teaching the gospel. In 1909 the Granite Stake started a weekly family home evening program. President Smith said the stake was inspired to do this. In 1915 he asked all members of the Church to adopt the program on a monthly basis and promised that great blessings would result. "Love at home and obedience to parents will increase. Faith will be developed in the hearts of the youth of Israel, and they will gain power to combat the evil influences and temptations that beset them." (*Improvement Era* Vol. XVIII, no. 8. June 1915.)

eternal nature of these relationships are a prominent explanation and expansion of the genealogical and temple ordinance work for the dead, which Joseph Smith introduced in Nauvoo. Joseph F. Smith's description of the family and its function is all encompassing. He marked the doctrinal boundaries of propriety and impropriety for men, women, and children. He described the temporal limitations of the family, as well as their spiritual and eternal possibilities. His message was sobering and elevating.

> We are living for eternity and not merely for the moment. Death does not part us from one another, if we have entered into sacred relationships with each other by virtue of the authority that God has revealed to the children of men. Our relationships are formed for eternity. We are immortal beings, and we are looking forward to the growth that is to be attained in an exalted life after we have proved ourselves faithful and true to covenants that we have entered into here, and then we will receive a fulness of joy.[52]

Joseph F. Smith helped prepare the members to gain the internal strength that could help move the Church, which is primarily an educational institution, forward onto a new level of righteousness and effectiveness. The key to this, he said, is strengthening the home and family. He firmly believed that the primary educational purposes of the Church were to be accomplished by developing strong and healthy families. This is the way he once expressed this perception.

> God is at the head of the human race; we look up to him as the Father of all. We cannot please him more than by regarding and respecting and honoring our fathers and our mothers, who are the means of our existence here upon the earth. I desire, therefore, to impress upon the officers of the Church the necessity of consulting fathers in all things that pertain to the calling of their sons to the Priesthood, and to the labors of the Church, that the respect and veneration which children should show for parents may not be disturbed by the Church, nor overstepped by its

---

[52]Joseph F. Smith, *Gospel Doctrine*, pp.377–378.

officers. In this way harmony and good will are made to prevail; and the sanction of the families and the family life, on which the government of the Church is based and perpetuated, will thus be added to the call of the holy Priesthood, insuring unity, strength and power in its every action.[53]

It is clear to see from statements like these how vital Joseph F. Smith felt the family was to all things, including education, if people were to experience success in their endeavors.

A Fatal Trade

Morality	**for**	**Ethics**
Sinai	**for**	**Babylon**

No other Gods	Whatever Makes Me Happy
Come Follow Me	OK with the Group, OK with Me
Keep My Commandments	Eat, Drink, and be Merry

---

[53]Joseph F. Smith, *Gospel Doctrine*, pp. 162–163.

David O. McKay

At mid-twentieth century, David O. McKay, who had worked closely with Joseph F. Smith and was instrumental in moving forward his family interests and correlating efforts, addressed the Relief Society Annual Conference in Salt Lake City. He told his audience that he felt the inspiration of the Lord to emphasize the need for more parental responsibility, such as the Prophet Joseph Smith had placed upon members of the Church, to teach and train their children. Then he reported the following:

> In 1850, the character and culture of the American people commanded the respect of all the world. European parents sent their sons and daughters to our institutions that they might imbibe this faith-inspiring atmosphere. The Sabbath was nationally recognized and observed. The churches were well-attended. Divorces were rare. Today . . . lawlessness is on the increase, the cost of crime at all levels is $22 billion, over $4 billion more than is spent for education. . . . The crime rate has increased thirty-four percent in the past five years, while the population has increased seven percent.

He then asked:

> Sisters, what has happened to change this Christian concord of 1850 into this criminal chaos of 1962?

And proceeded to offer this explanation to the question:

> One hundred years ago, Americans were still being reared in public schools which included religious instruction. The great *New England Primer*, which for more than a hundred and fifty years had been the textbook of American schools, was just passing into discard. Eighty-seven percent of the contents of this remarkable book, which had built the sturdy character of fathers, grandfathers, and great-grandfathers was the Bible. But from that time on, the Book of books ceased to be an important factor in public instruction.

Then President McKay explained that in the previous June, the Supreme Court of the United States, invoking the First Amendment to the U.S. Constitution regarding "Congress shall make no law respecting an establishment of religion, or prohibiting the free exercise thereof," by a vote of six to one, made *unconstitutional* the repeating of the following prayer: *"Almighty God, we acknowledge our dependence upon Thee, and we beg Thy blessings upon us, our parents, our teachers, and our country."*

> By making that [prayer] unconstitutional, the Supreme Court of the United States severs the connecting cord between the public schools of the United States and the source of divine intelligence, the Creator himself, "in whom we live and move and have our being."[54]

In 1965, as part of the correlation program, David O. McKay authorized the publication and distribution of *Family Home Evening Manuals* for every family, to assist them in teaching principles to protect family members and foster their development. His reemphasis of the early Church efforts to *prepare parents to prepare children to be effective parents* continues to this day. This aspect of the program has been a vital educational influence as circumstances and cultural changes have emerged which threaten the family. For example, in 1860 about 90 percent of the people lived in rural environments and 10 percent in urban settings; by 1960 these statistics were reversed—90 percent in urban settings and 10 percent in rural environments. This dramatic reversal changed the nature of how family members interacted and what values they were exposed to—such as the work ethics, use of leisure time, and devotion to religious values.

David O. McKay was a life-long leader and educator who was tutored by Joseph F. Smith and other earlier leaders of the Church. He was a classroom teacher and an administrator. His devotion to learning about and defending the foundations laid by Joseph Smith is unquestioned. His time to lead as President of the Church coincided with the readiness of the Church and its programs to become an *international* enterprise. Church education was planted in the Polynesian Islands of the Pacific and Mexico. Seminary training for high school age students was functioning, and institutes of religion were operating on or near

---

[54]*Relief Society Magazine* vol. 49, no. 12, pp. 877–878. December 1962.

numerous university campuses. The Church was poised to experience a phenomenal outreach to numerous other countries. David O. McKay made a world tour to assess the coming expansion. The remarkable and expansive vision of Joseph Smith was about to surge. President McKay declared,

> The responsibility of showing to the world that the gospel of Jesus Christ will solve its problems rests upon the men who make the claim, who believe that the declaration made by the Prophet Joseph is true. . . . The Church is so constituted that every human need may be supplied. I believe in [this] statement. I believe, too, that every world problem may be solved by obedience to the principles of the gospel of Jesus Christ. The solution of the great world problems is here in the Church of Jesus Christ. Ample provision is made not only for the needs of individuals, but also for the nation and groups of nations. I realize that is a great claim. I grant that we may seem to be arrogating to ourselves superior wisdom, but we are not. It is simply the application of God's plan to world problems. You who hold the priesthood have greater responsibility today, now that you live in this creative moment in the world's history, than ever the Church has had before. I repeat it. If we claim to hold the truth, it is obligatory upon every Latter-day Saint so to live, that when the people of the world come, in answer to the call, to test the fruit of the tree, they will find it wholesome and good.[55]

The Church had weathered the storms of political persecution, economic depression, two world wars, and the ever-increasing theories of academe which was moving further and further away from God and the moral codes he revealed. Yet there was more to come in the twenty-first century to follow. We are now immersed in these challenges; these are our burdens to bear.

---

[55]David O. McKay, *Gospel Ideals*, p.5.

Summary

So we come to the summary of this century-long bridge, symbolized by four men whose lives and contributions became pillars that helped move the educational vision, principles, and practices established by Joseph Smith into the mid-twentieth century. Many others have followed, refined, and expanded what these men believed, taught, and did; and the process continues. Brigham Young used what Joseph taught him to help establish a temporal footprint for the Lord's Kingdom on earth. John Taylor helped protect Joseph's teachings and doctrines from being polluted by "vain philosophies" of men. Joseph F. Smith further entrenched the integrity of Joseph's foundations for education in the families of the Church. And David O. McKay launched this ongoing movement to an international level that is still expanding into third-world countries in what has to be remarkable and marvelous ways. The educational organization of the Church with all its functions—temporal and spiritual—is now an international enterprise. And line upon line, precept by precept, here a little and there a little, the Kingdom is rolling forth and growing in a miraculous fashion.

PART XIII

JOSEPH'S EDUCATIONAL THOUGHT FOR THE 21ST CENTURY

The selected outline that follows is limited. It does not provide information regarding extensive international programs now functioning in the form of week-day religious education programs, colleges, a university with multiple campuses, and a multitude of auxiliary organizations and functions servicing a wide range of humanitarian concerns. Likewise, it does not mention the thousands of wards and stakes, hundreds of missions, and numerous welfare operations based upon Joseph Smith's foundational principles. What the next few pages do illustrate, is how Joseph's influence is now depicted in the attention currently given various age-groups drawn to the message Joseph Smith delivered. His educational doctrine and aims are clearly reflected in the mission statements or goals established for each age group. When one compares these aims or goals with the worldly educational enticements currently marketed in our culture, the validity and wisdom of Joseph's work are evident. The stark differences are readily apparent in various forms of media, malls, and texts; as well as in prominent programs, schools, and publications. The worldly alternatives continue to aggressively make their case, sometimes deviously and occasionally brutal. Documenting this rather well-known story is a topic for another discussion. Here, the focus remains on illustrating the ongoing positive influence of Joseph Smith's efforts to guide his people through a confused, distracting and disorderly world. The following charts help depict these differences quite clearly. The focus is on three age groups which were identified and used to structure Church curriculum in the 1960s.

Assessable Values—Cultural Conflicts

Joseph was a great educator because of the breadth and depth of his vision, and the integrity and practicality of his approach. His form of education is uplifting, motivational, and life changing. It has endless scope and cohesiveness. The breadth of his curriculum is simply extraordinary—addressing physical, mental, moral, and spiritual needs. The personal activity required is empowering to those who sincerely participate. The nature of the entire enterprise is ongoing and is not subject to a single personality for its continuance. The curriculum makes sense to those who embrace it and gives people a structure of knowledge that transcends the highs and lows of mortal life. Joseph's educational impetus withstands the test of time and relevance. The foundation of Joseph's teaching now sustains succeeding generations with an uncanny form of protection against the pitfalls of mortal life. The system is self-sustaining and offers both rebirth and renewal to anyone who wants to learn, feel, do and become. It builds on that which he taught: *learn it, act on it, and share it.* This is the drumbeat of modern Mormon learning. It is apparent that life on earth is life in the midst of opposition.

The following charts depict how the Church Joseph organized now acts to protect the family and each age-group connected with it. Each chart identifies specific goals, values, doctrines and principles relevant to a particular age-group or audience. Opposite each of these statements is a brief description of precepts now promoted in the counterculture that lead people in a different direction than the one Joseph Smith was taught to proclaim. The differences are self-evident.

Chart # 1: Goals established to serve children—ages 3–12

Chart # 2: Goals established to serve young women—ages 12–18

Chart # 3: Goals established to serve young men—ages 12–18

Chart # 4: Goals established to serve adult women

Chart # 5: Goals established to serve adult men

The cumulative message of these outlines is clear. Discussion can illuminate the circumstances, but the point to be made is simple: reflected in each of these programs is the genius of an educational vision and initial footprint established nearly two centuries ago. Consider the scope of this type of schooling. Today, it remains remarkably relevant and incredibly expansive—all by a young man who carved out of a crusty frontier environment an intellectual and spiritual blueprint that is still developing ways to implement its application. The positive consequences initiated by this young man are difficult to overemphasize; the number of individuals whose lives have been affected are nearly impossible for a person to enumerate. When one considers the evidence, there is reason to recommend an affirmative vote for Joseph Smith as "America's greatest educator."

Primary (Ages 3–12)

Church Instructional Focus	Alternative Views
Teach children they are children of God.	Teach children they are the sole product of biological evolution.
Help children learn to love Heavenly Father & Jesus Christ.	Help children learn to love toys, parties, possessions, recreational activities, and popular electronic games.
Help children grow in their understanding of the gospel plan of happiness.	Help children grow in their desire to be socially popular, successful at school, and accepted in the neighborhood.
Help boys prepare to receive the priesthood & be worthy to use this power to serve others.	Help boys obtain physical and intellectual skills that give them access to recognition, possessions, power, and leisure.
Help girls prepare to be righteous young women who understand the blessings of the priesthood, temple, and service to others. (*Church Handbook of Instructions*, Book 2)	Help girls prepare to attract the attention of boys and to use that attraction to fulfill their desires for love and security. (Popular Culture and Marketing Concepts)

Preparing *content*, establishing *process*, and implementing *structure* are essential elements in successful educational endeavors. Joseph Smith labored to lay the foundations for these elements. Those who built upon these foundations have made numerous refinements. The central factor, however, has remained constant: *Learn and teach the Lord's way,* not the way of the world. This requires *engaging the Holy Spirit* in whatever is to be accomplished. The Spirit is the unseen, absolutely necessary ingredient, to obtain maximum success in the transfer of vital information from one person to another; one truth to another; and the means of introducing light to achieve proper applications generation to generation. Brigham Young affirmed this element at Winter Quarters in 1846. He repeated the same view some thirty years later to Karl G. Maeser who was appointed to establish the Brigham Young Academy (later to become *Brigham Young University*) in Provo, Utah. At that time, Brigham Young's instruction was that all secular learning at the academy should be infused with teachings from the scriptures. Speaking to Academy Principal Karl G. Maeser, President Young said: "Brother Maeser, I want you to remember that you ought not to teach even the alphabet or the multiplication tables without the Spirit of God."[56] The temporal must be attached to the spiritual, or education is incomplete.

---

[56]Ernest L. Wilkinson and W. Cleon Skousen, *Brigham Young University: A School of Destiny*, (BYU Press, 1976) p. 67.

Young Women (Ages 12–18)

	Church Instructional Focus	Alternative Views
Faith	Embrace the Atonement of Christ.	Embrace the popular culture; have high expectations; hope to be lucky.
Divine Nature	Develop God-given talents and qualities.	Seek admiration, acceptance, and control by emphasizing physical and psychological attributes.
Individual Worth	Use personal talents to fulfill your divine mission.	Experience popularity and a sense of importance; emphasize sexual attraction; exhibit personal superiority—not inferiority.
Knowledge	Seek knowledge by faith and by study.	Achieve in school and at work in ways that generate wealth, power, and control.
Choice and Accountability	Do what God wants and accept the consequences.	Do what you want—regardless—and if it's legally wrong, don't get caught.
Good Works	Build the kingdom of God by obeying his commandments; willingly serve others.	Do whatever brings personal benefits, rewards, power, and gratification.
Integrity	Act consistently with right, not wrong, as revealed by God and his servants.	Act consistently with right and wrong as determined by your personal desires or your peer group.
Home & Family	Develop the disposition and commitment to strengthen the home and family. (Young Women Values)	Ignore home and family whenever they interfere with personal desires, pleasures, or goals. (Popular Culture and Marketing Concepts)

Young Men (Ages 12–18)

Church Instructional Focus	Alternative Views
Become converted to the gospel of Jesus Christ.	Become converted to objectives and activities that bring recognition from peers and personal gain to yourself and selected associates.
Magnify the Aaronic Priesthood and its callings.	Improve your acceptance, influence, and security; find a satisfying niche among your peers, male and female, whatever the cost.
Give meaningful, service to others.	Provide service to those who serve you and who can benefit your personal interests and goals.
Prepare to receive the Melchizedek Priesthood.	Prepare to receive the rewards and benefits that come from increased recognition and influence; exercise the power necessary to retain control of these advantages.
Commit to be worthy of and serve an honorable full-time mission.	Commit to those activities that sustain your personal interests and make your life more comfortable, pleasurable, and secure.
Live worthy to receive temple covenants and prepare to become a worthy husband and father. (Mission of the Aaronic Priesthood)	Live in a manner that commands respect and attracts those who can gratify your social appetites and physical desires. (Popular Culture and Marketing Concepts)

Relief Society (Adult Women)

Church Instructional Focus	Alternative Views
"We are beloved spirit daughters of God, . . . women of faith . . ." who:	Women are oppressed; they should recognize that:
"Increase our testimonies of Jesus Christ through prayer and scripture study."	Christianity is folklore, prayer is psychological, and scripture is myth.
"Seek spiritual strength by following the promptings of the Holy Ghost."	The physical body generates all mental energy; it is simply physical matter acting on matter.
"Dedicate ourselves to strengthening marriages, families, and homes."	Marriage is optional, families are temporary, and homes are incidental to personal desires.
"Find nobility in motherhood and joy in womanhood."	Motherhood is a burden; womanhood is defined by maximizing personal pleasure.
"Delight in service and good works."	There is value in seeking self-satisfaction, gender privilege, and combating male *chauvinism*.
"Love life and learning."	There is power and significance in fashion, personal recognition, and equality.
"Stand for truth and righteousness."	Keys to success are self-assertion, social tolerance, and situational ethics.
"Sustain the priesthood as the authority of God on earth."	Authority resides in the individual; group demands may be honored as necessary.
"Rejoice in the blessings of the temple, understand our divine destiny, and strive for exaltation." (*LDS Relief Society Declaration*)	There is no scientific evidence of life after death; eat, drink, and be merry is the pathway to happiness. (*Contemporary Social Curriculum/Media Messages*)

Melchizedek Priesthood (Adult Males)

Church Instructional Focus	Alternative Views
We are sons of God, our eternal Father—invited participants in the blessings and responsibilities of the Abrahamic covenant who:	**Men are confused about their proper role in a changing society. They must strive to be politically and socially correct and recognize that:**
Seek to worthily hold and exercise the Melchizedek priesthood and uphold the oath and covenant associated with that priesthood.	Power and authority are fleeting; it is necessary to compromise and learn to work the system in order to be successful.
Strive to become self-reliant sufficient to provide for a wife and children—physically and spiritually; by precept and example share righteous instruction, support, and refuge from harm and evil.	Temporal success comes sooner by learning to share in the wealth and power already possessed by others; this is accomplished faster and easier by avoiding legal or contractual family obligations.
Build the kingdom of God on the earth by obedience to the laws and ordinances of the gospel of Jesus Christ—including personal temple covenants.	Building a large estate, becoming wealthy, and achieving early retirement requires total personal dedication; get whatever, from whomever, as cheaply, as soon as you can.
Sacrifice for and serve those in need by following the Lord's plan and the leaders he calls to preside.	The objective of power, wealth, and possessions is pleasure, leisure, and personal gratification. Marriage and families are optional and secondary.
Honor all women as sisters of divine origin; assist them in righteously fulfilling their purposes on this earth and in eternity.	Women are biologically necessary; they may be useful, and can contribute either success or failure depending on their interests, attitudes, disposition, and talents.
Engage in redeeming those who died without a knowledge of the gospel of Jesus Christ. (Doctrines of the Restoration)	Life beyond death is questionable; do not let myth interfere with logic and reason. (Popular Culture and Marketing Concepts)

Joseph Smith spoke and wrote often of the conflicts in values between what God desired for his children, and what the world offered as alternative enticements. Centuries have come and gone but this challenge has not changed, as the foregoing charts indicate. In his day, Joseph championed the right of the individual to choose between these offerings. He said

> We deem it a just principle, . . . that all men are created equal, and that all have the privilege of thinking for themselves upon all matters relative to conscience. Consequently, then, we are not disposed, had we the power, to deprive any one of exercising that free independence of mind which heaven has so graciously bestowed upon the human family as one of his choicest gifts; but we take the liberty (this we have a right to do) of looking at this [worldly] order of things a few moments, and contrasting it with the order of God as we find it in the sacred scriptures.

Nevertheless, though people are free to choose, Joseph was prone to challenge the futility of going the way of the world. And he was not subject to the notion that these conditions were likely to change in his day or in the years ahead.

> Some may pretend to say the world in this age is fast increasing in righteousness; that the dark ages of superstition and blindness have passed, when the faith of Christ was known and held only by a few, when ecclesiastical power had an almost universal control over Christendom, and the consciences of men were bound by the strong chains of priestly power: but now the gloomy cloud is burst, and the Gospel is shining with all the resplendent glory of an apostolic day; and that the Gospel of our Lord is carried to divers nations of the earth, the Scriptures translated into different tongues; the ministers of truth crossing the vast deep to proclaim to men in darkness a risen Savior, and to erect the standard of Emmanuel where light has never shone; and the the idol is destroyed, the temple of images forsaken; and those who but a short time previous followed the traditions of their fathers and sacrificed their own flesh to appease the wrath of some imaginary god, are now raising their voices in the worship of the Most High, and are lifting their

thoughts to Him with the full expectation that one day they will meet with joyful reception in His everlasting kingdom.

Not so, Joseph said (he was adept at using contrast and comparison in his teaching),

A moment's candid reflection upon the principles of these systems, the manner in which they are conducted, the individual's employed, the apparent object held out as an inducement to cause them to act, we think, is sufficient for every candid man [or woman] to draw a conclusion in his [or her] own mind whether this is the order of heaven or not. (TPJS p. 48–49)

Writing later, explaining the parables of Christ, he cited the biblical warning:

The prophet [Jeremiah], foreseeing that they would thus harden their hearts, plainly declared it; and herein is the condemnation of the world; that light hath come into the world, and men choose darkness rather than light, because their deeds are evil. This is so plainly taught by the Savior, that a wayfaring man need not mistake it. (TPJS p. 96)

PART XIV

JOSEPH'S VIEW OF EDUCATION FOR ONE'S PERSONAL LIFE

The foregoing charts (Part XIII) clearly illustrate the differences that exist between the *purposes* of Joseph's teachings regarding education and the more prominent cultural *purposes* now dominating our society—particularly in its educational institutions. The contrasts are stark. Nevertheless, we are where we are, and we should not hide from the reality that envelopes. Ignorance is neither a good excuse nor adequate protection. What was most *valued* in the past by the prevailing society is not what is now most *dominant*. Yes, the transition from *there and then,* to *here and now* is an intermingled pattern. There is some good among the bad. However, the prevailing aims, both expressed and covert, that drive contemporary education are significantly different. It is essential to acknowledge the basic nature of this modern platform. Otherwise, the significant value of Joseph Smith's teachings will be less apparent to the individual, the family, and the larger community. This section emphasizes the fundamental value of what Joseph Smith was privileged to share with the world and links these values to the deeper and most lasting nature of the individual. Joseph's view transcended time as we know it; one implication is *that which transcends time is of greatest worth.* He not only stressed the need for literacy—*reading, writing, arithmetic, social skills,* and the refinement of the *arts*; he pressed for an education that was and is even more vital—*vision and character.*

Joseph emphasized that it is reasonable to believe that anything that transcends time is of greater value than that which does not. Our English language is full of words that reflect human imaginations of life *before* and *after* time as we mortals experience it. This is one form of very powerful evidence: the desire for human life to transcend both mortality and earth-time. Otherwise, why do words like *pre-earth, post-earth, forever, endless, infinite, everlasting* and *eternal* exist. Death or the finality of personal annihilation can be discomforting to most people. Clearly, Joseph Smith considered that the most important aspects of our lives on earth are those that endure beyond the world in which we now live. He was not alone in this judgment. Cultures from here to antiquity are filled with variant versions of this concept: evidence of things we cannot see and the substance of humanity's hope are manifest and valued by people in every known age. Hope for something beyond mortality is the belief of the majority—probably because that which transcends time really is of greatest worth. So thought the educator Joseph Smith. (D&C 132:7–8; 84:100; see also vss. 99–102)

Now to briefly summarize the history discussed previously in this essay, as it pertains to each of us personally:

Today, it is not difficult to recognize that the academic community in America (and Europe) has basically rejected what was once a *spiritual* cultural tradition, perhaps because the composite of that tradition itself seemed so flawed. Nevertheless, the present power structure in modern society has essentially denied in principle and practice the idea of a supernatural domain. The preference in the public sector is to ignore the spiritual or denigrate it in education. The prominent conclusion in public secular affairs now is that all legitimate knowledge ultimately is best explained by *physical matter acting on physical matter*—however refined by microscopes and mathematical theory or however expansive as projected by telescopic instruments and astronomical galactic theory. All other explanations are viewed as insignificant or inappropriate conjecture.

In most schools today, "Science" in some form or other is touted as the primary source of truth. This is the current foundation for the *secular religious order* that displaced conventional religious traditions in America a century ago. *The prime educational value now is making things*—computers, various digital devices, bridges, buildings, automobiles, airplanes, trains, medicines, music, art, literature, touchdowns and points on a basketball court. The great source of rewards is **making** *(the Modern view).* This perspective is in contrast to **knowing** *(the Greek view)* in order to revere and admire, which does have its adherents but is not dominant. And this is also different from **doing** *(the Hebrew view)* that which God requires of us in order to fulfill our eternal potential of

118

becoming more like he is. Today, both *knowing* and *doing,* in this descriptive sense, play lesser roles among significant contemporary cultural values, and the schooling that goes with it. Making things drives the culture at large and dictates the primary purposes of education.

The *modernists* have established secular schools and written a curriculum to match their new worldview. The once popular *Knowing* as a cultural goal and the *rhetorical mechanisms* that drove it have been pushed aside. So have the *revelations* and *prophets* of old who preached the doctrine of striving to seek and do God's will. Current textbooks, professional journals, and dominating political policy directly and indirectly suggest that God is irrelevant. God's moral code is considered by many to be obsolete and is increasingly considered a historical artifact. *Morality* has been redefined and become man-conceived *ethics*—personal conduct is now largely defined by either (a) history (Hegel's dialectics), (b) the group—the people, place, and period in which one lives (when in Rome do what the Roman's do), or by (c) the individual ("whatever is in my best interest or makes me feel good" is okay if it works for me). God is not part of the modern educational equation.

Traditional standards for conduct (the Ten Commandments) and biblical religion that teaches against sin promote the ideas of a Fall, a Redeemer, an Atonement, and a physical Resurrection can be ignored or denigrated. They are not important. These concepts are no longer considered necessary or particularly relevant in the public domain or the legal constructs in our society. In fact, there is a growing antipathy against such beliefs. In his day and time Joseph Smith was aware of these growing forces. He frequently reported that the circumstances now prevalent were imminent. He conveyed a message from Divinity which states that mankind had "strayed from mine ordinances, and have broken my everlasting covenant; . . . every man walketh in his own way, and after the image of his own god, whose image is in the likeness of the world (D&C 1:15–16). The prediction then was that "the day speedily cometh; the hour is not yet, but is nigh at hand, when peace shall be taken from the earth" (Ibid. 1:35). This certainly seems to be an apt description of our day; it is indicative of the personal challenges we now face individually and collectively. Humanist idolatry thrives in the core of contemporary education. Joseph Smith's educational effort was to thwart such undesirables.

Given the contemporary scene, it is very important to recognize how modern education has shuffled the *Reformation* of religion into the dusty backrooms of our libraries. All do not agree that that is where it belongs, but it is self-evident this is the case, particularly in the field of education. Religious *authority* for education in America is now primarily valid only in our homes and chapels, and even this is under attack. Such authority is no longer considered a viable civil endorsement. Our public universities abandoned their religious heritage a century ago, and the consequences have sifted down into the primary and secondary schools. Politicians skirt the issue, attorneys struggle with the concept, and *public educators* see it as a fear factor in their employment. Political correctness increasingly prevails.

The other two primary predecessors to our modern world—the *Renaissance* and *Enlightenment*—now known respectively as the *humanities* and the *sciences,* constitute the bulk of the curriculum. And the current trend is for *science* to control the major resources in some fashion or other. American education, organizationally, was "the Little Red School" or the chapel; it was basically n*eighborhood centered, parent controlled* and t*eacher supported*. This changed with the twentieth century consolidation movement—several little schools became a larger *central* school. Now the dominant pattern is a*rea centered, government/teacher controlled, parent assisted* schooling. Unions are re-enforcers of this trend. This transition of control and oversight has serious limitations and consequences. It is the focus of much contemporary discussion.

Valuing the Restoration—A Positive and Expanded Vision of Education

The two mega-disciplines of modern schooling (*humanities* and *sciences*) are locked in an ongoing squabble over budget and recognition; they are largely beyond parental control. Despite the efforts of numerous policy commissions to shore up shaky mergers between the two, confusion dominates. This brief snapshot of our contemporary society constitutes a historical backdrop against which the educational thought of

Joseph Smith should be considered. His ideas about the nature and purpose of education strike the modern enigma with laser-like floodlights. *An entirely new vision is revealed regarding what education should be about and the kind of authority needed to sustain it.* This penetrating perspective originated with Joseph's training—his tutoring regarding learning and teaching, following and leading. His unique preparation is exceeded only by the purposes of that preparation. Education from this vantage lifts people to new levels. I realize that entrenched social institutions can be stubborn and difficult to penetrate, but that should not be a barrier to considering a better way and nurturing it where possible.

The core of Joseph's educational teachings identify and address the most fundamental forces—(a) *the purpose of life,* (b) *the nature of death,* and (c) *the significance of love and trust—* all of which are mysteries and often irritants in modern educational literature. Nevertheless, these are basic constructs on which Joseph Smith formed his views of education. They continue to be preserved and illuminated by those who follow the teachings he was commissioned to establish and promote. What follows in this section is a cursory introduction to these educational fundamentals. As education in America has become more and more secular, the pattern of education perpetuated by those who embraced Joseph Smith's premises continue to formalize a defense against these worldly forces. In the Church he established, *chapel-centered, auxiliary directed, and priesthood supported* education was restructured in the twentieth century and tightened into a *family centered, priesthood directed, and auxiliary supported* system of instruction. This emphasis continues to expand. Administratively, the movement is nearly in the opposite direction of what has transpired in the public domain. The basics remain intact as the delivery pattern is modified to meet diverse social realities. It works.

Types of Salvation and Exaltation

All religious orders seem to address in some way the nature of human life beyond the mortal grave—whether and how it exists or doesn't. Christian denominations are very familiar with their concept of salvation. They understand and seek after this relationship with their God—through Jesus Christ. Joseph

Smith acknowledged and promoted the idea of Jesus as a Savior. He taught *salvation* as a twofold blessing. One part was a blessing bestowed upon all people. Because of Christ's mission everyone will receive a resurrected body and a continuation of personal life beyond the mortal grave. This was the gift of Jesus to all humanity. The other part is the opportunity to become a member of the Savior's *spiritual family*, his kingdom. The scriptures speak of him as the "bridegroom" and his Church as the "bride" (Isaiah 62:5; Rev. 19:9; D&C 58:11, 65:1–6). The blessing of joining this family requires an added degree of personal effort. *Salvation* as part of the *Savior's family* is obtained by "a spiritual rebirth," as Jesus explained to Nicodemus. This leader, a Pharisee, came to Jesus by night inquiring about membership in His kingdom. Jesus explained such membership was obtained by being "born of water (being baptized) and of the Spirit (receiving the Holy Ghost) by someone who had the proper authority (John 3:1–13.) This is the pattern established for a second level of *personal salvation*.

As part of the *restoration*, Joseph Smith *reintroduced* another dimension or degree of salvation that pertained to the temporal *family unit*. After receiving the initial instructions from Moroni and the sealing keys of the Priesthood from Elijah—as they had been given to Peter, James, and John on the Mount of Transfiguration—Joseph was able to explain to his followers that in addition to being preserved as *individuals*, they could also be saved as *family units*. This ancient sealing power was now returned to the earth. It is possible, with proper priesthood authority, for parents and children to be sealed together and perpetuate their family relationships and associations beyond mortality. This blessing, Joseph explained, required not only divinely bestowed authority but also *ordinances* that needed to be performed in *sacred space—a House of God, a Temple*—which would enable people to make formal covenants with their Creator that entitle them to this blessing. The promise was comforting, compelling and far more profound than what the world offered.

Priesthood Ordinances are Essential

That is why Joseph Smith was so focused on building temples for his followers. The great plan of happiness designed by God the Father and enabled by his only begotten Son in the flesh was both simple and infinite. And Joseph Smith further explained that a part of this plan included the invitation to men and women to be sealed together in marriage as husband and wife for this life and for the life to come. He was given the keys to a sealing power by Elijah the Prophet in 1836; it was an enabling process that could *exalt* those who desired to do so, to live as their Heavenly Father lives, and under the conditions that He lives. This seems to be what Paul the Apostle referred to when he spoke of the "third heaven" (2 Cor. 12:1–4) and which Joseph Smith was clearly taught as recorded in D&C 76:50–54; 132:15–17, 19. It is the ultimate, if not the primary, purpose for coming to this earth and mortal life. Education can serve no greater purpose than this.

The information and the procedures associated with temple instruction became the primary focus and the capstone of Joseph Smith's educational enterprise. The intent of all that is fundamental to learning and teaching is to help prepare people to seek after and embrace the light and truth of temple ordinances. It is *temple instruction* that gives concrete and confirmed meaning to the statement God made to Moses, when he asked about this earth and the mortals who inhabit it. Deity responded: *"This is my work and my glory to bring to pass the immortality and eternal life of man"* (Moses 1:39). Supporting this declaration appears to be the ultimate end of Joseph's educational policies and philosophy. His short but eventful life is filled with evidence that supports this commitment. It was this work that dominated his energy and resources during the final two years of his mortal life.

The core teachings of Joseph Smith are fused to priesthood ordinances—ordinances provided by God to enable his children, if they choose to accept the invitation, to become as He is and to live as He does. This aspirational vision, delivered to Joseph, directly shaped his educational desires for himself and for others. He persisted in steadily pursuing and sharing this aim, which gave meaning to the various elements that could engage others in seeking and acquiring the promised blessings. The message was *inclusive*, not *exclusive*, but it was also demanding and orderly. The desired outcome required the power of a series of covenant-based priesthood ordinances. [57] The phrase frequently expressed by Joseph which envelops the entire process was *"the fulness of the priesthood"* (D&C 124:28). The most driving message to his most intimate associates focused on this phrase. This was the ultimate goal to pursue.

The need to build temples—providing sacred space—was related to this goal. Joseph once likened the nature of these ordinances to the rungs of a ladder. *"When you climb a ladder, you must begin at the bottom [rung] and go on [a rung at a time] until you learn the last principle; it will be a great while before you have learned the last. It is not all to be comprehended in this world; it is a great thing to learn [exaltation] beyond the grave."*[58] But Joseph was adamant that that process needed to be pursued in this sphere of our existence. There were no shortcuts—the crucial, divine, and proper order of the ordinances (some only given in sacred space)—could be bestowed nowhere else:

> Therefore, in the ordinances thereof [the higher priesthood], the power of godliness is manifest. And without the ordinances thereof, and the authority of the priesthood, the power of godliness is not manifest unto men in the flesh; for without this no man can see the face of God, even the Father, and live (D&C 84:20–22).

The listing of the ordinances as rungs on a ladder include to be baptized, be confirmed, be endowed, be married for eternity, be accepted, and receive the blessings of a recognition attached to opportunities and responsibilities that come with conditional access to sealing powers and ultimate resources. This was the "fulness of the priesthood." Joseph wanted people to desire and embrace the promised blessings. The path was education. He knew this depended on their willingness to learn, to teach, and to be taught to be pure and to be faithful. It required knowledge because, he said, "knowledge does away with darkness, suspense and doubt; for these cannot exist where knowledge is. . . . In knowledge there is power. God has

---

[57]*Articles of Faith*, no. 3, 4, 5.

[58]General Conference address, April 6, 1844. *Times and Seasons* 5:612–617, published August 15, 1844.

more power than all other beings, because He has greater knowledge; and hence He knows how to subject all other beings to Him. He has power over all."[59] And he knew that voluntary submission and conversion was the rudimentary requirement to obtain this kind of learning. It requires personal choice and an agency with which to exercise that choice. This is what mortality was designed to help people accomplish. It was clear to Joseph, and he taught it to others, reverence for sacred ordinances. The "fulness of the priesthood" was intrinsically linked to ordinances. Ultimate personal character development is the bridge to true godliness, and as one of Joseph's successors carefully explained, "Godliness cannot be conferred but must be acquired, a fact of which the religious world seem[s] strangely and lamentably unconscious. Seek to benefit others, and others will seek to benefit you; and he that would be great, let him be good, studying the interests of the whole, becoming the servant of all."[60] Joseph Smith knew and taught that some things—very important things—are the result of personal choice and individual effort.

The Practical Purpose of Life

Joseph Smith taught that every person is the spiritual offspring of deity. This affects how one should view the nature and function of learning and teaching, following and leading. He testified, as noted, that we have a Heavenly Father who has made clear that his work and glory is indeed to "bring to pass the immortality and eternal life" of His offspring. The operational purpose of Deity's work in our behalf is to invite and prepare us to become like He is. Joseph believed that "happiness" was the *objective* and *design* of our existence and will be the end thereof—if we choose to qualify ourselves for such a state of being. This divine intent is defined by the statement "men [and women] are that they might have joy" if they so choose (2 Nephi 2:25). This precept and its application are the essence and the primary purpose of education. Each of us is free—permitted to act for ourselves, to know good from evil, and to choose righteousness or wickedness, life or death, in the eternal sense of these terms (Helaman 14:28–31). All of this

---

[59]HC 5:340.
[60]*Teachings of Presidents of the Church: Lorenzo Snow*, 2012, pp. 212–13.

is according to a "law, irrevocably decreed in heaven before the foundation of this world, upon which all blessings are predicated" (D&C 130:20).

Our personal existence is intended to flourish under the umbrella of this invitation. The parameters are set. The possibilities are enormous and eternal in nature. This reality has been extended to us, and by virtue of our agency we hold the key to accept or reject that invitation. It is our choice to qualify or not to qualify for the blessings proffered. Joseph's view was that to reject these propositions and substitute other premises in their place was to go the way of the world. The result of this rejection becomes an apostasy of our own making.

The Central Role of Family

Joseph made it clear that the origin and the fulfillment of this grand purpose unfolds within the enabling functions of what is called *family*. In our day, the term *family* has many referents. The English word itself, *family*, may have derived from a Latin word designating persons within a household with slaves: *famulus* for a male, *famula* for a female. The most fundamental form of *family* as it is now used refers to a unit resulting from a male and female who enter into a *marriage* relationship, which generally includes children. Whatever the English origin of this word might be (or like terms found in other cultures and languages), any unit within the various cultures composed of a male and female and their children may currently be considered a family.

Closely related to the word *family* is the other term, *marriage*. This word commonly connotes a mutually accepted agreement between a male and female that is permissible, accepted, recognized, and validated by external circumstances, laws, or mores, the natural result of which is to have children and perpetuate the species. Authentic family and marriage relationships have an eternal purpose. Today, both of these terms are currently under assault in our society. Some form of imitation, revision, or elimination seems to be the goal. This is not helpful and can be harmful.

Beyond the traditional, widely practiced, primary and self-evident social unit, the word *family* splinters into numerous applications with various connotations in our society. If one accepts the Hebrew story of the beginnings of the human family on this earth, as Joseph Smith did, there was an original purity in the basic model reported in the account of Adam and Eve and their immediate family unit. Since then a myriad of adaptations have emerged. Some of these applications are easily understood and validated; others appear to be the result of *confusion, corruption,* and *abuse.* We also now have various forms of genealogical families, *mafia* families, and a variety of organizational families relating to various *instrumental* relationships. These clusters of people based on instrumental relationships have little or nothing to do with the procreation or primary education of the individual as advocated by Joseph Smith.

Without attempting to describe all of these uses or applications of *family,* a simple pattern may help us recognize the diversity between three general elements applied to the way *family* is applied to social structures. This is useful in understanding Joseph Smith's view of this term in contrast to the other arrangements that have become associated with the word *family.* The three elements can be viewed along a continuum based on the nature of the relationships between the people involved: They can be distinguished as (a) *intimacy,* (b) *proximity,* and (c) *instrumental functionality.* For example, a family engaged in procreation is in the (a) *intimate* domain—where there are biological implications and social expectations; a *family* in the (b) *proximity* area could be a form of an extended biological family or some organization of individuals with purposes not so intimate—perhaps even nefarious or ganglike; finally, there are numerous associations of persons in the (c) *instrumental functionality* area where the social connections are simply instrumental such as the Wal-Mart family—or some other similar operation—individuals who see and speak of themselves as *family* but who have very limited associations. I stress these differences because it is important not to confuse the use of the word *family* as it applies to Joseph Smith's view of education. In his work, *family* was intrinsically related to procreation and education for purposes that exist in mortality and extend to eternity.

In Joseph's educational thought, the term *family* focuses on *three primary families.* Each plays a central role in his view of education: (1) a *Heavenly family*—where each individual became a person with a *spirit body*; (2) a *mortal or earthly family*—where each person obtained a *physical body* in which the spirit entity dwells, and (3) a *spiritual or adoptive family*—where individuals can be prepared to fulfill their ultimate destiny—to receive a *resurrected body with the same attributes as* their heavenly parents. Thus we each have a Heavenly Father and Mother who created our *spirit body*. We have an earthly father and mother who created our *physical body,* which our spirit body now inhabits during this temporary mortal experience. In addition, we are also invited to become a member of a *spiritual family* headed by Jehovah (Jesus Christ, the Savior), our Heavenly Father's Son, through which we obtain a *resurrected body suitable to our life beyond the grave.* Jehovah ministers to this family as a father—presiding, providing and protecting—while His Church organization functions as a mothering agency. Again, this is why scriptural references refer to Christ or Jesus as the *Bridegroom* and his Church as the *Bride* and its members as his *Sons and Daughters,* in a literal spiritual sense, as well as figuratively or metaphorically.

Each member of the Church of Jesus Christ, as a *spiritual* son or daughter, is entitled to become a joint heir with Christ, entitled to all the Father's blessings. As such they are invited to engage in the personal preparation that will enable them to receive a *resurrected body* capable of becoming a Heavenly Parent if they so choose. Joseph Smith's teachings suggests this extended concept of *family* is the pattern that all earthly education was intended to sustain (see references to *Bridegroom* and *Bride* in the biblical concordance; also Moses 6:58–62; Mosiah 5:6–10; 2 Corinthians 6:17–18; Romans 8:14; Galations 4:4–7).

The overall view of these family functions is now commonly referred to in Church literature as the *Plan of Happiness* or the *Plan of Salvation.* In this family, as in the two previous families, education is the driving force, and individual preservation the essential concern. All that pertains to learning, teaching, following, and leading is designed to sustain the central purpose of this family. What is commonly thought of as an educational curriculum becomes a means to a greater end: *Language/Arts, Mathematics, Science, Social Studies,* and various practical skills are important but remain subsidiary to the *character development* that will determine the nature of the resurrected body a person will receive and the privileges that come with it.

Our Heavenly Family

At present, we understand some generalities regarding our heavenly *spirit family*, but very few specifics. For example, we can know we had a father and a mother; we can know our father's name was Elohim, but we apparently do not know the name of our mother. These heavenly parents—a male and female—created our spirit body and prepared us to come to this earth, along with a great number of our brothers and sisters. We can know that each of us was taught and able to develop considerable knowledge, as well as the ability to use the gift of moral agency. We can know that two of our brothers, Jehovah and Michael, created this earth under the direction of our Father, Elohim. We can know that our large heavenly family was well organized according to the social order in which we then lived. We can know that Jehovah, our elder brother, had a specific calling to serve our family and provide leadership for us, and that He acted according to the will of our Father. We can know that our progress would be seriously limited if we did not choose to enter mortality and obtain a physical body. We can know we knew that this movement involved personal risk as well as rewards.

We can also know that another older brother in this family, Lucifer, rebelled against our Father and divided our heavenly family; when he rebelled against our Father he led away one-third of our brothers and sisters in an attempt to avoid the risks. We can know that none of these individuals who followed him were permitted to obtain a physical body on this earth, but they were allowed to reside in this domain with certain limitations. We can know that he, Lucifer, and those who followed him are still striving to destroy the rest of Elohim's posterity who did receive mortal bodies. We can know that Michael, who helped Jehovah create this earth, was given the mortal name Adam and the responsibility of being the first man in the flesh on this earth, and that he was given a wife named Eve. We can know these two were given the power of procreation in this realm and were assigned to be our first parents—to begin the human family on earth—to populate this earth and *teach their children* how to return to the realm of our Heavenly parents after this mortal probation was completed. We can know that a veil was placed upon our memories when we entered mortality. This suspension of memory enables us to be adequately tested in this mortal estate.

This much we can know about our Heavenly family and how it relates to our purposes during mortality.

Our Earthly Family

Joseph taught that it is intended to know more about our *earthly family*. We can usually know both our father and mother and both of their names. We can also be acquainted with our immediate ancestors and extended family and perhaps others of our progenitors, as well as many of our posterity. We can know who we are, why we chose to come to this earth to live, and generally speaking what our eternal destiny might be. We can know that we chose to come to this earth under the circumstances into which we were born. We can know that this process is not fate, chance, or impulse (Romans 17:16–34). We can know who the father and mother of our mortal posterity is, and that humanity was given the power of mortal procreation. We can also know that our mother, like all the mothers before her, prepared physical mortal bodies and gave birth to her children. We can know that each successful birth into this mortal estate involves three essentials: (a) *water*, (b) *blood*, and (c) *spirit*. We can know that it is vital for the welfare of all children to be taught and cared for until they are able to care for themselves. We can know that mortal children also need to be taught how to return to their Heavenly Parents. They need help to develop the kind of character necessary to participate in creating and perpetuating families of their own in mortality, and in their post-mortal existence. We can know that this information is all part of the plan we were taught before we were born on this earth. We can know that Jehovah is responsible for this personal preparation in our behalf; that it is he who shows us the way and will be our advocate with our Heavenly Father, Elohim, who wants us to return to live as he lives. This information is often considered suspect or even weird by many in the world culture that now exists. Such views, however, do not change the validity of the plan.

Our Spiritual Family

Finally, Joseph conveyed to those who live in this dispensation that they may also understand that part of our Heavenly Father's Plan is for Jehovah to invite us to become a member of his *spiritual family,* the one over which he presides, provides, and protects with the power, authority, principles, and ordinances necessary for us to become as He is. We can know that most of the responsibility for establishing, presiding over, and sustaining this third family, to which we may belong, was delegated by Elohim, our Father in Heaven, to Jehovah his only begotten Son in the flesh. Thus, our eldest brother in our Heavenly family, Jehovah, was commissioned to serve as our *spiritual* Father on this earth. We can know that to become a member of this family requires that we choose to be born again—in a special way (John 3:3–7)—and that this birth to be successful also requires three essential elements: (a) *water*, (b) *blood*, and (c) *spirit*. (Moses 6:59–60.) We can know that Jehovah is the Father of this organization that functions as a Church—a nurturing "mother" to all who accept and sustain membership therein. And thus, as mentioned previously, our Savior, Jehovah, is called the Father (Bridegroom) of this spiritual family. The Church organized in Christ's name and powered by Him is the symbolic Mother (Bride) of this special family, of which all are invited to become members.

We can know that in order to be a worthy son or daughter in this family of Jesus Christ (Jehovah) and fulfill our ultimate destiny, it is necessary for us to willingly choose and continually sustain our membership. This entails essential and continuous education and also (1) being born again of the *water* (*repentance*—a willingness to commit to standards and signified by baptism through immersion under proper authority); (2) always remembering to accept and partake of the fruits of the Atonement of Christ (accepting *forgiveness* through the shedding of his (our Savior Father's *blood*); (3) receiving and abiding by the teachings of the *Spirit* (Holy Ghost), which will lead us and teach us to make all the covenants and receive all the ordinances and sealing necessary to be saved, resurrected with a celestial body, and exalted. This process is referred to as *conversion*—living in the world but not being of the world, and refusing to adhere to its false and wicked beliefs and practices. The partaking of symbolic sacraments weekly is part of this conversion process.

We can know that this is what it means to become a member of Christ's family—to always remember him, keep his commandments and endure (remain faithful) to the end. This is the gospel (good news) of Jesus Christ. However, we must complete the training and character development necessary by partaking of the sacrament, attending the temple and receiving the necessary ordinances, endowments and sealing to accomplish the purposes in full. This is what this family provides—namely, to secure for us as husband and wife a resurrected body capable of (a) residing in the celestial order where our Heavenly Parents reside and (b) becoming entitled and empowered to procreate spiritual offspring of our own. Herein is the ultimate purpose of this *spiritual* family of Christ—to qualify individuals capable of creating spirit children of their own in their own family. This is the work and glory of God and all who become as He is. This, Joseph taught, is why we need to pursue education and seek after all that will contribute to our fulfilling these purposes. He summarized the practical nature of this endeavor in these words:

> We believe in being honest, true, chaste, benevolent, virtuous, and in doing good to all men; indeed, we may say that we follow the admonition of Paul—We believe all things, we hope all things, we have endured many things, and hope to be able to endure all things. If there is anything virtuous, lovely, or of good report or praiseworthy, we seek after these things. (PGP Article of Faith 13)

Herein lies the operational foundation and expansive nature of Joseph Smith's philosophy of education. These elements reflect educational aims of his view regarding (a) *who we are*, (b) *why we are here on this earth*, and (c) *what our destiny can be*. They are the aspirations toward which essential learning and teaching should strive. They create the atmosphere and tone for productive instruction and all forms of curriculum associated therewith. Whether that instruction be reading, writing, or arithmetic; art, music, or dance; science, social studies, or recreation, they are worthy educational standards against which to compare and consider content. *The best education* includes and is shaped by a knowledge of correct answers to the three great issues above. And this kind of education is controlled by, and dispenses the truth about, other elements and attributes such as those which follow: the nature of life, death, love, trust, service, respect, civility, agency and charity. These attributes are safeguards; they enable, protect, and help preserve the knowledge and skills that are transmitted in the process and curricula that we call education. Without such safeguards the educational process can become a liability rather than an asset. It can be harmful rather than helpful to humankind.

In a moment of reflection, Joseph once made the observation that perhaps he was meant to swim in "deep waters," but he thought that was better than "shallow." I do not know exactly what this phrase meant, but it could refer to some of his insights into the nature of life's most important and intriguing topics. His teachings do impact such vital subjects and relationships as *Life and Death; Love and Trust; Love and Light; Love and Service; Trust and Civility; and Charity, Respect, and Agency.* I do not know how Joseph would briefly explain each of these terms, but I do know he has influenced how I think about them. I also know it is difficult to put into words the deeper meanings these words represent. The next few pages are an attempt to give a brief explanation of how his teachings have caused me to think and feel about these basic elements of human life. Joseph's teachings can affect our personal perceptions.

The Nature of Life and Death

Just as life is largely a mystery to mortals, so it seems is death. The conjecturing about life and death goes on generation after generation. The explanations and the expressed preferences are not in agreement. Discussions, books, articles, and college courses continue to be created to explore these topics, because life and death are so universal and personal. Nevertheless, there is little or no widespread agreement among generalizations, let alone specific details. Ultimately, the choices are reduced to *naming explanations,* such as "Death is the end of life," or "Death is the cessation of biological functions that sustain life," etc. Or *explaining explanations* that provide ritual descriptions such as those involving what some categorize as mythologies; for example mummification;

reincarnation or theologies, like purgatory. Widespread differences along either of these paths remain. People in every culture continue to struggle with the implications of death—both their own and other's. What is death? Where does it lead? What can we do to avoid it? What is its purpose? Conjecture prevails, consensus is non-existent. It is apparent that humankind does not have a complete knowledge of life and death.

Joseph Smith confronted the foregoing dilemma by simply extending the application of the propositions inherent in the view of *family* that was revealed to him and the limitations associated therein. He did not try to explain the secrets associated with "life" or "death." He just allowed what he did know to be true and could understand to shed light on what we experience with life and with death. He turned his back on the numbing influence of *fate* and fully embraced *faith*—the generating source of hope. Embracing the truths he knew to be true and sensible, he illuminated the nature of death and its purpose in a positive context. His explanation was lighted by many propositions which he accepted as factually relevant to our purposes for being in mortality. He knew fundamentally why we were here. This knowledge enabled him to understand and help others to understand the necessity of death as a doorway to continuing life. He knew people who had experienced death. He met and conversed with them.

His key to applying this information as the means for understanding the nature of death was to define *death* as a *separation*. This simple concept makes many otherwise troubling and difficult circumstances much easier to deal with. This view of death wasn't to make the process easy or pleasant, but it was more positive than most, if not all, of the alternative proposals that are entertained by people. His view was a logical and comforting extension consistent with birth. For example, if one accepts the notion that we existed as functioning persons with a spirit body before we were born on earth, it is sensible to understand how that spirit body could animate—give life—to our mortal body. Likewise, when that spirit body leaves its mortal tabernacle, the physical body can no longer function—it dies; this is mortal death, *the separation of the spirit body from the physical body.* It is the counterpart of life which becomes evident when a person is born. This perspective is highly relevant to education.

He knew that a similar application can be given to the term *death* as a *separation* when applied to the warning given to Adam and Eve. They were told that if they partook of the forbidden fruit they would surely die, meaning they would surely be *separated* from the presence of God. They did partake, and they were separated. In this view of death, it is apparent that we can suffer both *physical death and spiritual death*. It all fits neatly in the description of the Plan of Salvation and Exaltation that Joseph Smith outlined for the people he served. Mortal death is as universal as mortal birth. Spiritual death is likewise as universal as *spiritual life*—if one understands that spiritual life enables one to live in the presence of and not be separated from the comfort, opportunities and satisfactions of becoming like and living with our Heavenly Parents. From this perspective our physical death is simply a means to a greater end. Without physical death to help set us free from our spiritual separation from God, we are locked into undesirable and destructive circumstances (see Alma 12:12–37; 2 Nephi 9:6–10). The detailed nature of death may be missing, but its vital purposes are clear and understandable.

The Significance of Love and Trust

Love and trust are mercurial when it comes to stipulating their meaning—both transcend the limitations of language. They refuse to be solely reduced to either definition or attribution. Everyone has a claim on them and a unique manifestation of their expression. In the most generous sense, neither can be separated from the personality that houses them. Thus, no writer can actually describe love or trust as they would be manifest in word or deed by Joseph Smith. This is something they would have to experience by interacting with him. The best one could do with a description would be fragmented, because the meanings involve feelings and these can be strangely elusive. The closest one might come to portraying these two qualities by the written word is, I believe, by association. To represent love and trust as they might fit in Joseph's educational thought requires sensing their relation to other concepts or qualities in which he believed and precepts which he taught. Even this may be problematic. It is easier to

135

write some of this explanation in first-person form, as if what I am writing is close to what Joseph would say, based on my understanding of his beliefs and teachings.

I believe Joseph would readily agree that everyone has a personality and everyone is unique. I think he believed that each person is a source of light that reveals truth through the way that person acts. I think it is clear that he believed *personality* has a continuance, and this eternal existence of the individual is the essence of meaning. Where there is no personality there can be no meaning. I see *personality* as something like the filament in a light-globe, which glows when powered by electricity. Personality is the filament in our body that glows when powered by the energy of life. Personality is the light globe of life; it is the manifestation of *life-light* by comparison to *electric light*. Without that filament, that innate intelligence, or as one might say, *consciousness*, all is darkness. Where there is no personality there can be no light. The death of the physical body confirms this. Eliminate personality and there is no way to make truth known; it cannot be manifest. Awareness of our own *being* constitutes the nucleus of our personality and drives the activity in our day-to-day affairs. These premises permeate Joseph's teachings.

Personality is the unit from which and through which light and truth radiate, but so does error, Joseph observed. Consequently, truth and error can be encountered wherever there is personality—in ourselves and in others. It is through our personality that skills, emotions, and characteristics come into existence. And the use to which they are put can be good or bad. These observations are not hidden, exclusive, or restricted. They are available to every person; once embraced, their confirmation and their fruits are self-evident. They do not need scientific experiments or academic experts for validation, though these may apply and confirm what I am saying. Evidence of the validity of these propositions is available to every parent, teacher, and child. We can all know when we experience love and trust and when these are absent.

Everyone may be a witness of this growth in awareness and the manifest uniqueness of each child. The intrinsic developmental process is pervasive in all humanity. However, Joseph made clear that it is only through God's personality that *all* truth and no errors are obtained, and *all* light and no

136

darkness manifest. Our individual destiny is to become like our Creator, in whose image and likeness we are and can become. This is a primary opportunity and challenge inherent in mortality; it is part of the pathway that leads toward our potential destiny. It is the core of education. What greater cause could there be? What better aim for education? This message is evident both in what Joseph believed and how he lived and taught; it is what he encouraged others to believe, live and teach. We are all capable of this; we can love and trust.

Personality is essential to the notion of *human agency— where there is no personality there can be no human agency—* because such an entity *cannot act, it can only be acted upon.* Consider a stone—it has no basis for acting; it can only be acted upon. Other people are also important to this agency-based dynamic; they are fountains of truth from which we nourish our very being. Hence it is not good for man or woman to be alone; people need each other. Individuals have inherent value; they are not expendable items. Great is the worth of the individual; people manifest truth to each other; there is light within each personality. For this reason alone, if for no other, it is important to care about each other.

This fact can be readily observed from the moment a mother cradles a newborn child in her arms. Everything about us attests to this truth, including death, which marks the departure of the personality and its light from the mortal body to pursue the next stage of its destiny in another dimension. Death, as previously mentioned, is the unmistakable witness that we are more than our physical being. Every mortuary houses this silent testimony, this compelling witness. Joseph taught with conviction that death is not the end of life. Personality has a continuance, and this eternal existence is the essence of meaning. It is easy to recognize that to believe less than this is to set ourselves up as less than what we are and to be proven wrong. These sentiments form an essential part of the foundation for love and for trust. Without any doubt, Joseph Smith held and expressed these convictions. He was a champion of love and trust.

The denial of life without end is a substitute belief put forth in the face of numerous witnesses who have testified otherwise. For me, this is unworthy. Believing I will cease to exist sells myself short for no good reason—unless one assumes that some form of self-justification can be considered a good reason. Self-annihilation, were it possible, may be an argument that could obliterate personal accountability. But what comfort is there in this rationale? What gain is there in self-destruction to avoid accountability? The notion itself is a dark and negative thought, void of compelling evidence. Accountability is meaningless if the end of our existence is evaporation into nothingness. Who can generate enthusiasm to embark on a trip to nowhere? Can you? Joseph didn't seem to think so either. All he lived for, he died for; and he did so with confidence that life goes on for everyone.

Love Sustains Light

This brings into sharper focus another fundamental, the purpose of *love*. In order for little children to grow up in the light, they need to be loved. Love is a fundamental element in the nurture of every human being. Love is governing oneself in ways that nurture the disposition to care about others—to do for them that which they cannot do for themselves, usually without expecting anything in return. This is love. Love and light are natural companions. Parents and teachers are sources of light for children—not all light, but a very significant source. Love is a major vehicle for conveying light to others. Love and light are what make knowledge worthwhile. What good is knowledge if there is no love or light? The key to properly *acquiring* and *applying* truth (knowledge) seems to reside in continuously seeking more *light*—divine light that enables one to see the truth and understand how to properly act upon it. Light ennobles and enhances; darkness shrinks and distorts human personality and the truths manifest through it. And love facilitates light. Joseph's biography is replete with examples of this fact as it operated in his relationships with others. He suffered unjust accusations, afflictions, persecutions and numerous ill-founded lawsuits. On average he faced a lawsuit every month of his ministry, charges that took his liberty, his assets and ultimately his life. N*ot once* was he found legally guilty of *any* of these charges. Yet his life was also filled with acts of kindness, service, and contributions that drew incalculable admiration from the multitudes who knew him. He was loved because he loved others, and he was hated because of this love—strange as that may seem.

My focus here is on the presence or absence of the light associated with the personality. I believe, as Joseph did, that people are moved into the shadows of life by nurturing the spirit of disobedience and by the nurture of false traditions. This is confirmed by my own experience; I know when I move toward or away from light, and I see this same pattern in other people. We are all aware of this phenomenon in our personal lives (D&C 93:29–40). We may deny it, but we know it. I can choose the direction; light and dark, physical and spiritual, are plainly manifest to me—as I believe they are to all people. What we sense or experience may vary because of ignorance or education. But the options are there, and the process is pervasive.

True, it is possible to make choices that move us into the dark until we disdain the light and try to blink it away—in a manner of speaking. But it is also possible to choose to live in the light until one takes no pleasure at all in the dark. The evidence is in us and around us. Light and love are companions; they attract each other. So do darkness and selfish gratification. You do not need anyone to prove this to yourself or to prove this to anyone else. It is self-evident. Understanding and accepting this context enhances and fortifies learning, teaching, following and leading. It is a boon to parents and the sustenance of healthy social associations in any setting. It is better to live in the light than it is to be lost in the dark. This is a platform on which Joseph Smith endeavored to form education. He knew that where there is no vision the people tend to perish. Conveying this vision from one generation to the next is the province of education.

Adults are edified when they reside in light and truth, because there is always a measure of *love* under such conditions. Children deserve to be reared under this umbrella of both light and truth; they naturally elicit love. Likewise, parents by nature are capable of generating love if they don't hide or shield it with bad choices. Were it not so, there could be no enduring relationships, because there would be insufficient love to sustain the necessary light to produce happy associations. Love, that precious form of appreciation, is a fruit of truth when it is accompanied by light. That is why education needs to be more than just a love of learning; it must be a love of learning *what is true*—which includes a fundamental respect for others.

Truth without light is incapable of eliciting love; it is limited to the application of mechanics, of physical pleasure, of self-interest, of impulsive self-serving passion, and is blind to many important consequences. Nowhere is this more evident than in our most intimate relationships. Abuse of children, spouses, the aged, the disabled, and the disadvantaged can all be traced to some application of the mechanics of truth devoid of light; it is therefore an application estranged from true love. Without light we do not have eyes that see or ears that hear. We become subject to a self-inflicted handicap of social blindness and insensitivity. We become potentially dangerous to ourselves as well as to others. Ignorance is not a safe path to follow; true education is.

Love is Manifest in Service

Light and truth, properly combined, both inform and sustain productive love. I say "productive love or true love" because there are *counterfeits*, which are not love at all. Selfishness has long been known to masquerade as love. Selfishness is the great pretender. It will don any number of costumes as a means of seduction in order to satisfy its self-serving objectives. This is not love. Literature and movies derived from literature are filled with examples of seduction driven by selfishness; so are too many personal lives. Joseph pointed out that light cleaves unto light; it seems to follow naturally that love, which is a product of light, would both seek and attract light. True love enlightens, it does not blind; darkness does blind, and darkness also cleaves unto darkness. We cannot be fully free without love and light. We may be deceived by counterfeits, but they bring no reward, only less liberty. And they leave us more vulnerable, like fish that swim in murky and muddy waters. We are blessed by love and cursed by its opposites.

Love is manifest through service. It is in service that love is most commonly encountered. Service is a form of giving: a manner of thinking, feeling, and doing in behalf of others. Service enhances both the giver and the receiver. Without service beyond self, love is not clearly manifest. Love allows us to live beyond ourselves—beyond selfishness—by inviting us to serve. Love is born in illuminated thought, nurtured in feeling, and demonstrated by action.

Thoughts are the seeds that precede our actions. It follows that the purpose of learning, teaching, following, and leading is to implant in the mind *right thoughts*, *pure motives*, and *noble ideals*; right words and actions will inevitably follow. This is the lubrication of true education. It is unfortunate that modern schooling has drifted away from this emphasis. Character education is no longer a central theme. To ignore, contaminate, or prohibit this ennobling purpose restricts learning, corrupts teaching, subverts following, and compromises leading. The educational enterprise is jeopardized and can cripple the human soul. It is not good when *parents* and *teachers* lose sight of this great responsibility that is worthy of our best efforts. There are many testaments by people who have said they felt these positive qualities in their relationship with Joseph Smith. He would desire that this be a mark in everyone's life. He made it a visible mark in his own life and encouraged others to do likewise.

Trust and Civility Enhance Human Agency

The dynamics of *human agency*—the presence of life and the capacity to act within the light of one's awareness—is an ever-present process. Legitimate learning and teaching, following and leading, extend beyond the temporal to the moral and the spiritual. *It is in the moral and spiritual domains that trust is nurtured and where civility emerges and matures. Love and trust form the essential foundation for enduring civility. Without love and trust, civility cannot survive.*

Temporal activity, physical or mental, can be fully self-serving. We can function temporally without the tempering influences of the trust that undergirds moral and spiritual order. When this occurs the consequences are potentially destructive. It is only in the moral and spiritual domains where real safety for those beyond the self can be found. There is no enduring safety for the soul, or the souls of others, in the physical and intellectual arenas devoid of moral and spiritual oversight. They constitute an essential environment. Only when the self is subjected to principles that protect others can there be the safety that some call civility. It is civility, born of trust, that fulfills the goal of helping children to walk uprightly. If we are to avoid abuse, mayhem, and murder, we must invoke the trust that cultivates civility. And lest we forget, there can be no real civility without moral and spiritual input. Physical and intellectual substitutes may be useful but are sorely inadequate to bring to pass what matters most. Education must be measured against these inherent standards of mortality.

Civility requires a foundation of positive character—trustworthiness in character—which is governed by a moral order. Joseph taught that light and truth, consistently pursued, can preserve people from the ignorance and error that block the development of character that sustains civility. *This is why character development is the primary purpose of true education* and God's character is the proper example. As Joseph said, "It is the first principle of the Gospel to know for a certainty the character of God. (TPJS p. 345). True education utilizes both light and truth to develop the personal character that promotes civility. The love that issues forth from service is the soil in which trust and civility are nurtured, developed and enabled to flourish. One may be forced to serve without love, but one cannot really love and not feel a desire to serve. It could be a personal aphorism to say, *Where there is no personal service there is no love, and where there is no love there will be little or no trust or civility.*

The positive improvement of one's character expands the opportunity to choose and act; it makes people free—free to encounter more truth, greater light, and an increased abundance of love. Proper choices foster the trust and civility that make possible life in a higher order. This perception supports the biblical exhortation "Know the truth and the truth shall make you free." The views of love, trust and civility described are an example of the rest of that little story. The statement itself is a worthy exhortation. And it is designed to begin in our families and will be manifest in productive education as well as in the lives we strive to live. These observations follow Joseph Smith's premises.

Charity is the Canopy for Love, Trust, Respect

It has been said that it is a greater compliment to be *trusted* than to be *loved*. Perhaps that is because love itself can so easily be a one-way street. A person can be loved but not love in return. *Love properly bestowed and properly received generates respect.* As love, trust and respect flourish in human affairs, there is an opportunity to foster lifestyles that encourage their expansion and continuation in the form of respect. When this occurs and is sustained, ultimately an environment of charity will prevail. The absence of selfish and destructive motives and behaviors seems to invite into one's life what one could call *charity*.

Joseph Smith embraced the definition of *charity* to be the "the pure love of Christ." He felt this was the ultimate aim of the best education. Our Savior is filled with and freely dispenses pure love. He encourages all who will, to the extent they are able, to follow his example. Faith and hope are the foundation upon which such love is born and bestowed. One might conclude, as Joseph did, that where there is no faith there can be no hope and where there is no hope there can be no charity. Charity is the pure love that enables a person to voluntarily do for others what they cannot do for themselves. Here are the words he translated and shared with all who would receive them:

> And charity suffereth long, and is kind, and envieth not, and is not puffed up, seeketh not her own, is not easily provoked, thinketh no evil, and rejoiceth not in iniquity but rejoiceth in the truth, beareth all things, believeth all things, hopeth all things, endureth all things. Wherefore, my beloved brethrern, if ye have not charity, ye are nothing, for charity never faileth, Wherefore, cleave unto charity, which the greatest of all, for things must fail—But charity is the pure love of Christ, and it endureth forever; and whoso is found possessed of it at the last day, it shall be well with him. (Moroni 7:45–47)

PART XV

JOSEPH'S INSPIRED VIEW OF LEARNING AND TEACHING

The Spiritual Core of Education

Perhaps the most unique aspect of the pattern for learning and teaching given to Joseph Smith is the role ascribed to the spiritual core of how the best education occurs. In 1832 and 1833, about a year after the Saints moved from New York to Kirtland, Ohio, the Lord gave specific instructions to Joseph regarding the role of the teacher and the learner in His lay operated Church. There was no professional clergy as such, His organization was to be manned and sustained by converted and dedicated members. This meant that an educated membership was essential. Following a period of pondering and praying concerning the education of the Saints, the following process was received and recorded.

> I give unto you a commandment that ye shall continue in prayer and fasting from this time forth. . . . you shall teach one another the doctrine of the kingdom. Teach ye diligently and my grace shall attend you, that you may be instructed more perfectly in theory, in principle, in doctrine, in the law of the gospel, in all things that pertain unto the kingdom of God, that are expedient for you to understand; of things both in heaven and in the earth, and under the earth; things that have been, things which are, things which must shortly come to pass; things which are at home, things which are abroad; the wars and the perplexities of the nations, and the judgments which are on the land; and a knowledge also of countries and of kingdoms—That ye may be prepared in all things when I shall send you again to magnify the calling whereunto I have called you, and the mission which I have commissioned you. (D&C 88:77–80)

This was to be the content and scope of the curriculum. The instructions continued regarding the process of implementation. Among other things, the nature of the learning/teaching relationship was explained.

Therefore, verily I say unto you, my friends, call your solemn assembly, as I have commanded you. And as all have not faith, seek ye diligently and teach one another words of wisdom; yea, seek ye out of the best books words of wisdom; seek learning, even by study and also by faith. Organize yourselves; prepare every needful thing; and establish a house, even a house of prayer, a house of fasting, a house of faith, a house of learning, a house of glory, a house of order, a house of God; . . . Appoint among yourselves a teacher, and let not all be spokesmen at once; but let one speak at a time and let all listen unto his sayings, that when all have spoken that all may be edified of all, and that every man [person] may have an equal privilege. See that ye love one another; cease to be covetous; learn to impart one to another as the gospel requires. (D&C 88:119–123)

Previously, Joseph had been instructed to teach his people to live lives worthy of the companionship of the Spirit—both the Spirit of Christ and the Holy Ghost. These admonitions included:

And they shall observe the covenants and the church articles to do them, and these shall be their teachings, as they shall be directed by the Spirit. And the Spirit shall be given unto you by the prayer of faith; and if ye receive not the Spirit ye shall not teach. (D&C 43:13–14)

In other words, *why* learners and teachers do *what* they do when they seek to learn and teach is very important. It is essential that if one wants the best results, it is important to engage in the educational process with the right intentions and in the right way. A positive and worthy disposition by both learner and teacher is critical. Otherwise, the results will not be what they otherwise might have been. The learning and teaching will be less than what it could be; it will be substandard by comparison regardless of where it takes place.

146

This counsel applies to all learners and teachers in all settings. Though not always reached, it is a worthy standard and invites us to strive to become better learners and teachers. It represents a beneficial disposition.

Assessing Joseph Smith's Educational Views

The basic principles of learning and teaching espoused by Joseph Smith are readily available. They have been articulated, adapted, and re-adapted for nearly two centuries. This lengthy history of application and refinement continues in the present and touches nearly everyone's stewardship: *parents and children, followers and leaders, preachers and hearers, learners and teachers.* As technology has changed, the adaptations have been modified to match the times and resources. The dynamic nature of Joseph Smith's educational vision is remarkable. It is easily understood and applied. The doctrines and principles remain stable and unchanged. Most of the information is contained in the standard works of The Church of Jesus Christ of Latter-day Saints and the prophetic commentary associated with their use. *I will conclude this essay with a summary of how these principles and pro-positions might be embraced and applied to enhance our personal educational quest.* Others will articulate their own versions. Because Joseph left so much to work with, this is not very difficult to do. But it does require some *desire*—enough to create *attention*, and the attention must develop into *interest*, and the interest must result in a *commitment to act*. Otherwise progress stalls. When there is no commitment, no willingness, there can be no fruitful progress.

It is apparent that time and circumstances will continue to refine the processes of implementing Joseph's kind of education. But the doctrines and principles will remain constant, as they have been in the past. It is simply our personal understanding of these principles and doctrines that will continue to develop generation upon generation. I feel confident that applying this inspired guidance will improve learning and teaching in our homes and classrooms. The instructions can be adapted to any teaching situation; they are simple truths that enable each person both young and old to grow and serve. Studying the scriptures by the Spirit will help us think the right thoughts, feel the right feelings, say the right words, and do the right deeds. This is why Jesus was such a powerful teacher. Part XV *explains Joseph Smith's inspired view of learning and teaching.* Part XVI *describes Joseph Smith's scriptural record on how to prepare and present learning and teaching consistent with that inspired view.*

This part (Part XV) of the monograph begins by reviewing *Joseph Smith's and Elijah the Prophet's respective missions.* Their missions are part of the structure in which we now live. They have very important complementary roles. The assignments given to these two individuals were linked at the very beginning of the latter-day restoration of the gospel of Jesus Christ. Understanding Joseph Smith as an educator cannot be fully appreciated without also understanding the role of Elijah, who gave Joseph *the keys of the sealing powers of the priesthood.*[61] The keys of this power are the enabling factors that connect education on earth with education in the spirit world. The *Spirit of Elijah* helps drive this connection, facilitates its function and insures the fulfillment of its eternal purposes. The sealing ordinances made possible by Elijah's visit pertained to both the living and the dead. They envelop what Joseph referred to as the *fulness of the priesthood.*[62]

This section ends with an examination of *the four elements that constitute the framework of most if not all intentional education.* They are evident in most educational endeavors. These elements are apparent in the writings and the descriptive accounts of Joseph's educational interactions, particularly with the people among whom he lived and endeavored to teach. Modern terms that describe these four elements are *context*

---

[61]"The spirit, power, and calling of Elijah is, that ye have power to hold the key of the revelation, ordinances, oracles, powers and endowments of the fullness of the Melchizedek Priesthood and of the kingdom of God on the earth; and to receive, obtain, and perform all the ordinances belonging to the kingdom of God, even unto the turning of the hearts of the fathers unto the children, and the hearts of the children unto the fathers, even those who are in heaven." HC 6:251 (spelling modernized).

[62]Without disclosing details, Joseph made this comment regarding the apostle Peter's admonition to "make your calling and election sure" (2 Peter 1:10). He offered the saints three keys: "1st key: knowledge is the power of salvation. 2nd key: make your calling and election sure. 3rd key: it is one thing to be on the mount and hear the excellent voice, etc., and another to hear the voice declare to you, 'You have a part and lot in that kingdom'" (TPJS p.306, May 21, 1843; HC 5:401–403).

(why), *content* (what), *structure* (where), and *process* (how). My intent is to illustrate how these elements influence the learning/teaching relationship. I will begin with a comment about the nature of the *context*. In this case, *context* is inseparably linked to and built upon the work of Joseph and Elijah and their respective missions in this dispensation.

Joseph Smith and Elijah: Companions in an Educational Mission

When Moroni introduced Joseph to his earthly educational mission, he explained that the boundaries of this assignment were to extend beyond the mortal veil. It is important to grasp this thought and keep it in mind. Moroni repeated the message to Joseph three times. A primary objective of Joseph's mission was to inform the human family of their opportunity to maximize each individual's eternal potential. Joseph was told that this seemingly daunting task was to be accomplished by and through the "Spirit of Elijah." Resources were to be provided and disseminated on both sides of the veil to make this happen. It was a pattern that included an invitation for each of us to partner with the Savior in his great work of serving others—becoming "Saviors on Mt. Zion" is a phrase that denotes this invitation.[63]

---

[63]President Howard W. Hunter (testifying of Elijah's mission) said, "I bear witness that the same prophet who was fed by the ravens, by the never-depleting handful of meal and cruse of oil, who brought back life to the widow's son, whose sacrifice was consumed by an unkindled fire, who was taken into heaven in a chariot of fire, has appeared in this day, as foretold by Malachi. He is turning the hearts of this and the past generations toward each other. Prior to the building of temples in this dispensation and the appearance of Elijah, there was little interest in seeking out and identifying families of the past. Since temples have been built, genealogical interest in the world has increased at an accelerating rate. The gathering of hundreds of people to Salt Lake City, representing forty-five nations, for the World Conference on Records is a demonstration of this great interest. . . . Revelation in this day has given us the true meaning. Let me read to you the words of Joseph Smith in answer to the question: '. . . this is the spirit of Elijah, that we redeem our dead, and connect ourselves with our fathers which are in heaven, and seal up our dead to come forth in the first *resurrection*.' (HC vol. 6, p. 252.) May the spirit of Elijah burn deep into our hearts and turn us toward the temples, I humbly pray, in the name of *Jesus Christ*. Amen." (CR, 1971. See also D&C sections 127 and 128.)

Moroni outlined this process for Joseph by referencing several Old Testament scriptural accounts. He confirmed the Prophet Malachi's prophecy that the Lord would send the Holy Ghost to be his messenger and prepare the way by covenant for his return to rule and reign on the earth. (Joseph was reminded of this later—see D&C 45:9.) Moroni then expanded the biblical version of this information by telling Joseph that the Lord would reveal to him "the Priesthood [keys] by the hand of Elijah the prophet, . . . [and] he [Elijah] would plant in the hearts of the children the promises made to the fathers, and the hearts of the children shall turn to their fathers." Otherwise, "the whole earth would be utterly wasted at his coming" (see JSH 1:36–39; D&C 2:1–3).

It was obvious such an undertaking was to be gradual and ongoing, and would extend beyond Joseph's mortal life. It was to be pervasive and envelop every kindred, tongue, and people. Joseph received the priesthood keys from Elijah in the Kirtland Temple that enabled him to administer the *sealing ordinances* that could bind family relationships on earth and in heaven. These sealing ordinances were to extend earthly priesthood blessings and link them to a spirit-world program affecting individual and family *exaltation*. Joseph understood the importance of this process. [64] He recognized that Elijah, a prophet of miracles while he lived on the earth, was to lend his Spirit to a temple-based religious education work that operated on both sides of the veil. Elijah's mission was to reconcile families—children to their fathers, fathers to their children—

---

[64]Joseph Smith said, "I wish you to understand this subject, for it is important; and if you will receive it, this is the *Spirit of Elijah*, that we redeem our dead [ancestors], and connect ourselves with our fathers [and mothers] which are in heaven, and seal up our dead [relatives] to come forth in the first resurrection; . . . we want the power of Elijah to seal those who dwell on earth to those who dwell in heaven. This is the power of Elijah and the keys of the kingdom of Jehovah" (TPJS pp. 337–38). Joseph also explained, "What you seal on earth, by the keys of Elijah, is sealed in heaven; and this is the power of Elijah, and this is the difference between the spirit and power of Elias and Elijah; for while the spirit of Elias is a forerunner, the power of Elijah is sufficient to make our calling and election sure; and the same doctrine, where we are exhorted to go on to perfection . . . We cannot be perfect without the fathers etc. We must have revelation from them, and we can see that the doctrine of revelation far transcends the doctrine of no revelation. . . . Here is the [correct] doctrine of election that the world has quarreled so much about." (Ibid., p. 338)

according to the divine pattern. The sealing ordinances are the means of connecting the living with the dead in eternal relationships that accomplish their destiny and fulfill our Heavenly Father's work (PGP Moses 1:39).[65] In a very real sense this work was to unfold as a miraculous process. It was going to happen and we wouldn't understand exactly how, but we would see that it was.

Thus the foundation for education was to be laid by Joseph who would initiate the great work of building temples to provide information and ordinances for what is now unfolding as a world-wide family history and genealogical movement. This quiet but world-encompassing process is spreading in every land and culture; it is a spiritual labor of the greatest significance. It is evident that miraculous and unimaginable events, technologies, interests and interventions are combining to touch the lives of millions of people—both living and dead. It is so massive an influence as to be only partially comprehended by any single individual or group. For example, the increasing rate of development in these educational matters can boggle the human mind. One source notes it required "over 80 years to make 1 billion records easily search-able online, but volunteers have completed another billion" in just seven years. "The speed at which family history work is being completed is unprecedented" (*Church News*, August 4, 2013, p. 4.). We may

---

[65]Russell M. Nelson, a latter-day Apostle, summarized this unique educational companionship in these words: "In 1844, Joseph Smith asked, 'What is this office and work of Elijah?' The prophet promptly answered his own question: 'It is one of the greatest and most important subjects that God has revealed. . . . This is the spirit of Elijah, that we redeem our dead, and connect ourselves with our fathers which are in heaven. . . . This is the power of Elijah and the keys of the kingdom of Jehovah.' Some among us still have neither perceived the Spirit of Elijah nor its power. Yet, we are bound by this warning: 'These are principles in relation to the dead and the living that cannot be lightly passed over. . . . For their salvation is necessary and essential to our salvation . . . they without us cannot be made perfect—neither can we without our dead be made perfect.' Joseph Smith's responsibility was to 'lay the foundation' for this great work. Important details were to be revealed later. At April conference 1894, President Wilford Woodruff announced this revelation: 'We want the Latter-day Saints from this time to trace their genealogies as far as they can, and to be sealed to their fathers and mothers. Have children sealed to their parents, and run this chain through as far as you can get it. . . . This is the will of the Lord to his people.'" General Conference address, "The Spirit of Elijah" October 1994.

151

not *fully* understand how or why such things like this occur, but they do.

A personal affirmation of this phenomenon was apparent in a recent experience in our own family. And this type of anecdote is not unique; it's remarkably common—among all peoples. Briefly stated, our experience unfolded like this: My wife, a convert to the Church in her early twenties, has been diligently striving for decades to establish accurate records for her progenitors. Her family genealogical information ended when her immigrant forebears arrived in America near the turn of the twentieth century from Europe and the British Isles. In an effort to bridge this genealogical dead-end, she recently joined a daughter and son-in-law on a trip to Poland and Austria. The rumors were that many if not most of the records in those areas had been lost or destroyed during the wars. Her relatives in America knew little or nothing about what had happened to family members who had not migrated. And those who stayed behind generally lost touch with those who left— each was essentially a mystery to the other.

The trip was largely to be a search in the dark, so to speak. Nevertheless, with the help of an unusually sensitive genealogist in Warsaw, Poland arrangements were made to visit an archive in Suwalki—a town in northern Poland, an area where some of my wife's relatives had formerly lived. Upon arriving there, they were fortunate to have an entire day to search what they discovered were many volumes of old and beautifully kept records in which they found many important family names. All the records had *not* been destroyed by the wars. Later that afternoon, they made a subsequent blind visit to a very small village and church—some twenty miles distant— in a town named Krasnopol. My wife had some evidence that her family members had lived in this village.

My wife had an old letter, originally written in 1947, from that town to a distant relative in America. She had kept this letter for decades. The postmark was the clue. When translated to English it revealed that a younger brother, named Bronsilaw, had written from this location to his sister who had migrated to Pennsylvania, asking if she knew what had happened to their brother, Antoni (my wife's grandfather). The family name was Sosnowski, and my wife's grandfather's given name was Antoni. In Krasnopol these traveling Americans, with their interpreter, met a priest. They asked him if he knew of any Sosnowski families living in the area. He gestured in a general direction that led to a dirt road into a rural farm district some distance from the town. They traveled in that direction and began knocking on farmhouse doors. It was raining and beginning to get dark. Finally, they came to a house where the person living there pointed to a specific farm house in the distance. They went to that house, knocked, and an elderly lady opened the door. The genealogist guide asked if this was a Sosnowski residence and if they knew of an Adam Sosnowski. She answered, "Yes, that was my husband's grandfather's name." The translator then told her she had some people in the car who had come from America to meet them, and they were related to that Adam. The woman then clapped her hands in excitement and invited them all to come into the house. She told them that she had often prayed that someone would come from America and tell them what had happened to their family who left Poland so long ago. This eighty-year-old couple then explained how she and her husband, Antoni, a son of Bronsilaw, had been named after his brother, my wife's grandfather, Antoni, who had migrated to America in 1907. Thus began an emotional reunion with tears of joy and continues today despite distance and language barriers.

There is more to the story, but all this happened in less than 48 hours after my wife arrived in Poland, with little thought that meeting her family relatives was even possible. A similar but equally unusual set of circumstances resulted when she left Poland and arrived in Vienna, Austria, to seek similar information about another of her genealogical lines. Pages could be written describing remarkable "coincidences" that occurred in the area known as Burgenland. What transpired there was similar to the unexpected experiences in Poland— each resulting in multiple generational extensions of her genealogy. It was not only unexpected, it was unpredictable. Yet these remarkable accounts are not uncommon. The unique *educational companionship of Joseph Smith and the Spirit of Elijah* is alive; it is operating well throughout the earth, as Joseph was told it would, and as hundreds and thousands can now readily testify.

Joseph Embraced and Enhanced the Spirit of Elijah

Joseph Smith manifested an inclusive invitation for people to obtain and feel the blessings of Elijah's continuing miracles in their personal lives. He said *"We don't ask any people to throw away any good they have got; we only ask them to come and get more. What if all the world should embrace this gospel? They would then see eye to eye, and the blessings of God would be poured out upon the people, which is the desire of my whole soul."*[66] Joseph's view of the individual's capacity was equally enveloping. He described the process in these words:

> When we understand the character of God, and know how to come to Him, he begins to unfold the heavens to us, and to tell us all about it. When we are ready to come to him, he is ready to come to us (HC 6:308). We consider that God has created man with a mind capable of instruction, and a faculty which may be enlarged in proportion to the heed and diligence given to the light communicated from heaven to the intellect; and that the nearer a man approaches perfection, the clearer are his views, and the greater his enjoyments, till he has overcome the evils of his life and lost every desire for sin; and like the ancients, arrives at that point of faith where he is wrapped in the power and glory of his Maker, and is caught up to dwell with Him. (HC 2:8)

Joseph fully understood the general breadth and depth of his mission. He often spoke of his assigned role, sometimes emphasizing that responsibility in graphic expressions. For example, he once said "I calculate to be one of the instruments of setting up the kingdom of Daniel by the word of the Lord, and I intend *to lay a foundation* that will revolutionize the whole world. . . . It will not be by sword or gun that this kingdom will roll on: the power of truth is such that all nations will be under the necessity of obeying the Gospel" (HC 6:365). In his moments of reflection he would refer back to his initial calling:

---

[66]HC 5:259.

154

This messenger [Moroni] proclaimed himself to be an angel of God, sent to bring the joyful tidings that the covenant which God made with ancient Israel was at hand to be fulfilled, that the preparatory work for the second coming of the Messiah was speedily to commence; that the time was at hand for the Gospel in all its fullness to be preached in power, unto all nations that a people might be prepared for the Millennial reign. I was informed that I was chosen to be an instrument in the hands of God to bring about some of His purposes in this glorious dispensation. (HC 4:536–37)

This spirit of inevitable destiny emanated from Joseph as he interacted with the people. It was motivational and was confirmed in the lives and deeds of many of his followers. This process continues to function today—the veil can be very thin between the work of Joseph and the work of Elijah—and it is interfacing on a much wider scale and with greater and greater intensity.[67] We may not understand all the details, but we do understand the purposes and some of the challenges.

Joseph's Unfolding Educational Program—A Continuous Process

It was evident to Joseph in the months and weeks before his untimely death that the growth and development of his restoration mission would occur in the Rocky Mountains. He

---

[67]Joseph Smith explained that, "The spirit, power, and calling of Elijah is, that ye have power to hold the key of the revelations, ordinances, oracles, powers and endowments of the fulness of the Melchizedek Priesthood and of the kingdom of God on the earth; and to receive, obtain, and perform all the ordinances belonging to the kingdom of God.... What you seal on earth, by the keys of Elijah, is sealed in heaven; and this is the power of Elijah" (TPJS pp. 337–38).

The Prophet Joseph Smith also offered the following explanation: The spirit of Elijah is to come, the Gospel to be established, . . . and the Saints to come up as saviors on Mount Zion. But how are they to become saviors on Mount Zion? By building their temples, erecting their baptismal fonts, and going forth and receiving all the ordinances, baptisms, confirmations, washings, anointings, ordinations and sealing powers upon their heads, in behalf of all their progenitors who are dead, and redeem them; . . . and herein is the chain that binds the hearts of the fathers to the children and the children to the fathers, which fulfills the mission of Elijah (TPJS p. 330).

sensed the work was to fall on the shoulders of those with whom he had shared his aims and teachings. He did what he could to prepare them for what was to come. This would involve a modern exodus to an environment more conducive to their success. Plans were made and pursued. Persecution threatened the city of Nauvoo and its environs. The martyrdom of Joseph and his brother Hyrum intensified these difficult circumstances. The Saints would have to leave this social and physical setting and find a place more suitable to do their work. They did what they needed to do and the long trek west began in 1846. Nevertheless, education remained a visible and viable objective over the ensuing decades. It was a central concern of both leaders and families, despite the painful physical suffering and sacrifice in yet another primitive setting that demanded and taxed their physical resources. It was hard but it was successful.

The Long Trek West

The ultimate purpose of this educational program involving family relationships was revealed to President Brigham Young by the Prophet Joseph Smith, who appeared to him in a vision while the Saints were gathered at Winter Quarters in Nebraska. Among the instructions Joseph gave his immediate successor were these:

> Be sure and tell the people to keep the Spirit of the Lord; and if they will, they will find themselves just as they were organized by our Father in Heaven before they came into the world. Our Father in Heaven organized the human family, but they are all disorganized and in great confusion. (Ms. History of Brigham Young, 1846–47)

Brigham Young then added, "Joseph then showed me the pattern, how they were in the beginning." Years later, President Young spoke of this revelation in these words:

> I will now say to my brethren and sisters, that while we were in Winter Quarters, the Lord gave to me a revelation just as much as he ever gave one to anybody. He opened my mind, and showed me the organization of the Kingdom of God in a family capacity. I talked to my brethren; I would throw out a few words here, and few words there, to my first counselor, to my second counselor and to the Twelve Apostles, but with the

exception of one or two of the Twelve, it would not touch a man. (JD 18:244)

These comments affirm the fact that the educational program envisioned and initiated by Joseph is ongoing; it unfolds line upon line, here a little and there a little, according to the Lord's own time table. And it is designed to bring to pass "the immortality and eternal life" of humankind. It is all about education in the broadest sense of that term.

Joseph Smith taught that this *reorganization* of the *disorganized* human family was an essential element of the educational process. Properly understood, the family is the core of education, both the nuclear and generational families. What happens in the home is vital to what happens everywhere else. A critical key to ultimate personal progress is embedded in and facilitated by the function and structure of the family. The "big picture," Joseph maintained, involves the family—parents and children and grandchildren, progenitors and posterity, the living and the dead. His teachings were passed on to those who followed him in the pursuit and fulfilling of the work to which he was appointed. This continuity is attested to in the writings and teachings of each of his successors, whose stewardship it was to perpetuate the work and lead the Church and pursue the purposes that Joseph was called to establish.

President John Taylor, who presided over this work after the death of Brigham Young, expressed the continuity of Joseph's educational thought in these words:

> Joseph Smith in the first place was set apart by the Almighty according to the counsels of the gods in the eternal worlds, to introduce the principles of life among the people, of which the Gospel is the grand power and influence, and through which salvation can extend to all peoples, all nations, all kindreds, all tongues and all worlds. It is the principle that brings life and immortality to light, and places us in communication with God. God selected him [Joseph] for that purpose, and he fulfilled his mission and lived honorably and died honorably. I know of what I speak for I was very well acquainted with him and was with him a great deal during his life, and was with him when he died. The principles which he had, placed him

in communication with the Lord, and not only with the Lord, but with the ancient apostles and prophets; such men, for instance as Abraham, Isaac, Jacob, Noah, Adam, Seth, Enoch, and Jesus and the Father, and the apostles that lived on this continent as well as those who lived on the Asiatic continent. He seemed to be as familiar with these people as we are with one another. Why? Because he had to introduce a dispensation which was called the dispensation of the fulness of times, and it was known as such by the ancient servants of God. What is meant by the dispensation of the fulness of times? It is a dispensation in which all other dispensations are merged or concentrated. It embraces and embodies all the other dispensations that have existed upon the earth wherein God communicated himself to the human family. Did they have the Aaronic priesthood in former times? Yes. So have we. Did they have the Melchizedek priesthood in former times? Yes. So have we. Did they have a gathering dispensation in former times, when Moses led the children of Israel out of Egypt? Yes. So have we, just as it was predicted by the prophet Jeremiah.

President Taylor continued, reminding those over whom he presided during his stewardship of this continuity as follows:

We are now gathered together to Zion. For what? To build up Zion, and to accomplish the purposes of the Lord pertaining to the human family upon the earth. And being gathered together we are organized with apostles and prophets, with presidents and their counselors, with bishops and their counselors, with elders, priests teachers and deacons. We are organized according to the order of God, and these very principles that look small to us emanate from God. We have seventies and high priests, and all these men hold certain positions which it is expected of them that they will fulfill and magnify, here in the flesh, in the interests of truth and righteousness; in the interests of the kingdom of God and in the establishment of correct principles among the Saints of the Most High. We are here to co-operate with God in the salvation of the living, in the redemption of the dead, in the

159

blessings of our ancestors, in the pouring out blessings upon our children; we are here for the purpose of redeeming and regenerating the earth on which we live, and God has placed his authority and his counsels here upon the earth for that purpose, that men may learn to do the will of God on the earth as it is done in heaven. This is the object of our existence; and it is for us to comprehend the position. (John Taylor, JD 21:94, April 13, 1879)

This is the inspiring view of education in its larger (macroscopic) perspective as held by Joseph Smith. The details of organizing and implementing the various *educational elements*, the practices, processes, and performances have steadily evolved. The *why, what, where, when,* and *how* of preparing the succeeding generations have emerged, and merged in ways that suit the realities of the times and circumstances. Revelation is ongoing, not static; so are refinements in policies and methodologies—adapting to the needs, resources, and readiness of the people to embrace them. Contemporary technological advances and expanding temporal and human resources are currently pushing forward previous boundaries that were not possible in past centuries. Increasing membership and additional revelation continue to challenge each generation. *The larger the island of knowledge and achievement, the longer and more exciting has become the shoreline* of Joseph's educational vision. The doctrines and principles remain the same today as they were in the past. It is the processes and performances that continue to be modified, refined, and magnified. Why not?

Origins of Instructional Curriculum

Following the pattern established by Adam and Eve, Joseph Smith encouraged, stressed, and set a personal example of self-driven, lifelong learning from his childhood until his untimely death. Literacy was emphasized, a knowledge of numbers was considered essential, and social applications in various forms were popularized and admired throughout his life. He knew that Adam and Eve were commanded to teach their children to read and write. He knew that the basic purpose of these skills was to keep a record—a sacred record designed to preserve the family and the social order on earth and in heaven, for time and eternity. It was clear that temporal knowledge and skills were to serve spiritual purposes as well as the practical needs for safety, food, shelter, and clothing. Joseph had personally recorded in English the latter-day form of the Lord's initial instructions regarding education:

> And a book of remembrance was kept, in the which was recorded, in the language of Adam, for it was given unto as many as called upon God to write by the spirit of inspiration; and by them their children were taught to read and write, having a language which was pure and undefiled. . . . Therefore I give unto you a commandment to teach these things freely unto your children. (Moses 6:5–6, 58)

Before the restored Church was even organized, Joseph had also translated Mormon's account of the destructive role that *corrupt* and *distorted* education had brought upon an earlier civilization in the western hemisphere. He knew well the devastation that formed as a vigorous counterculture gained power and influence. The nature of the kind of education this culture pursued is aptly described in the Book of Mormon:

> And he [Amulon] appointed teachers of the brethren of Amulon in every land which was possessed by his [the Lamanite King's] people; and thus the language of Nephi began to be taught among all the people of the Lamanites. And they were a friendly people one with another; nevertheless they knew not God; neither did the brethren of Amulon teach them anything concerning the Lord their God, neither the law of Moses; nor did they teach them the words of Abinadi [who taught the mission of Jesus Christ]; but they taught them that they should keep their record, and that they might write one to another. And thus the Lamanites began to increase in riches, and began to wax great, and began to be a cunning and wise people, as to the wisdom of the world, yea, a very cunning people, delighting in all manner of wickedness and plunder, except it were among their own brethren. (Mosiah 24:4–7)

Joseph was quite aware of the consequences that come from education that leaves (1) God, (2) the Ten Commandments, and (3) the mission of Christ out of the curriculum. He stressed the importance of *not separating literacy in word and numbers from character and integrity* in whatever type of schooling was being pursued. This emphasis is equally valid today. Learning and teaching information and skills solely at the physical and mental levels of instruction may produce important and impressive results. But, such education can be entirely selfish unless it is supported by and fused with moral and spiritual values. Education without these moral and spiritual supports is not safe; it is dangerous and destructive. Joseph knew that pursuing physical and intellectual goals alone was not the same kind of education as striving for moral and spiritual excellence. And, unless each of the four domains is included in what we learn and teach, our character will not be what it ought to be. This is the major message in the account of Amulon's schooling program versus the teachings of Alma described in the Book of Mormon.

Cultural and political decadence, it seems, also morphed out of this initial educational innovation by Amulon and his associates. What gets taught makes a difference. Although Mormon does not give details in his record—the relationship between Amulon's schools and the rise of a subsequent variant known as the Order of Nehor—he does make the connection (Alma 21:4; 24:28–29). It is clear that a professional social *order* developed from this agnostic and materialistic kind of schooling; Mormon identifies it as the *"order of Nehor."* It is apparent that those who fostered and maintained this special society and its unique curriculum were primarily dissidents who left the Nephite communities and went to live among the Lamanites. The professionals who belonged to this order were well educated according to the standards of their school system. They had apparently studied a number of disciplines and become influential lawyers, priests, and teachers. Mormon describes the teachers and students in this system as those who "loved the vain things of the world" and sought after "riches and honors" (Alma 1:16). He identifies the basic beliefs, policies, and practices of these professionals; their general strategies are also described in several instances involving Alma and his associates as they interacted with these people. Names like Ammonihah, Amlici, Zeezrom, and Korihor may be familiar. I conclude that there are lessons to be learned from the scriptural accounts of those who have preceded us.

Content, Process, Structure, and Context

Comprehending what we call *education* requires some understanding of *four general elements* that shape the learning/teaching relationship. The presence of these four elements is abundant in Joseph's writings and educational endeavors. Regardless of what words are used to identify these four pillars, their presence and function should be acknowledged:

1. There has to be identified *content*—whatever the subject matter might be.
2. There is always a *process* involved in using or sharing the content.
3. *Structure* ought to be created or provided if one wants the best results.
4. *Context* nearly always influences content, process, and structure.

Because these terms may seem somewhat abstract, it may be helpful to consider how they function in a simple, concrete example. Consider the illustration of a ship constructed inside a bottle. This novel item is often seen in curio shops—particular along seacoast towns or villages.

Learning or being taught how to build a ship in a bottle requires all four of the elements mentioned. There has to be identified *content*—some materials. A *process* is required to accomplish the task—some method and skills. A *structure* is necessary in order to facilitate or in this case create a recognizable object. The object—the ship—being created has to fit into the bottle—which is the *context* in this example. The next step will be to compare what is obvious in this illustration and show how it relates to or applies to education.

In this example the *materials*—the *content*—involved, in educational terms, can be called *curriculum*. The curriculum is the primary *content* in education. The *process* for constructing the ship requires skills and techniques; in educational language this is usually known as *methodology*—people take courses in *methods* when they train to become teachers. They practice the skills and techniques of teaching. The person who made the ship in this example, had to imagine the ship and how to construct it so it would fit into the bottle. He or she had to create a *structure*—in thought and then physical reality. In education, how one uses his or her skills to organize the materials and sequence them is known as *structure*. *Structure* is supposed to facilitate learning and promote understandable communication between the learner and the teacher. In the example of the ship in the bottle, the bottle itself is the *context*. The *context* has a great influence on (a) what is considered to be *content*, (b) the *methods* applied to the content, and (c) how it is structured. In our example, for instance, the ship as it exists in the picture could not have been built in some radically different shaped bottle. The *context* would not have allowed it. *Context* not only can affect, it actually determines *content, process,* and *structures* in education—for good or ill.

Joseph Smith was very conscious of *context* in his educational endeavors. He wanted to keep the context as large as it needed to be in order to facilitate the learning and teaching he wanted to share with others. A similar pattern is evidenced in the learning and teaching that Jesus fostered in his day. A good example is the way he explained the nature and need for parables to his disciples and the multitudes who came to listen.

The writers of the gospels of Matthew and Mark offer an explanation in their accounts.

> He, Jesus, began to teach by the seaside. . . . He taught them many things by parables, and said unto them in his doctrine, hearken . . . (Mark 4:1–3; see Matthew 13:6–43).

Then Jesus told the parable of the sower. This story is about a farmer who had some seeds and wanted to raise a crop of grain. This was his goal, plan, and objective—in another word, the *structure*. The farmer went out into the field with his seeds (the content, curricular materials). He scattered (sowed) the seeds—the *content*—on the ground in different places. Some fell on a pathway, some on rocky soil, some in the weeds and thorns, and some on good (fertile) soil. This was the way the farmer planted his seeds—the *process* or method he used.

So this temporal farmer in Jesus's story had utilized (a) the *content* (seeds, the *word* of the gospel), (b) the *process* (his methods), and (c) the *structure* (his goals, plans, objectives)— three of the four elements—but the farmer had misjudged or failed to recognize much of (d) the *context*. Jesus pointedly went on to explain very clearly the outcomes of these applications and to point out what happened because of the *context* (the environment of the field, the soil, heat, birds, thorns, and perhaps moisture). It is easy to ignore the *context* when we become preoccupied with the *content, process,* and *structure*. This is a common failing in modern education. What were formerly considered the *means* often have become the *ends;* and the consequences—the real, sometimes surprising outcomes—so often overlooked, prove to be disastrous.

Jesus finished his story to the multitude by explaining how these *context* factors influenced the yield of the farmer's efforts. Some seeds yielded nothing, and others thirty, sixty, and some a hundred fold. It was possibly discouraging and less than what he had hoped for. After the sermon was over and the disciples were alone with Jesus, they asked for a further explanation. He answered "Unto you it is given to know the *mystery of the kingdom of God:* but unto them that are without, all these things are done in parables. (Mark 4:11.) Then he said, in effect, you know the *spiritual context,* you should be able to understand the *spiritual message.* He then proceeded to explain some of the symbolism. (see Mark 4:14–20)

Joseph Smith was given even more of an added insight when he was working on the translation of the Bible in 1832. It was made clear to him that "the field was the world, and the apostles were the sowers of the seed; and after they have fallen asleep (died), a terrible apostasy was to occur." And he, Joseph, was to help fulfill this parable through the restoration of the gospel "in the last days" (D&C 86:1–11). And Joseph was sensitized to the importance of context. He often emphasized this in his teachings: using a wedding ring—which has no beginning or end—to symbolize eternity; the rungs on a ladder—to emphasize order in progressive development; the temple—to emphasize living that connects the mortal to the spiritual.

Summary

Attention has now been given to some of the reasons Joseph Smith developed an inspired view of learning and teaching. Much more could be written, but these *four segments* illustrate a skeletal view of the umbrella of ideas that shelter his unique philosophy of education:

- The prophet Joseph's mission was linked to the prophet Elijah's work.
- The continuity of Joseph's unfolding educational program is remarkable.
- The origins of instructional curriculum preceded and influenced his ideas.
- The role of *content, process, structure,* and *context* in his educational endeavors and in his educational thought are apparent, as they are in most serious forms of education. His use of *context* is quite extraordinary.

166

The final Part (XVI) in this monograph examines the scriptural foundations of effective instruction: (a) its *preparation* and (b) its *implementation*. These functions are the practical issues for all who intentionally engage in the learning/teaching process—in the home or in the classroom.

SCRIPTURAL FOUNDATIONS OF EFFECTIVE INSTRUCTION

Embracing the Holy Spirit—an Antidote for a Decadent Society

Joseph Smith's teachings regarding education were both specific and comprehensive. He was a practical and realistic educator. Theory was not sufficient; he wanted to share principles that would demonstrate success in both the *temporal* and *spiritual* domains. He acknowledged that doing something well requires effort and diligence. He translated his vision and aspirations into concrete standards. This is evident in his writings as well as in his labors—whether the focus was on learning or building temples. The following information is one attempt to present some of his observations and expectations. A particular view of education revealed in these selections is still governing most of what is espoused by those who share his lofty goals. Learning and teaching like Joseph Smith is an ongoing operation—one that is worthy of the most serious examination and application. These foundations are composed of two general elements—(a) *preparation* and (b) *implementation*. It is a matter of intentionally embracing the task and then organizing and presenting the information. Effective education requires a serious effort.

(A) Preparation

Why we need to improve Instruction. The Lord said, "Zion cannot be built up unless it is by the principles of the law of the celestial kingdom." (D&C 105:5.) He desires that his people be "taught more perfectly, and have experience, and know more perfectly concerning their duty," including all that he requires at their hands. This includes improving our ability to teach one another the doctrines of the kingdom. (D&C 88:77; 105:10.) The lifestyle and education of the Saints should be unique— "not after the manner of the world." (D&C 95:13–14; 94:2.) Joseph was sensitive to these instructions. He tried hard to follow them. And he desired attentive learners. There is a story that illustrates this expectation. One day, while teaching a large audience in an outdoor setting in Nauvoo, the congregation became overly interested in a flock of geese circling above them. Joseph tried to keep the audience focused on his message to little avail. Finally, he said: *"If you are more interested in those geese than you are in what I am saying, go ahead and watch them."* He then abruptly left the podium and went home.

Instructions from the scriptures about learning and teaching have been compiled in this document to support the goal of "perfecting the saints." The scriptures proclaim that proper spiritually based instruction must occur under the direction and by the power of the Holy Spirit (D&C 42:13–14; 50:13–22). To use this information effectively we must prayerfully read and ponder the citations. As these scriptures are studied, personally and with others, the Holy Spirit may act upon each participant according to individual needs. In order to comply with scriptural counsel, an improved understanding of the role and responsibility of the learner as well as the teacher is necessary. Learners must be trained, as well as teachers. We are informed that Church members can rise above some levels upon which we have paused too long. There is room for improvement in each generation.

Sample Statements Regarding Instruction. Introductions to approved Church curriculum manuals contain guidelines for learners and teachers. The emphasis in these instructions is consistent with the counsel on learning and teaching found in the scriptures. As a sacred and spiritual approach, it differs from traditional learning and teaching practices. The Prophet Joseph Smith said, "To become a joint heir of the heir-ship of the Son, one must put away all his false traditions." (TPJS p. 321.) This applies to educational traditions and principles. The material that follows is an expansion of the brief guidelines currently found in Church manuals. When these instructions are prayerfully and conscientiously learned, applied, and shared, they will enhance and edify the learning and teaching in our homes, Church, and elsewhere. Consider, for example, the following excerpts:

> Instead of providing lesson objectives and step-by-step outlines, this manual provides resources to help *you* formulate objectives and outlines that meet the needs of class members. Seek inspiration about how to help

class members understand the scriptures and apply the principles in their lives: pray for the Spirit's guidance, use the scriptures, bear testimony, use sacred music, express love, and share spiritual experiences.

For classes to be most effective, members should read and ponder the assigned scriptures at home before coming to class. . . . Having studied the scriptures, *class members should teach and edify one another* (see D&C 88: 118, 122). Their participation helps invite the Spirit into the class and encourages them to apply and live scriptural principles. It also enables class members to benefit from each other's gifts, knowledge, and experience.

Remember that *the Holy Spirit is the teacher* in your class. When you teach by the Spirit, you can expect some significant results. . . . Some of the fruits to be enjoyed when you teach and learn under the direction of the Holy Ghost are humility, prayer, faith, repentance, and covenant keeping. (from *Previous Sunday School and Relief Society manuals: Guidelines for Teachers.*)

How Learning and Teaching Occur. Learning and teaching occur "precept upon precept, . . . line upon line. here a little, and there a little" (Isaiah 28: 10). As we live and have experience, the process unfolds. The desire to improve is important. Studying the scriptures with the intent to develop our learning and teaching skills will help us connect preservice, inservice, and supervisory experience. Both learning and teaching play an important role; neither should say of the other "I have no need of thee" (1 Cor. 12:21). Becoming a willing learner is the best preparation to be an effective teacher. We can all improve our abilities to learn and teach. All of us can grow in light and truth as we seek, knock, ask, and receive under the influence of the Spirit. Like Jesus, we too can increase in wisdom and in favor with God and man (Luke 2:52).

A Pattern for Successful Learning and Teaching. Soon after the gospel was restored, the Lord revealed a simple pattern for successful learning and teaching in his Church. In summary he said:

a) "Instruct and edify each other" (D&C 43:8).
b) "Act in all holiness before me. . . . Sanctify yourselves and ye shall be endowed with power" (D&C 43:9, 16).
c) "Teach . . . the things which I have put into your hands" (D&C 43:15).
d) "Treasure these things up in your hearts, and let the solemnities of eternity rest upon your mind" (D&C 43:34).

These same instructions are emphasized in other revelations.

Instruct and Edify Each Other

Read examples of this principle found in D&C 88:122; 43:8; Alma 1:26	We learn from and teach one another.
Read D&C 4:3, 5; 28: 16; 60:2; Moroni 7:47– 48; 8:16–17; D&C 12:7–9	Fear often blocks our desire and willingness to share with each other. Love overcomes fear.

Act in All Holiness

Read John 14:16–17, 26; D&C 42:13–14; 46:28; 50:17–22.	To teach one another, we need his Spirit to be with us. There is a three-way partnership: the Holy Ghost, the learner, and the teacher.
Read D&C 88:34–35, 121, 124–126.	The Holy Spirit does assist those who strive to be worthy and those who seek to teach that which is acceptable to God.
Read I Nephi 3:7	The Lord does not ask us to do things we cannot do. He will provide what we need after we have done all that we can with what he has already given us

Teach What I Put into Your Hands

Read 1 Nephi 13:25–26; D&C 107:89; 43:15;	Formal instruction in the Church is under the direction of the Savior. Course outlines are prepared and approved under the direction of his priesthood officers. Those who teach in the Church are expected to "teach according to the covenants" and from the resources that are "put in their hands."
Read D&C 43:15	The teacher's responsibility is to prepare and present the principles and ideas provided in the authorized materials adapted to meet the needs of class members as the Spirit directs. All may share personal testimony to support these principles and ideas. The authorized materials should not be set aside and something else substituted in their place without priesthood approval.
Read D&C 84:54–58	When we ignore or treat lightly the things the Lord expects us to teach, we come under condemnation.

Treasure These Things in Your Hearts and Minds

Read D&C 88:128–131; 84:85	The teacher takes the lead as an example of a willing learner and sets a positive classroom mood. Teachers should not monopolize classroom instructional time, but they should establish and maintain classroom order in a gospel atmosphere. The same principle applies to parents in the home.
Read D&C 88:63–64; 88:40	The disposition of the teacher is essential to uplifting and edifying lessons. A teacher's positive spiritual attitude encourages positive spiritual attitudes among class members. This kind of attitude comes from the teacher's relationship with the Lord.
Read D&C 121:39–46	Teaching in Church classes is an extension of priesthood authority. Personal and class prayers are essential. Order precedes effective instruction.

All Can Learn, All Can Teach

Heavenly Father wants every person to be a learner and a teacher: We are under strict commandment to learn the plan of salvation and teach it to our children (Moses 6:58–62). Successful *learning* and *teaching* are both based on the same simple skills and resources. The fundamental skills of learning and teaching are loving God and others, serving God and others, and sharing with others the gifts and resources God has given us. These skills are developed in the everyday activities of life—living in a family, being a friend, hosting and being hosted by others as we visit with relatives, friends, and strangers. Both learners and teachers express these skills when they encourage, involve, show interest, commend, and respond.

Successful learning and teaching are supported by resources that are given to every person by Heavenly Father.

Read D&C 138:56; see references in the Topical Guide; read and ponder your patriarchal blessing.	We were prepared before we came to this earth in our "pre-mortal life" to do the things we are called to do.
Read Luke 2:40, 52; 2 Nephi 28:30; D&C 98:12	Since our birth we have learned many things. We have the capacity to continually learn new things.
Read D&C 11:21; 12:8	As we learn to be effective students, we prepare ourselves to be effective teachers.
Read Mosiah 4:14–15; Alma 1:26	Learning and teaching are companions that need one another; both are intended to be forms of service to God and others. As we learn, we receive something that someone else has learned. Because we have learned many things, we have many things to share with others. When we share something we have learned with someone else, we teach. Examine priesthood and relief society manuals. Note the scriptural insights and prophetic witnesses to gospel truths. We also teach when we share something someone else has learned with others.

Charity Never Fails; It Edifies

Charity is the pure love of Christ. We have charity when we place our will in subjection to God's will—when we desire to see and treat others as he would see and treat them (Moroni 7:45–47; Luke 22:39–46; 1 Cor. 8:1). Charity helps us learn and teach. Edification is experiencing light and truth; it is a feeling we should have when we teach and when we learn. It is through charity that we are spiritually edified—nourished and enriched (Mosiah 23: 15–18; D&C 93:36–37).

Read Luke 24:32	Jesus provides an example for edifying others in his experience with two of his disciples on the road to Emmaus. We also can open the scriptures with the help of the Holy Spirit and cause hearts to feel warm and uplifted.
Read D&C 46:11–12, 26; Moroni 10:8–24	We are edified by the gifts of God, gifts that reside in each of us. Moroni warned that we should not deny the gifts of God. He explained that these gifts are many, but they all come from God. This is one reason we are commanded to serve one another—to share the gifts he has given to us. "There are different ways that these gifts are administered" to profit us. Because each of these gifts is given to a specific individual, there is uniqueness in the way the gifts are delivered.
Read D&C 18:10; 60:2	When we refuse to participate or act to prevent others from participating in our classes, are we not denying the operation of the gifts of God? Is not the individual more important to God than the gifts?

Directed by the Spirit

Our learning and teaching can be directed by the Spirit. The Gift of the Holy Ghost is bestowed after baptism. The companionship of the Spirit is retained by keeping the commandments of God, by seeking the Spirit's guidance, and by heeding its promptings (D&C 33:11–18; 20:71–79; Moses 6:59–60; Mosiah 2:36–37). The Holy Spirit is a sure guide: It testifies of the truth and can lead us to know the truth of all things (D&C 45:57; Moroni 10:4–6). The Holy Ghost teaches in a variety of ways: visions, the still small voice, thoughts that come into our minds, dreams—and all can be valid.

Each person should seek to understand the messages of the Spirit. Understanding comes as we pray, study, ponder, and apply truth; eyes will see, ears will hear, and hearts will understand (Proverbs 4:18; D&C 50:24, 40–41; Matt. 13:43; D&C 93:31–32, 36).

We can avoid being deceived—thinking we are directed by the Spirit when we are not (D&C 43:1–7; 46:7–9; 52:14–19).

In the Church, both the learner and the teacher may have the Gift of the Holy Ghost. This creates a unique teaching/learning setting. The teacher can be inspired in preparing and delivering the message. The class member can be inspired to receive and confirm the message and witness to its truthfulness. Both the learner and the teacher may be instruments in the hands of the Lord to bless others (Mosiah 23: 10; 27:36; see "Instrument" in the Topical Guide).

Unlike some instructional patterns, where the practice is to simply sit in classes while teachers dispense gospel information and doctrines, the better way is interactive. As learners we are to actively gather in these eternal truths, pray for the Spirit to be with us, and willingly share our witness to these truths with others in the class. It is this kind of interactive relationship that should characterize education. Though order must prevail, we are all to be both learners and teachers. There is a time to preach but this should not be prevail in the classroom. Teaching and preaching may be similar in some ways but they are not synonyms.

Our Heart, Mind, Might, and Strength

How learners and teachers view each other is important. The scriptures describe people in terms of *heart, mind, might,* and *strength* (D&C 4:2; Isaiah 55:8–11). This is in distinct contrast to most popular educational and psychological descriptions. Humans are now commonly portrayed as physical organisms who think, have needs and appetites, and respond to their environment. We are more than this: We are children of God with a spirit body and a physical body that together constitute our soul (D&C 88:15). We lived before our birth on this earth, and we will live after we pass from this mortal life. Our learning and teaching will improve if we understand and relate to each other in the way people are described in the scriptures.

The term *heart* refers to our innermost self, where our basic decisions and commitments are made. What we think in our hearts is the true index of our character. This should be the focus of education at all levels—child, youth, and adult (Proverbs 23:7; Mosiah 2:9; see "Heart" in the Topical Guide). The term *mind* refers to our capacity to become aware of things—as they are, as they have been, or as they may be; it is the system we use to attract, select, categorize, classify, and store information. The mind is subject to the management and control of the heart (D&C 64:34). The term *might* refers to our temporal and spiritual resources—whatever we legitimately possess or own. Wealth, property, and other physical objects are examples of might (D&C 76:94–96). The term *strength* refers to the properties associated with our individual bodies. Strength includes generative powers in the form of muscle, bone, and tissue and regenerative powers such as our bodily systems—circulatory, respiratory, neural, and glandular (D&C 59:9; Alma 26:12; Moroni 9:18, 10:32). Many of the lyrics in our hymnbook reflect this scriptural view of humankind.

(B) Implementation

Prepare Every Needful Thing

Humans are both spirit and physical beings (D&C 93:33; Abraham 5:7). We exist in both temporal and spiritual domains (D&C 29:31–35). Teaching temporal principles and ideas is important. But teaching moral and spiritual principles and ideas goes beyond temporal instruction. The common pattern for teaching about the temporal world is often expressed in the terms *show, tell,* and *do.* Mothers, fathers, and professional teachers soon learn that this pattern helps them teach others. They show them what they want them to understand, tell or explain what to do with it, and then help them do it for themselves. This process is not difficult; we all use it in our daily lives. Moral and spiritual instruction may include, but must extend beyond, temporal instruction.

When we teach about moral or spiritual matters, a more refined pattern applies. Joseph Smith portrayed this pattern for teaching moral and spiritual lessons clearly. It can be expressed in three simple principles. As indicated previously, we are admonished to

1. *Teach according to the covenants* (D&C 107:89): show truths of the plan of salvation.
2. *Teach by the Spirit* (D&C 42:13–14): tell these truths under the influence of the Holy Spirit.
3. *Teach as a witness* (Mosiah 18:8–10): express a personal witness to affirm these truths in both word and action.

Jesus demonstrated this pattern when he used experiences, incidents, stories, or parables to teach others. A parable, for example, is an earthly story with a heavenly meaning. Jesus would describe an earthly or temporal experience that his listeners understood (even though they usually didn't grasp the full meaning), then he would use this real-life event to help those who would see and hear to understand a *moral* or *spiritual* ideal (Matt 13:3–52). The earthly helps us learn and teach about the heavenly. Elder Orson F. Whitney said, *"Man, earth, and time are symbols of God, heaven, and eternity. They lift our thoughts from man to God, from earth to Heaven, and from time to eternity."* (*Improvement Era*, August 1927, p. 851.)

We are preparing to live in a celestial kingdom. These laws or principles of teaching moral and spiritual lessons enable us to teach one another the doctrines of the celestial kingdom. The process is not difficult to understand. We can all apply moral and spiritual instruction in our daily lives. The Lord taught Moses to use earthly symbols to teach spiritual lessons (Exodus 12:21–27; Deut. 6:4–9). But the method of Moses, like the law of Moses, was to prepare us for more spiritual instruction. When we are spiritually prepared we can receive spiritual teachings directly.

There are major barriers that prevent us from applying these laws of spiritual learning: failure to "see" the spiritual (John 3:3–5) and failure to "understand" because of unbelief (Mosiah 26:3), not opening our eyes to see and our ears to hear (3 Nephi 11:5). These barriers can be overcome by humbly seeking divine assistance (D&C 136:32). Each person who does this can know how to proceed (Luke 24:32). This preparation is more significant than the physical circumstances in which we teach—helpful as these might be.

Important Steps in Preparing and Presenting Moral and Spiritual Lessons.

Read D&C 11:21–22	Read the resource material prayerfully; preparation precedes both presentation and reception.
Read Jacob 1: 17	Obtain your errand from the Lord; identify ideas that come to you as you prepare that most needed by the particular people you are to teach.
Read D&C 93:43, 50; 132:8	Place these ideas in order; prioritize their importance. Teach the most important ideas first. As time for teaching in the Church is often limited, this approach insures that you will always have used whatever time is available to teach the most important ideas.
Read D&C 43:15; 52:4; 88:77; 107:85–89	Relate each idea you are to teach *to a gospel principle or ordinance*; if the idea cannot be supported by a gospel principle or ordinance, don't teach it. Strive to keep instruction connected to basic gospel principles.
Read D&C 6:31	Be a personal witness of what you teach. Testify of the truths you teach.
Read D&C 6:28	Add the witness of the scriptures and of present-day prophets to the truths you teach.
Read D&C 88: 122	Invite and assist class members to share their personal witnesses and insights. This enables the Spirit to use the gifts of all to edify all.

Learning and Teaching as a Witness

As teachers, we must recognize that the contribution of the learner is vital to effective classroom instruction in the Church. Heavenly Father has bestowed special gifts on each of his children. Each individual has unique experiences in life.

Everyone has something important to contribute to others because of these gifts and experiences. Each class member has the obligation to be a witness to the principles that are taught in Church classes (D&C 60:2), and each should be given the opportunity to do so. As learners in a class, we must improve our abilities to respond in helpful ways without using too much time. Teachers need helpful learners, and learners need each other. When we respond as class members, the Holy Ghost is able to use not only the instructor's talents but the class members' talents to edify and uplift all the participants.

As mentioned earlier, preparing and teaching temporal lessons, focuses on *showing, telling,* and *doing.* The physical world is comprehended best when it is encountered directly, explained simply, and experienced personally. Moral and spiritual teaching may go beyond this to focus on *teaching according to the covenants, teaching by the Spirit,* and *teaching as a witness.* Moral and spiritual lessons, like temporal lessons, may be more readily received when they start with the concrete and move to the abstract, begin with the simple and move to the complex, and then let the learner confirm the lesson by becoming a witness—one who can testify to the veracity of what they have been taught. *Joseph Smith lived as a learner and taught as a teacher in this manner.* Today we are encouraged to do the same by his successors.

Understanding Children, Youth, and Adults

It is apparent in the teachings of prophet leaders who followed Joseph Smith's pattern of understanding, that effective instruction is subject to the age level and readiness of those who are doing the learning and the teaching. This process is easier to facilitate when people understand what the Lord has revealed regarding children, youth, and adults. They do differ. Joseph Smith helped preserve some of this counsel in the scriptural records with which he worked. It is helpful to understand and shape our instruction to match these recorded differences. Such information can improve both our learning and teaching. For example, consider the following illustrations and commentary related to some of the differences between children and youth that may influence instruction.

Concerning Children

Read D&C 29:46–48; 1 Cor. 13:11; Moroni 8:8–12; 3 Nephi 22:13–14; D&C 68:25–26	Before little children begin to become accountable, they experience authority primarily in the form of another person: e.g., whatever mother or father says is right or wrong is easily accepted as right or wrong. Little children depend on the values of others in making their moral choices. There are numerous implications associated with this fact.
Read D&C 68:28–32	President David O. McKay taught that proper example and instruction in the early years will fortify a child against "the doubts, questions, and yearnings that will stir his soul when the real period of religious awakening comes at 12 or 14 years of age" (*Man May Know for Himself*, p. 296). After children begin to become accountable, they are able to experience authority in the form of rules or commandments—independent of personality. As they develop increasingly broad intellectual curiosity, they become interested in how other people respond to rules or commandments that govern right and wrong choices. Then comes puberty and adolescence when the powers of procreation develop.

Concerning Youth

Read JS 2:28; Alma 36:3; 37:32–35; 38:2; 39:10; Mormon 1:1–6; 1 Timothy 4:12; 2 Timothy 2:22.	As youth enter puberty, the capability and desire develops to understand principles that support rules or commands. They want to know, "Why?" They have a deep spiritual yearning to understand the principles upon which requests are made. President McKay explained, "You can be in this world, but not of the world . . . . In that period of life in which your physical nature manifests itself, . . . God has given you . . . power of reasoning; he has given you the power of judgment, discretion, and self-control, and these for a divine purpose" (Ibid. p. 257). This counsel is consistent with the differences between youth and adults that Joseph recognized in the earliest period of the Restoration.
	Teenagers and adults can experience authority in the form of principles that govern both the words people say and the rules they make. Youth sense the importance of self-mastery, and if they are not deceived by the influences of the adversary, they want to learn the principles that govern it. The Prophet Joseph Smith viewed this process as the key to good government for human beings. Said he, *"I teach them correct principles and let them govern themselves"* (MS vol. 13, p. 339).
	Preparing and presenting lessons consistent with the age level and readiness of those we teach will improve our instruction. 4-year-olds, 9-year-olds, and 17-year-olds are different. Our instruction should be compatible with these differences.

Love them, Correct Them, and Provide a Way for Them

This was the pattern the Lord taught Joseph Smith (D&C 95:1). It is the key to a positive instructional relationship. Effective classroom conduct for both parents and teachers can be summarized in this simple three-step pattern: *Love those you teach, correct them* when necessary, and *provide a way for them* to accomplish the purposes of the instruction. (Ponder D&C 95:1; 1 John 4:19; D&C 130:20–21; 2 Nephi 2:10–13; 1 Nephi 3:7.) A phrase from one of Elizabeth Barrett Browning's sonnets suggests that this is a personal task: "How Do I love thee, Let me count the ways." Each teacher will love, correct, and provide according to his or her unique gifts and personality. Likewise, each learner will respond to love, correction, and provision according to his or her personal uniqueness. A teacher often needs to pray, ponder, and actually write a list of specific, personal ways to show love, correction, and provision for a particular person to enhance learning and teaching. Effective discipline resides in the people involved; it develops as positive personal relationships are governed by correct principles, leading to action. Constructive action results when attention develops into interest, and observation is transformed into participation.

Preventing problems by appropriate involvement is better than trying to correct problems arising from a lack of involvement. Those who teach should understand: *Attention* is brief, transitory, and tentative. *Interest* is sustained, continuous, and compelling. Effective teaching seeks the *attention* of class members but leads them to develop *interest*. When learners progress from observer to participant, the likelihood of interest increases. Observation may be passive and temporary; participation is active and committing. *Personal application* is the goal of effective learners and teachers.

Children, youth, and adults who learn the doctrines of the kingdom as participant learners will be better prepared, know more perfectly, and have a greater desire to fulfill their duties. Parents, teachers, and leaders who involve those they teach in the instructional process will find more success and greater joy in their labors. As we embrace these scriptural instructions and make them the pattern for our learning and teaching, we will become better prepared to magnify our callings and fulfill our respective personal missions in this life. Like Joseph, we can embrace and apply the principles and processes that enable a person to become a better learner and more skilled teacher. He was a personal example of one who responded to sharing the Savior's invitation "Come unto me and be saved" (3 Nephi 12:20). By responding to that invitation he became a valiant servant to many other people. Therefore, "how great shall be [his] joy" in the kingdom of the Father with "many souls" because he brought them to the Savior (D&C 18:15–16). This is a promise to all; it is a goal worthy to pursue.

Thus we approach the end of a brief review of some of the elements which I believe qualify Joseph Smith to be recognized as America's greatest educator.

As indicated in the concluding question of the Prologue to this monograph, if someone asks, *What was the book about anyway?* I repeat: one simple answer to this question could be, *This book is about seeking to understand how to learn and teach like Joseph Smith was taught to learn and teach.* I believe such an endeavor is a very worthy pursuit and most certainly, it is timely.

APPENDIX A

(Note: These appendices could not exist without the work of Joseph Smith.)

This appendix is a more complete explanation of common educational options when they are considered in light of three continuums: (1) One continuum runs from *belief* to *nonbelief* in both the natural and supernatural domains of reality. If one assumes there is both a natural and a supernatural domain in reality, it is quite different from assuming there is only the physical domain and nothing else. This distinction has significant impact on how one defines and pursues education—learning and teaching. (2) A second continuum of belief is between whether the individual or the group should have the primary emphasis. If one believes that the person and his or her needs, wants, and preferences are the most important, it is quite opposite from placing a similar emphasis on what the group thinks, needs or wants. This too has important implication for what education should be like. (3) The same tension exists between what one believes about the role of nature and nurture. Some people believe the basic nature of the child is fixed and this should determine how you go about learning and teaching. Others feel that a child is flexible and subject to becoming, within limits, by nurturing whatever one might desire. The first view is somewhat akin to assuming that people are like seeds, and whatever the seed is that is what will be the outcome—apple seeds grow apple trees. The second view is that a child is like a blank slate, and any reasonable expectation can shape that child by nurturing it into whatever one might desire. Learning and teaching are both affected by which you believe.

Where one chooses to stand in relation to these optional belief patterns does make a difference. The distinctions become much more evident when a person looks at the answers he or she provides to these basic educational questions:

What is education?

What is humankind?

What is learning?

What is teaching?

What should be taught?

What is God's role?

The diagram below depicts four different quadrants when the axes of these continuum's interface. When educational programs are created and implemented they take on the characteristics of the assumptions one makes. Where one stands in relation to these continuums determines which quadrant one is in, and how this influences the answers to the six questions above. There is considerable flexibility within each quadrant, but the differences are stark between the quadrants. The do seriously influence how learners feel, teachers teach, what will be taught. These factors have been present for centuries. They were functioning in Joseph Smith's day, and they are all alive and well today.

Where a person stands on these matters largely determines what type of educator he or she will endeavor to be. Every father and mother is affected. It makes a difference if a person believes there is a supernatural domain or there isn't. It makes a difference who one believes should be in charge of and control the educational process—the individual or the society— regardless whether that society is a church or a secular institution. Proponents and opponents to these differing views have been very active in the history of American education, as well as in other nations. Below are examples of educators who have adopted different positions along these divergent continuums and the four flex-models of education they represent. It is evident to those who work in the field of education that fundamental assumptions influence how people view learning and teaching and how they structure the schooling that will occur. (Additional explanation is available in N. J. Flinders, *Teach the Children*, chapter 7 and Appendix A.)

The Agency Model	The Individualist Model
Johann Gottlieb Fichte	Jean Jacque Rousseau
Friedrich Froebel	A. S. Neill
C. Stephan Evans	John Holt
Emmanuel Mounier	Abraham H. Maslow
Robert Ulich	Carl Rogers
Rudolph Steiner	Lawrence Kohlberg
David O. McKay	

The Theological Model	The Society Model
Plato	Emile Durkheim
Socrates	Charles Hubbard Judd
	St. Augustine
	Edward L. Thorndike
John Calvin	B. F. Skinner
	Jean Baptiste de La Salle
	Samuel Bowles and Herbert Gintis
Pope Pius XI	Mortimer J. Adler

Notwithstanding the considerable variety of programs that may appear in each of the quadrants, the basic premises are easy to discern. We have a long history and many examples of schools that fall roughly into four different categories. This can be visualized in a simple chart.

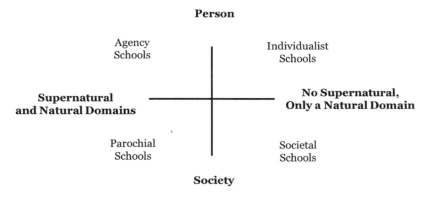

1. The *lower left quadrant* of authority sponsored the traditional form of schooling in early American history. It was religious or parochial in nature. Those who favor this realm believe there is both a natural and supernatural dimension to existence. They also presume that the authority of the church or some similar social institution takes precedence over the preferences of the individual. These assumptions are manifest in the organization, implementation, and methodology of instruction that are created, promoted, and used. Hence, authority is manifest in a hierarchal pattern:

God	(empowers the church or social order)
↓	
Church	(empowers the school, selects curriculum and teachers)
↓	
Teacher	(directs and evaluates the student)
↓	
Student	(is accountable to the line of authority)

2. In the *lower right quadrant,* people reject the notion of a supernatural dimension to existence and presume reality is simply a natural or physical domain. The assumption is clothed in a purely secular, naturalistic wardrobe. In this realm society also prevails over the individual as the primary source of authority. *The society, not the individual, controls education.*

Society	(empowers the government and the school)
↓	
School	(selects the curriculum and the teacher)
↓	
Teacher	(teacher directs and evaluates the student)
↓	
Student	(student is accountable to the line of authority)

3. In the *upper right quadrant,* people also reject the notion of a supernatural dimension to existence and presume that reality is simply a natural or physical domain. In this realm *the individual, not the society, is the primary source of authority.* The individual dictates his or her education. The function of the child is to live his or her own life, not the life that his government, anxious parents, or some teacher who thinks he knows best or feels that the child should so live. The teacher, school, and government exist to serve the individual's desires. Autonomy and self-determination reign supreme—not institutions. This type of education is often discussed, occasionally pursued, but seldom broadly established.

Student   (directs his or her own learning)

↓

Teacher   (serves and enhances the students
↓   interests)

School   (provides teacher facilities and
↓   resources)

Society   (endorses and supports the
             educational program)

4. In the *upper left hand quadrant*, people accept the reality of both a supernatural and a natural domain. They may also acknowledge that each individual is composed of both a spiritual and physical dimension. In this realm, *primary authority and responsibility for personal education reside with the individual, but limitations and external expectations need to be acknowledged.* The individual is subject to and has an imperative interactive relationship with God. The individual may also have a vital, interactive, and responsible relationship with other persons who may assist in the teaching/learning process. Individuals also may have an interactive relationship with society—but society exists to serve and support rather than dictate in educational matters. Authority is derived from and is manifest through each of these relationships. The family institution may play a vital role in this approach to education (D&C 68:25–34). It is in this quadrant that Joseph Smith's views of education fit most comfortably.

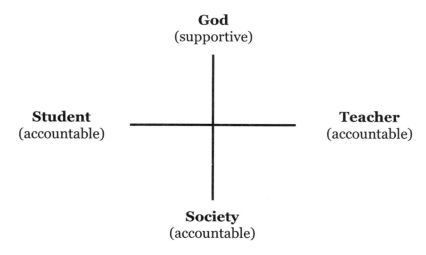

God
(supportive)

Student   **Teacher**
(accountable)   (accountable)

Society
(accountable)

In this quadrant, the individual is viewed as an *agent* with inherent freedoms for self-determination. But he or she also acknowledges a *supernatural influence* that gives context to his or her actions. Individuals are not autonomous; they are independent but have a shared relationship with authority. An individual in this domain also accepts and honors the fact that others who may be the teachers are also accountable as individuals to the superior influence of supernatural authority. Therefore, all individuals stand on equal ground, each perceiving that social institutions exist to serve the interests of the individual and not the other way around.

Joseph Smith endorsed the belief that "We believe that governments were instituted of God for the benefit of man; and that he holds men accountable for their acts in relation to them, both in making laws and administering them, for the good and safety of society. We believe that no governments can exist in peace, except such laws are framed and held inviolate as will secure to each individual the free exercise of conscience, the right and control of property, and the protection of life" (D&C 134:1–2). It is evident that Joseph believed that institutions exist to serve the individual; people are the end, organizations are the means to that end, and care should be taken not to confuse the two.

A *third axis* could be added to this pattern for thinking about education: the *Nature* versus *Nurture* axis. The question underlying this axis is: Are individuals basically determined by their *nature* to become whatever they become, or are they basically *nurtured* into what they can become, within wide and varied possibilities? Are people basically formed by some *genetic* or by *acquired* functions? Where one positions oneself on this third teeter-totter, which also intersects the previous two concerns, does influence the kind of educational path one will travel. (I will forego adding that visual complexity to this discussion; it would be a great topic in another forum.) Suffice it to say, these three axes raise fundamental questions that affect educational practice.

Recognizing different and often conflicting answers to these questions and propositions helps one understand Joseph Smith's views of education and the foundations upon which these respective views rest. He was aware that no educational enterprise can safely extend beyond the foundation upon which it is built. The foundations of an educational program do invite inevitable consequences; they are significant. And in the final analysis it is *authority* that *validates* or *invalidates* the presuppositions that frame the foundations. It is folly to assume otherwise. Joseph Smith was well aware of this phenomenon in all aspects of our lives.

APPENDIX B

	Korihor (74 B.C.) Alma chapter 30	August Comte (1798 - 1857)	Karl Marx & Friedrich Engles (1818 - 1895)	Friedrich Nietzsche (1844 - 1900)	Sigmund Freud (1856 - 1939)	John Dewey (1859 - 1952)	Humanist Manifesto (1933, 1973)
Religious doctrines are foolish traditions of our ancestors.		Religious doctrines are merely the result of an immature evolutionary stage which society will outgrow.	Religious doctrines are merely an economic invention of the ruling class.	Religious doctrines are the moralities for the herd animal—the free spirit makes his own morality.	Religious doctrines are the shared neurotic illusions of a culture.	Religious doctrines are the inflexible dogmas of an outmoded institution.	Religious doctrines are outmoded and cannot meet today's needs.
You cannot know what you cannot see. You cannot know that God exists.		Science is the sole means of obtaining true knowledge.	Only the natural, the material, is knowable and therefore real.	"All credibility, good conscience, all evidence of truth comes only from the senses."	Science is the only road to true knowledge.	Patient cooperative scientific inquiry is the only sure road to facts, truth, and progress.	All claims should be able to pass the tests of science. No credible scientific evidence exists for the belief in a supernatural.
Religious convictions are the result of a deranged mind.		Religious convictions are the result of an immature and untrained mind.	Religious convictions are the fantastic reflections of a fearful mind.	Religious convictions are the evil instincts of a diseased soul.	Religious convictions are the hopeful illusions of a neurotic mind.	Religious convictions are misinterpretations of real experience by an insecure mind.	Religious convictions are the harmful illusions of an unreasonable mind.
God does not intervene in our behalf, we survive in life by our own efforts. There is no punishment for sin.		Progress requires that the old notion of "God" be replaced with "Humanity"—the supreme natural phenomenon.	When the Proletariat (the worker class) realizes there is no other world than this, they will use force to set themselves free.	For the free spirit, God is dead. He creates his own morality.	The belief in a supernatural God is an illusion—We grow the most when we realize we must rely strictly upon our own resources.	We progress not by faith in some supernatural being, but by cooperative scientific inquiry.	"No deity will save us, we must save ourselves."
Churches and religions place people in bondage, chaining them to ideas and authorities.		Nonscientific churches are intolerant and feed upon the immaturity of people.	Religions are like an opiate, lulling people into ignoring the injustices of this life, in hopes of heavenly justice and reward.	Christian "believers" are the saddest prisoners of all.	Like a sleeping potion, religion acts to bind the mind from free intellectual growth and society from flexible progress.	Churches sap the genuinely religious with their foolish doctrines.	Traditional religions do a disservice to the human species by holding them back.

APPENDIX C

The popularity of modern secular philosophy in today's schools has, like those in medieval times, created equally serious but almost opposite doctrinal conflicts. Three examples are:

(1) Because modern thought defines existence as *monistic*—that physical matter is the only building block in the universe—it is unthinkable that man also has a spiritual body. The psychologist John Watson, arguing against man having a supernatural dimension, wrote, "One example of such a [false] concept is . . . that every individual has a soul which is separate and distinct from the body. . . .[but] no one has ever touched a soul, or has seen one in a test tube, or has in any way come into relationship with it as he has with the other objects of his daily experience" (John B. Watson, *Behaviorism*, 1924, p. 4).

(2) Because modern thought defines existence as monistic, it is unthinkable that "God" can be anything more than a property of physical matter, or that a spirit demon (the devil) could exist. John Dewey, the famous American educator, explained "God" in these words: "What I have been criticizing is the identification of the ideal with a particular Being, especially when that identification makes necessary the conclusion that this Being is outside of nature, and what I have tried to show is that the ideal itself has roots in natural conditions; it emerges when the imagination idealizes existence by laying hold of the possibilities offered to thought and action . . . . It is the active relation between the ideal and actual to which I would give the name 'God.' I would not insist that the name must be given" (John Dewey, *A Common Faith*, 1934, pp. 48, 51). Albert Einstein added his supportive perspective when he said, "The more a man is imbued with the ordered regularity of all events, the firmer becomes his conviction that there is no room left by the side of this ordered regularity for causes of a different nature. For him [the informed thinking person], neither the rule of human nor the rule of divine

will exist as an independent cause of natural events. . . . In their struggle for the ethical good, teachers of religion must have the stature to give up the doctrine of a personal God" (Albert Einstein, *Out of My Later Years,* 1950, pp. 29–33).

(3) Because modern thought defines existence as monistic, it is convenient to attribute to physical matter (and the social environment derived from it) the responsibility for social evil. The psychologist B. F. Skinner taught, "In the traditional view a person responds to the world around him in the sense of acting upon it. . . . The opposing view—common, I believe, to all versions of behaviorism—is that the initiating action is taken by the environment rather than by the perceiver. . . . The environment stays where it is and where it has always been—outside the body. . . . There is no place in the scientific position for a self as a true originator or initiator of action." (B. F. Skinner, *About Behaviorism,* 1974, pp. 72–73, 225). "After the reign of Henry VIII in England many sinful acts were formally declared to be not only immoral but illegal, . . . making what were once dealt with as sins into crimes rendered the designation of sin increasingly pointless . . . . Gradually the effects of 'the new psychology,' . . . began to be apparent. . . . Some crime was being viewed as symptomatic. Sins had become crimes and now crimes were becoming illnesses; in other words whereas the police and judges had taken over from the clergy, the doctors and psychologists were now taking over from the police and judges" (Karl Menninger, *Whatever Became of Sin,* 1973). The results of this transition are obvious: you do not punish people for being sick because of exposure to a faulty environment or a malfunctioning nature—even their own nature. Morality was redefined as ethical relativism. The environment or genetics became the cause of behavior; the individual was deemed legally less and less responsible for his or her behavior.

The teachings of Joseph Smith reject the foregoing propositions. He taught that (1) the universe is composed of two building blocks—spirit stuff and physical or temporal stuff. "For man is spirit. The elements are eternal, and spirit and element, inseparably connected, receive a fullness of joy" (D&C 93:33). (2) Regarding God and the devil, Joseph foresaw the time when people would "deny the power of God, the Holy One of Israel, and [would] say unto the people, . . . hear ye our precept; for behold there is no God today, for the Lord and the Redeemer hath done his work, and he hath given his power unto men" (2 Nephi 28:5). Likewise, he noted, concerning the Adversary, that "he [the devil] saith unto them: I am no devil, for there is none. . . . thus he whispereth in their ears, until he grasps them with his awful chains, from whence, there is no deliverance" (2 Nephi 28:22). (3) As to the moral consequences of these doctrines, Joseph proclaimed, "The children of men . . . are redeemed from the fall, they have become free forever, knowing good from evil; to act for themselves and not to be acted upon, save it be by the punishment of the law at the great and last day, according to the commandments which God hath given" (2 Nephi 2:26). "We believe that men will be punished for their own sins, and not for Adam's transgression" (PGP Article of Faith 2). Morality is doing what God says is in the best interest of his children.

APPENDIX D

(Adapted from Neil J Flinders, My Decision: An Act of Faith or a Piece of Cowardice, 1989)

Everyone's Choice:
An Act of Faith or a Piece of Cowardice

The issue of submitting to God—the true God—is the central issue in human history; it is the primary test of mortality. This choice is an underlying element in nearly all major social, political, educational, religious, and cultural controversies. The evidence bearing on this issue is abundant in both the factual and fabled histories. Consequently, it is a message of history that clearly appears in the broader outline of events in the Western World. In a sense, one could say this choice constitutes the story of how the modern world in which Americans and Europeans now live, got to be like it is— "without God, without Creed."[68] This view is simply an example of many stories—stories of different people, living at various times in history, in different settings. Each of the stories, however, contributes to a common theme: man's struggle with the issue of obedience to God.

Modern men like Sigmund Freud, John Dewey, and Walter Lippmann clearly posed this issue.[69] Notwithstanding these different perspectives, the underlying subject of this essay remains the issue of submission—or not. The issue addressed here is the willingness or unwillingness of man to submit to the true God of creation when he is made manifest. As Cicero so eloquently proclaimed, "There is no race either so highly civilized or so savage as not to know that it must believe in a god, even if it does not know in what sort of god it ought to believe. Thus it is clear that man recognizes God because, in a way, he remembers and recognizes the source from which he sprang."[70] An extension of the question of personal submission

---

[68]James Turner, *Without God, Without Creed: The Origins of Unbelief in America*, 1985.

[69]Walter Lippmann, *A Preface to Morals*, 1929, p. 144; Sigmund Freud, *The Future of an Illusion*, 1927; John Dewey, *A Common Faith*, 1934.

[70]LAWS I. VIII, 24. As quoted in *Lynchburg College Symposium Readings*,

to God, and equally critical, is the willingness of men who choose not to acknowledge God, to allow other men, who do acknowledge God, the freedom to submit to Him. This too, tests the nature and character of mankind.

Although Joseph Smith was born into a family influenced by a biblical environment, he still faced this ancient choice. New England was noted as a religious society. Ironically, at the turn of the 19th century, the specific environs of Sharon, Windsor County, Vermont by some measures shared with a location in Switzerland the distinction of being the two most literate spots on the earth. Colonial America was familiar with the bible—particularly the Old Testament. Included in this book of beginnings was a provocative collection of Proverbs, considered by many to be the closest document to a teacher training manual then available. The awareness associated with this knowledge base caused many people to consider the welfare or jeopardy of their personal soul. This interest often became quite intense and fed the fire of many revival meetings.

Like others in his day, Joseph Smith had to decide whether he was going to *act on faith* or to consider belief in a higher power as an *"act of cowardice."* Josephus, the Jewish historian, notes that choice was evident in the life and exploits of Nimrod, a great-grandson of Noah, who was credited as the political engineer of the Tower of Babel. He it was, Josephus claims, that led the people of his day into disbelief. Nimrod's aim was to convince the people they could get along without God—that they were sufficient in their own power—thus the building of his famous tower in Babel. Nimrod's claim was that he would guide the people in building a tower so high it would be above any future flood. And once it was built, he would personally "avenge God for destroying their forefathers."[71] Josephus adds, "Now the multitude were very ready to follow the determination of Nimrod, and to esteem it *a piece of cowardice* to submit to God; and they built a tower, neither sparing any pains, nor being in any degree negligent about the work."[72] (see Pieter Bruegels' illustration, a 16th century artist.)

Classical Selections on Great Issues, The Nature of Man, Vol. I (London: University Press of America Inc., 1982) p. 7.

[71]*Flavius Josephus: Antiquities of the Jews*, Vol. IV, 2, p. 39.
[72]Ibid. 3.

Pieter Bruegels, a 16th century artist, painted three versions of the *Tower of Babel*. The one shown here details the consuming nature of human pride. It portrays the ultimate vanity of even the boldest of human endeavors. Nimrod is depicted in his royal splendor, accompanied by a retinue of guards and subordinates, surveying the work of some stonecutters.

Nimrod, according to modern scholars, is described in many ancient documents. Reportedly, he was a giant in physical stature. He is credited with establishing the towns of Babel, Erech, and Accad in the land of Shinar (Sumer) in southern Mesopotamia, and also the northern Mesopotamian cities of Ninevah, Rehoboth-Ir, Calah, and Resen. The Nimrod legend is connected by the Jews, Greeks, and Persians to the constellation called Orion by the Greeks. This group of stars symbolizes the ancient and mighty hunter-warrior. Apparently, Nimrod was a real historical figure widely known and noted for his Kingship, conquests, and his building enterprise.

Simply stated, the issue was: Does man need God, or can he go it alone? Nimrod himself seemed convinced not only that man could go it alone, but that God could be replaced. This aggressive position was fueled with a specific attitude that has since come to dominate many societies, including our own. The intimidating taunt in every corner and clime, from the sleazy side of societies to the ivied halls of academia, has been and still is: It's *a piece of cowardice to submit to God.*

Joseph Smith was not only familiar with the book of Genesis, he understood the story line in the rest of the Old Testament. He knew of Moses' experience with the Pharaoh of Egypt, a sophisticated, worldly and wicked man—another example of how men struggle against submitting to God by substiting various counterfeits. Pharaoh, on hearing Moses' report of his experiences with God in the Sinai, made light of Moses. His response was typical of the pattern: "Who is the Lord, that I should obey his voice to let Israel go? I know not the Lord, neither will I let Israel go."[73] He chided Moses, saying it was naive to think that Pharaoh could be fooled by mere tricks and magic, ascribed to some divine power. The Egyptians, he said, were also skilled in this kind of learning; Moses could only hope to find believers among the ignorant and uneducated.[74]

This confrontation and denial is followed by the sequence of events described in Exodus chapters 5–12. Ten plagues came upon the Egyptians. Great physical and social distress resulted from these plagues, but it wasn't until the firstborn children all died that Pharaoh would consent to release the Israelites from their bondage. Even then his decision was temporary. He changed his mind soon after and led his army in pursuit of the Hebrews, who were gathered at the borders of the Red Sea.

Every generation, one individual at a time, faces the question of submission to God. It is the pattern of rejecting God that has created a need for prophets. The Old Testament is composed of three types of literature: the Law, the Prophets, and the Writings. The law was established to direct the believers, the Writings are testimonials from believers, and the

---

[73]Exodus 5:2.
[74]*Antiquities* Bk. 11, Ch. XIII 2, 3. p. 81.

Prophets are voices of warning to those who seek the path of disbelief. Israel's family history is largely an account of the prophets who pleaded with the people against the drift toward disbelief. Joseph Smith knew and understood this story line. He clearly distinguished between the two stories—you might say *Story A* and *Story B*.

Moses, the author credited with the best known version of *Story A*, begins his account with a description of the events which transpired in a Garden in Eden. Rich in symbolic meaning, this episode clearly defines the capacities and priorities of mankind. The central theme of this story revolves around the difficulties man has experienced in maintaining a proper relationship with his Creator—his Father in Heaven. Essentially, the record states that all men and women were the spiritual offspring of Heavenly parentage and lived as individual personalities with spirit bodies before becoming mortal beings on this earth.[75] Mortality for these children of God is a brief but important test designed to qualify them, according to their desires, for different types of experiences in their post-mortal existence.[76] In order to successfully fulfill the purpose of mortality it was necessary for mankind to experience a fall and the redemption of an atonement.

Two characters, Adam and Eve, are placed in a beautiful garden. They are told to enjoy its comfort and its produce—with one exception: they are not to partake of the fruit of the tree of knowledge of good and evil. The violation of this instruction, they are told, will result in a change in their nature: they will become mortal, subject to death, and personally responsible for many other conditions associated with mortality. An adversary, Satan, in the form of a serpent beguiles Eve into partaking of the forbidden fruit; she in turn persuades Adam to partake, lest they be separated from each other and thereby be unable to fulfill a prior instruction to multiply and fill the earth with other of God's children. This transgression by Adam and Eve results in their being removed from the Garden with its many pleasantries and placed in the harsher, telestial environment of this earth.

---

[75]Genesis 2:5; Jeremiah 1:5; Hebrews 12:9.
[76]1 Corinthians 15:40–42; 2 Corinthians 12:2.

In Moses' description of the conditions existing in the Garden of Eden, he preserves for mankind a simple but excellent explanation of the essential principles that govern living and learning—the core of human experience. He recounts that God breathed into Adam and Eve the "breath of life," symbolized by the "tree of life" in the Garden of Eden. In addition to becoming living souls capable of expressing desire, Adam and Eve also received their agency—the capacity and opportunity to make choices within the realm in which they were placed. In his narrative account, Moses also describes a second tree in the Garden whose fruit Adam and Eve were warned not to eat. This second tree is identified as the "tree of knowledge of good and evil". Choosing between right and wrong, making moral decisions, is thus identified as the focal point—the essence of mortal experience. Learning to choose good over evil is the basic purpose of mortal life. Success in doing this, they are informed, requires that they voluntarily submit their desires to God's instructions—his commandments.

Adam and Eve were living, acting, choosing and learning souls, existing without a knowledge of good and evil—without conscience until they partook of the forbidden fruit. When they chose to eat of the fruit of the tree of knowledge of good and evil their condition changed. They became moral agents, accountable (as are all men) for their own sins in the day of judgment.[77] To their former capacities was added an awareness of the difference between good and evil, between right and wrong. They acquired the capacity of conscience. Then Adam and Eve were removed from the Garden of Eden and placed in a world of opposition. Their choices now resulted in the process of creating personal values, values that in turn would shape and direct their lives. The energy of life within them, often referred to in scriptural literature as *desire,* found expression in this new world, according to the agency God had given them. Their choices became investments—right or wrong —of time, energy and other resources. These investments became their values. Diagrammed, the process might be considered a simple formula:

Life + Agency + Moral Knowledge + Choice = Value

---

[77]1 Corinthians 15:19–23; Revelations 20:12.

This appears to be the Mosaic description of what values are and how we acquire them. It is a simple but comprehensive explanation. People's values are the results of their choices: their commitments of time, energy, interest, allegiance, money, effort, and other resources. These personal values uniquely sculpture each individual's personality, lifestyle, and purposes. Responsibility, for example, is merely a reflection of a person's desire to protect and preserve his or her investments. Not all people do this with the same intensity. And there is a tendency to rate people along this line. People are commonly considered irresponsible when they fail to protect their investments (values), or the investments that someone else feels should be protected. The cause of most human controversy seems related to these differing views of responsibility.

Character is a reflection of the consistency with which a person acts to protect his or her investments—his or her choices. Character implies predictability. The Hebrew-Christian position is that when a person acts to preserve and protect what God considers to be positive values (e.g., the Ten Commandments), he is exhibiting good character. If a person consistently (predictably) acts to protect what the Creator considers to be negative values—poor investments—he exhibits undesirable character. In a nutshell, this is the message from Moses. Man may make choices in harmony with the guidelines (commandments) revealed by God and experience growth and development. Or, he may make choices in opposition to these guidelines and experience decadence and deprivation.

Story B, in all its varied forms is the rejection of Story A and the act of substituting some counterfeit version of one's own making in the place thereof. It is in this context that Joseph Smith lived and pursued the fulfillment of his mission as a Prophet and a Minister of Education.

About the Author

Neil J Flinders

A lifelong student and professional educator (b. July 11, 1934)
Reared on a farm and served in the U.S. Army Medical Corps

Earned degrees:
Bachelor's (Sociology/Journalism)
Master's (Religious Education/Ed. Philosophy)
Doctorate (Administration/Human Relations)

Vocation Experience:
U.S. Army Medical Corps, Lab Technician
Seminary and Institute teacher, teacher trainer, lecturer,
educational consultant
CES Director of Research
Professor, School of Education, Brigham Young University
President of Far Western Philosophy of Education Society

Church Service:
LDS Sunday School General Board, stake president, bishop,
high councilor, elders quorum president, missionary, temple
ordinance worker, teacher

Author:
Numerous articles; professional papers; monographs; several
books, including the following notable books:
- *Personal Communication: How to Understand and be
  Understood*
- *Teach the Children: An Agency Approach to Education*
- *Leadership and Human Relations: A Handbook for Parents,
  Teachers and Administrators*
- *The Next Generation: A Grandfather's View of Self-Evident
  Truths: Truth and Error, Values and Principles, Relationships
  and Skills (limited family distribution)*

Family:
Married to Joan D. Robertson
Parents of 7 Children; 37 Grandchildren; 5 Great-
Grandchildren

INDEX

213

S